Baroque in Back

Contemporary Shakespeare Production

Studies in Shakespeare

Robert F. Willson, Jr.
General Editor

Vol. 20

PETER LANG
New York • Washington, D.C./Baltimore • Bern
Frankfurt • Berlin • Brussels • Vienna • Oxford

H. R. Coursen

Contemporary Shakespeare Production

PETER LANG
New York • Washington, D.C./Baltimore • Bern
Frankfurt • Berlin • Brussels • Vienna • Oxford

Library of Congress Cataloging-in-Publication Data

Coursen, Herbert R.
Contemporary Shakespeare production / H. R. Coursen.
p. cm. — (Studies in Shakespeare; v. 20)
Includes bibliographical references and index.
1. Shakespeare, William, 1564–1616—Dramatic production.
2. Shakespeare, William, 1564–1616—Film and video adaptations. I. Title.
PR3091.C666   792.9'5—dc22   2009049006
ISBN 978-1-4331-0924-9
ISSN 1067-0823

Bibliographic information published by **Die Deutsche Nationalbibliothek**.
Die Deutsche Nationalbibliothek lists this publication in the "Deutsche
Nationalbibliografie"; detailed bibliographic data is available
on the Internet at http://dnb.d-nb.de/.

© 2010 Peter Lang Publishing, Inc., New York
29 Broadway, 18th floor, New York, NY 10006
www.peterlang.com

Printed in Germany

Table of Contents

Illustrations

All illustrations are from the author's personal photo collection of Shakespearean publicity material from press kits.

The Polonius family: A. Bromley Davenport, Robert Holmes, and Muriel Hewitt in Barry Jackson's 1925 'Plus-fours' Hamlet.

Introduction

Responsible performance criticism can only emerge from an analysis of the components of specific productions. It cannot come from the practice of "theorizing" performance. How do you theorize a decision that a director makes? Or that an actor makes within a line of iambic pentameter? The actor and director are not working with theory or emerging from theory. They are coping with how to make a particular script comprehensible to an audience. It is practice, not theory that must inform performance criticism. And it is performance that provides the data for criticism of the plays. And they are *plays*, that is, words set down to be spoken by actors before an audience. Whatever "Shakespeare" may be, it exists within the continuum between the stage and where a spectator sits in the fifth row.

I am not claiming that "literary" approaches to the plays are useless. They often help us understand the issues of the script and guide directors in selecting what to emphasize and, with longer scripts, what to edit. Margreta de Grazia's brilliant recent book on *Hamlet*, though not performance based, can inform productions of that play in useful ways. She chronicles the play's concern with lost kingdoms, its focus on plots of ground, and its emphasis on interrupted inheritance. Each of these strains of thought can be retained in the editing of a long script for production, and thus certain emphases that the script makes can be included within the space that a spectator's imagination is given to explore. (Coursen, 2008)

I disagree, then, with Cynthia Lewis that "a performance approach constitutes a completely different paradigm from that of teaching the play as literature." (2005, 122) I am suggesting that the play *as* literature can inform the play as script, by suggesting what the play is all about. That "all aboutness" will be different for different directors, of course, but reading the play must be an a priori act within the continuum of creating a performance. Plot, as Aristotle says, is the basic element of drama. It is important, for example, to notice that both *Richard II* and *Hamlet* begin after a secret murder. That secret trembles under the opening scenes of each play and dictates the tonality of the "world of the play" and, certainly, argues some tectonic insecurity beneath the seemingly confident courts of Richard and Claudius.

William Worthen indicts the New Criticism for isolating the intrinsic elements of the text and thus denying the "interpretative free play" of performance critics. (1997, 154) I would suggest, though, that a "literary" reading of the text can be a useful prelude to an editing of that text for performance. In one of the paradigms of the New Criticism, Reuben Brower discusses the key metaphoric groupings in *The Tempest*: "strange-wondrous... sleep-and-dream...sea-tempest...music-and-noise...earth-air...slavery-freedom...and sovereignty-conspiracy." (1951, 184) Brower argues that these linkages tend to appear at the most dramatic moments of the play. While this is a short script requiring little editing, Brower suggests what lines to leave in or, at least, what moments in the poetic fabric of the script to emphasize. I have argued that Prospero's "fellowly drops" at the sight of Gonzalo are the culmination of a process of compassion and grief—Miranda's tears for those on the ship, Ferdinand's for his father's apparent death, Alonso's for Ferdinand's apparent death, Miranda's for Ferdinand's labors, Ariel's grasp of "human" compassion, and, finally, Gonzalo's tears for the King and his party. That action, when it finds involuntary expression in Prospero, is the play's emotional climax. And it is a "literary" analysis that can be realized in performance. (Coursen 2000, 59-60)

I agree with Paul J. Hecht about the "tide of scholarship that every year seems to distance itself from 'literature' in any centralized, commonly held sense." (2005, 127) In denying literature, "theory," whatever it may be, says little or nothing to the process of producing the plays and responding to productions.

In addition to "returning" to a sense of "unity" in literature—though we will disagree about that "unity" in every specific instance—I suggest that "contemporizing." productions is usually a mistake. Too often, productions brought into some similitude with the "times in which we live" merely reflect what the audience already knows. If political language merely reinforces what the speaker thinks the public already believes, many productions do the same. I once had an educated woman say to me that she would not read a novel about a woman written by a man. It did no good for me to suggest that she was ruling out work by Joseph Conrad, Henry James and William Faulkner. By contemporizing a script, directors often rule out the imaginations of their own audiences.

Directors are influenced by the bombardment of news and the avalanche of new media, and it is those elements that, too often, creep into production. And directors are notorious imitators of other directors. As soon as *Henry V* encompasses modern weaponry, all designers seem to hit the local salvage stores for costumes and props.

My critical methodology is simple, some will say simplistic, even "reactionary." (Traister, 1999) It is simply to suggest how the script works *as* script—that is, a text meant to be performed. And that understanding is not some independent thesis awaiting activation, but has itself been informed by performances, good and bad. Reviews of individual productions, which I include here, are part of the process—the raw data and immediate critique which, in conjunction with the play text, contribute both to methodology and result.

I admit to having no idea what people mean when they claim to "theorize" performance. Performance is an interpretation of the script, and our effort should be to try to understand what directors and actors are doing and to evaluate the relative success of their efforts. I place that admittedly subjective judgment against my understanding of the script, so there's an ur-text lurking there, but how does one avoid that? My audience, I assume, would be those who teach undergraduates, students for whom the Shakespeare course may be their only academic contact with Shakespeare. My own sense, after fifty years of doing that, is that the jargon packaged along with theory is not useful in an undergraduate class, except for the purposes of parody, and that getting students to productions is the best way to teach Shakespeare.

What follows, then, is far more in line with Paul Nelson and June Schlueter's *Acts of Criticism: Performance of Shakespeare and His Contemporaries: Essays in Honor of James P. Lusardi* (2006) than with Peter Holland and W. B. Worthen's *Theorizing Practice: Redefining Theatre History* (2003), much as I admire the brilliance often displayed in the latter sector. I doubt that directors are reading criticism that "theorizes" production and I have no idea how it translates into effective dramaturgy. I do know that a careful "old-fashioned" reading of the script can provide useful dramaturgy. I have performed that role for productions of *Hamlet, As You Like It* and *Measure for Measure*. As different as those scripts may be, I doubt that any of them was written according to postmodernist critical tenets.

Barbara Hodgdon asks, "How do we use performance? As pleasurable memory, as potentially generative of critical materials, or as fragments for the margins, punctuating literary, textual, or historical arguments, relegated to footnotes?" (2007, 3)

I place myself squarely in the middle category, performance as *directly* generative of critical materials, and, for the dramaturge, as potentially influencing further performances themselves.

I have dealt in detail with modern re-interpretations of the plays. They tend to diminish the original, as in the case of *O*, the story of a tiny and inarticulate basketball player at a prep school. His link with the Moor is jealousy. It is a shame, for example, that Patrick Stewart did not consider his huge following and remarkable skills to give us a "straight" *King Lear*. Instead, he appeared in *King of Texas*, a transfer of the Lear story to the 19th century Southwest. Lear's of "less than the middle height" can be powerful (Yuri Jarvet and Ian Holm, for example), but this production found Stewart imitating a Texas accent and reduced the dynastic issues of the play to a quarrel about a cattle ranch. As I said at the time, the production resembled one of Shakespeare's "sources." A person would have wondered, were that the case, how Shakespeare had shaped a masterpiece from such unpromising material. Stewart as King Lear would have been an event that would have attracted first-time viewers to Shakespeare's masterpiece. (Coursen 2005, 127-131)

I am not a fan of productions that "modernize" or "westernize" or "far-easternize" Shakespeare. Such approaches tend to distort the way the scripts work and draw our attention away from the issues they explore, as we ooh and aah about how cleverly the director has fitted the script to his concept. But it is an issue deeper than anachronism. Shakespeare has striking clocks in Rome and Elizabethan sprites in Athens. A production that specifies a time and place other than "Elizabethan" or "Roman" or, say, Victorian England, or a generalized modern and thus neutral setting lures us toward the production's metaphor. Those of us who know the play tic off similarities and differences. Those who don't know the play are convinced that, somehow, it works and "means" in its invented environment. We are told—see how much Shakespeare is like us! It is the Sarah Palin effect. But I suggest that its seduction also leads to a falsification. Regardless of our familiarity with the script, we will invariably be pulled in the direction of the visual metaphor—the costumes, the set, the props. In a *Richard III* set in 1937, we will wonder why, at the outset, a modern army has forgotten the old habit of placing guards around the encampment and, at the end, why Richard's mechanized force has not developed an air force. Air Marshall Stanley has the only B-25 ever built! In other words, the time chosen demands an accurate modeling, particularly when it is a time close to ours. And the closer to our time it is, the more difficult it is to wrench the Shakespearean script into the selected format. Richard wants a horse because his motorized vehicle has become stuck in the mud. How did the director resist having some passing Tommy shout "Get a horse!" at him? And Richard's confrontation with his guilty soul—an Augustinian moment in a play full of religious allusions, usages, and misapplications—simply does not fit into the fascist climate of 1937. Instead of emerging from something the script provides, the director takes what a given culture provides and jams it down on the inherited language and worldview. The praxis—the basic story the play tries to tell—is distorted out of recognition to anything other than the concept the director has chosen.

Shakespeare wrote at a time when the "chain of being" could still be employed as an archetype underlying a play's action. As late as *Macbeth* (1605-06) Shakespeare could use the concept to emphasize the heinousness of killing a king. That was how the great preachers of the time—Lancelot Andrewes and John Donne, for example—were depicting it: a crime against God. I would argue that an audience can still be educated to that antique configuration by a production. Otherwise, suddenly empowered mousing owls make no sense. A director might as well cut the line that shows how the world order, as the play depicts it, has been turned topsy-turvy. I may be, as Traister says, a "reactionary," but so is the play. A contemporary setting for the play will erase a significant element of the inherited script. *Hamlet* is set in a post-sacramental world, a reformation by regicide, but the characters do not realize that. It is a world to which the sacraments were recently available. But, with a king-killer on the throne, funerals merge with marriages, efforts at prayer must fail, a prime minister is buried "in hugger-mugger," his daughter, having drowned in a reverse-baptism, receives "maimed rites," poisoned wine is forced down the throat of a dying man—is thy [comm]union here?, and so on. A contemporary version of the play set in New York's low rent district cannot convey this sudden disconnect with the grace of God. But a production like John Caird's (2001) can do so. It was a non-specific modern production, but the world of the play was tugged at by older values that had only recently been functioning and the destruction of people and purpose was accompanied by liturgical music. The effect was eerie, as if Elsinore were haunted not just by a walking Ghost but by the spectral imagery of a lost world.

I am hardly arguing for a return to Shakespeare's time and techniques, even if either were recoverable. I am suggesting that we must respect the moment of the script and recreate it effectively for a modern audience. The force that was Shakespeare does not exist in the 21st century, but we can recreate it. Certainly a culture that enjoys fantasy and science fiction has the imagination to appreciate another time and another place that just happen to mirror our own deepest fears and wishes. To flatten the script into "relevance" by showing us how much it is like our world is to rob the script of its own metaphor. It is "unlike" our world in ways that permit us to breathe within the world achieved there—not here. The process encourages our own imaginations and frees us to perceive the psychic mirror that is held up in various ways to a variety of natures, even within a single human being. Can an African American understand only *The Invisible Man* or *Native Son*? Is *The American* inevitably a closed book to an African American? Can a woman grasp only *Jane Eyre*? Is *The Great Gatsby*, narrated by a male about a male character, an impossible reach for her? The scripts are accessible without having to translate them completely into Shakespearean contexts, as if the plays existed behind a museum's velvet ropes, though it helps for students to know about "the king's two bodies" and the great chain of being. And it is not necessary for program notes to educate an audience. A spectator can sense the illegitimacy of Lear's "while we unburden'd crawl toward death" and the order implicit in the disorder represented by that mousing owl downing a falcon, "towering in her pride of place." Modernizations, however, tend to lose those meanings—though the concept of two bodies does inhere in any political office. I am suggesting that a relatively "traditional" production of Shakespeare asks only that we suspend our disbelief, not that we believe. The necessary suspension then permits our "negative capability" to function. We can enjoy living for a time within the continuum that the metaphor creates.

To modernize is not just to simplify, but to lie. I do not believe that Shakespeare was writing in the template of post-modernist critical theory. We can deconstruct. And we can apply feminist critiques. But modernized productions tend to deny us that process by doing the imaginative work for us. And such productions conflict with the way I understand the scripts and with the way that I teach them. I teach them with as full an awareness of how modern staging techniques and modern media shape and condition performance as I can muster, but also with a sense of what the scripts might have meant to their original audiences. That involves an awareness of the transitive power of metaphor—the link between unlike things: Shakespeare's time and our own. Production, however modern, becomes immediately trapped in its time. It plunges backward in time at the moment of its emergence, passing the script seeking production, which is going in the other direction. The script is also, inevitably, a product of its time. *A Midsummer Night's Dream* and *Richard II* find much of their resonance in late-Elizabethan England, while *Macbeth* discovered its original audience in the court of King James. We have then a complicated exercise in history and chronology. That means that the metaphor—the comparison of two unlike epistemes—demands an imaginative leap from the spectator over an increasingly widening chasm. That also means that a director must respect both times and, particularly, should not force a present moment down upon the script. Present moments have a habit of changing rapidly. The original play text, as far as we can ascertain it, is inevitably part of what Robert Weimann calls *locus*, as opposed to *platea*, which is the way the play is produced. (1988) As Worthern says, the texts are "vessels of authority, of canonical values, of hegemonic consensus." (1997, 6)

John Styan argues that Shakespeare and his contemporaries had to adjust their techniques to many different stages during the Elizabethan-Jacobean period. (Styan, 1967, 7) The stages themselves dictated what could happen on them. If *A Midsummer Night's Dream*, for example, were written originally for a wedding celebration in a great hall, that eliminated an "above" and a "discovery space." The play functions without those playing areas already prominent in the early scripts. Styan, then, argues that *locus* and *platea* were interdependent entities even early in Shakespeare's career. The plasticity of the scripts owes much to the variable conditions that existed as they were created and helps explain their continued adaptability through time, even their constriction into proscenium formats.

Another determinant, Styan argues, was "the shape into which the spectators were mustered and their relationship to the players." (1967, 14) If we extend the element of "shape" forward in time, we glimpse the ways in which

conceptual space—the various shapings and expectations of different theaters, and of film and television—conditions what Styan calls "the emotional
range" that production can achieve. (1967, 14) Much of what we say today
about Shakespeare in any medium is explicit in Styan's meticulous analysis of
Shakespeare's techniques.

The plays are constantly reconceived. Even a production that pursued with
precision the design of a production of, say, the mid-1980s, would emerge as
a different production today. The audience would have changed. Even a person who had attended the identical production some two decades ago would
respond to it differently. His or her own experience would have shaped a different psychology of perception than pertained at some prior moment in his
or her ontogeny. And productions that attempted to reproduce Elizabethan
techniques look dated today. William Poel's useful attempts, for example, look,
as they must, like the early twentieth century.

Evaluating production, then, is an on-going activity and emerges within a
Zeitgeist that conditions the way a particular production achieves its meanings.
The analysis of two competing points of view—that of the script and that of
the culture into which the script is being projected, and of their differences and
similarities—becomes, then, the basis of Shakespeare criticism.

Nicholas Jones says that "readers [of criticism know *Hamlet*] well enough
so that description can be dispensed with." (2006, 72) That is true. But description is necessary in reviewing productions of *Hamlet*. The space itself—size of
the stage and the auditorium, or TV, or film—conditions and shapes the content. The play as Platonic form takes on a local habitation that can include the
editing of the script. The production makes the inherited script distinct from
any other production of the same script. And it is in these distinctions that we
learn not just the script's infinite variety but also how it communicates to its
audience in time, or, in the case of film or TV, how it communicated then and
what it says in any given now.

In referring to the "authority" of the Royal Shakespeare Company and
Shakespeare as "national playwright," William Worthen says, "By allowing
Shakespeare such authority, we reify Shakespearean drama—and the tradition
it represents—as sacred text, as silent hieroglyphics we can only scan, interpret,
struggle to decode: we impoverish the work of our own performances and the
work of the plays in our makings of the world." (1996, 25) If I understand

Worthen correctly, we impoverish our own imaginations by claiming that one way exists to "do" Shakespeare, and that we spectators submit to that claim, silently and humbly, as if at an Anglican high communion. We are not meant to respond spontaneously or individually but only in a General Confession that has been written out for us. Above all, we are not meant to enjoy. Indeed, we are meant to feel guilty when we go to *Hamlet*. Kenneth Branagh, in 1993, indicated the Barbican audience with a sweep of his right hand when he said "guilty creatures sitting at a play."[1]

If, as Royal Shakespeare Company (RSC) actor David Toughton says, "a character first emerges from the language" (Smallwood 1998, 77), any production evolves gradually. For the actor, the process involves an interplay between specific words—"their very sound and shape" (Toughton, Smallwood, 77) and an emerging conception of who the character is within the developing production surrounding and implicating that character. Prior to the actor's process, though, a director must decide on "plot"—the shape of the action. Aristotle has always been right about the primacy of plot—what happens, the order in which things happen, the causes of what happens, and the concatenation of action and response. Silent films, with only images and title cards to work with, prove the point. (Coursen 2002, 95-111) It follows that a "bright idea" can emerge only from deep consideration—not from a sudden insight like, "It's like this in India!"

It also follows that "house style"—BBC, RSC, or the in-group smugness that sometimes characterized Joseph Papp's productions in New York (*Paramus* for *Pyramus*, for example)—also deadens the ability of a script to communicate with an audience. Expectations are confirmed by the visual codes, not challenged toward the discovery of new perceptions. And "house style" migrates as directors copy the ideas of other directors. Let's do *Henry V* with modern weapons! The director, bereft of ideas, forces his concept down on the actors. Why should the actors develop any sense of who they are in this script? In Ron Daniels's awful *Henry V* in Cambridge, Mass. (1995), for example, Williams was a first lieutenant, that is an officer, perhaps of equal rank with Davy Gam, Esquire, and thus within the social level of the aristocracy. That's just wrong. The director, having chosen a current military milieu, had no idea how it worked and could only count on an equivalent ignorance within his audience. (Coursen 1996)

In his discussion of scenic design, Dennis Kennedy defines two codes of signification: the metonymic and the metaphoric. The metonymic is consistent with "the absence it represents." (193, 13) In other words, if Gertrude wears a "medieval Danish costume" or "a seventeenth-century English costume," or whether "a fully detailed illusion of Elsinore" or the Danish court is represented by "a single throne," the "codes require no special effort to read since they remain similar to the process of deciphering that we use in ordinary life, and are within the visual expectations western audiences customarily bring to *Hamlet*." (13)

"An actor wears a metal circle on his head and the audience understands that Claudius is the king." (13) The metonymic code is "iconic." (13)

The metaphoric is "symbolic," as in a "*Hamlet* before a towering monolith, *Richard III* on a giant staircase, *The Winter's Tale* on a floor of green slime." (14) "The metaphoric method of visual encoding reminds us powerfully of the place of the audience in theatrical activity." (14) True, Aristotle's fourth cause is too often neglected as a dynamic component of the dramatic continuum. We figure out what that monolith is. The staircase represents the up and down nature of politics and perhaps the chain-of-being that the "hedgehog" Richard perverts. Green slime for *The Winter's Tale*? Perhaps it represents the nasty algae washing up lately on the seacoast of Bohemia. My own sense is that a bare stage might have been better than some of these "symbols." At least with a bare stage we are free to make our own metaphors.

Kennedy goes on to say that "directors and designers [must] discover new and appropriate performance styles that illuminate the texts yet ring true in a world almost totally transformed, both in and out of the theatre, since their composition." (15)

An element of that transformation, of course, is the production of the plays in media undreamed of in 1600. Each imposes different limitations to scripts designed for three or four specific stages in Shakespeare's time. TV, emerging from radio, can incorporate more language than can film, which derives from the expressive but non-verbal photograph. But TV's limited field of depth makes it a close-up medium. And TV is seldom "live." The source of power is a plug in the wall behind the set, not an audience within the space where the action is happening. Film can give us Agincourt in chivalric combat or muddy slaughter. But film relies on images, and language is only an adjunct to what we see, whether in title cards or words spoken by an actor. TV is a literal medium, but can be stylized into a metadramatic space, as Jane Howell showed brilliantly in her BBC *Henry VI* sequence. Film is flexible enough to combine the literal and the suggestive, as Olivier does in wafting a Disney-scape outward from the gaze of Princess Katherine after her English lesson and in creating the Book of Hours distance into which the victors of Agincourt trudge.

Kennedy's metonymic mode incorporates productions that place the plays in contemporary settings. In such productions our decoding is no decoding at all, merely an inability to go anywhere, imaginatively. Such productions replicate our own worldview as captured in objects and restrict the script to our time. The same shriveling and narrowing occurs when the director says, as he does too often, let's set the play in the Wild West! That is a time distinct from our own, but we have learned its codes and manners from a thousand films and TV shows. The same familiarity—and thus lack of imaginative engagement— does not pertain when a script is placed in an early Victorian setting. There the distinctions between setting and where we sit are clear and the setting, props and costumes will not automatically erase our imaginative engagement with action, character, and language. Class distinctions endemic to both Shakespeare's time and the mid-19th century are also easy to define. Yet the Crystal Palace and Dodge City are contemporaries. Crucially, early Victorian England does not rule out the older ways of looking at the world encoded in the script. The Wild West substitutes its worldview for whatever the script's may be. The "old world" of the Wild West has no history and is being erased as "civilization" marches toward the sunset.

I will argue, then, for productions that retain a link with what the language dictates. Set *Hamlet* where you will, but it must be a world where "foils" exist and where their length is significant when it comes to a duel. And the world of *Hamlet* must have a residual trace of what ritual was—since it vividly does not work in the Elsinore we experience in production. I don't believe that the references to ritual can be edited out of the script, so in a production set in a specific historical moment they can be merely puzzling or can explain why people profess not to understand Shakespeare. When I saw Liviu Ciulei's *Hamlet* in 1978 at the Arena Stage in DC, set in a late 19th century Bismarkian Germany, I understood why Ciulei cut the graveyard scene. Elizabethan burial practices did not translate to this steel world. But why were these post-Darwinians crossing themselves all the time? Concept and script were colliding with each other at some deep level. But the production achieved a brilliant moment when mad Ophelia (Christine Estabrook) intruded upon a state dinner party and used the flowers from the center piece for her distribution of blossoms. It was a powerful collision between formality and the forces that were destroying the appearance of a well-conducted court. The four-sided Arena Stage gave the play a sense of other things happening, particularly when Hamlet paused to soliloquize. Pirates were still marauding on the high seas, Fortinbras was still marching briskly in search of paltry conquests, and plots were being constructed in the shadows of Elsinore. And, when a door was opened in the auditorium, Kristoffer Tabori's Hamlet paused to shout, "Will you please shut that door!" The production definitely intersected with the busy world surrounding it.

In their description of Henryk Tomaszewski's *Hamlet: Ironia and Zoloba,* a pantomime performed in Poland in 1979, Halina Filipowicz and Gary Mead say:

> The whole of Eastern Europe has been involved in a struggle since the death of Stalin to liberate itself politically and culturally, and it is important to place this *Hamlet* not only in the context of Shakespearean performance, but also in the of the effort to achieve artistic freedom... Tomaszewski consciously sought to elaborate... the real political power of the court, its ruthlessness; the paradox of life in the midst of death; and the ultimate success of art in opposition to the dictates of politics. None of this was made so explicit in the performance as to reduce it to a doctrinaire travesty of the original, a reading of the present into the past of the sort that so often flaws attempts to make previous art speak for contemporary society. One of the intellectual beauties of this production was the success with it drew forth the latent contemporary potentialities of *Hamlet* without destroying or distorting the text... The perennial struggle between political will and artistic autonomy focused the production, but without crushing the interest we have in Hamlet's personal tragedy. The two themes were so tightly interwoven as to suggest a revaluation of *Hamlet* that returns it to a more pristine state. (1981, 377)

I am not sure about "pristininity," but I would argue that most efforts to make a script "relevant" by placing it in a perceived present render it instantly irrelevant. The past explains itself to us only in its language and forms, not in our own. The past may help us understand the present, but only if we engage in the making of metaphors, not if we merely reframe a prior culture as if it were our own. It is so only when our imaginations link that world to the potentialities latent in our own lives and the world in which we attempt to live them.

What follows will a) focus on specific productions, that is, on the immediacy from which more considered insights about the scripts can emerge—though the critical process over time incorporates more and more past experience; b) look at some interpretative issues in *Richard II, Henry V, Hamlet* and the question of Ophelia, [2] and *The Tempest* that must, at least, be considered before a production is launched; and c) consider allusions to Shakespeare in films, ancient and current, with particular emphasis on the prevalence of *Romeo and Juliet* in those films. Shakespeare is a strong but often unremarked undercurrent in contemporary film, a voice reminding us of our linguistic and artistic past and projecting that past into a contemporary moment. I continue to be surprised by the number of times that a film will reach back to touch that ongoing flow of energy known as Shakespeare. The instant in the film becomes a brief contact with something at once elusive but also very present in a culture far removed from Elizabethan-Jacobean England. It creates a metaphor between those unlike things—a line from a play by Shakespeare and a film made some 350 or 400 years later. In the case of films, Shakespeare becomes "our own" in surprising ways, sometimes by expanding and illuminating the film in which an allusion appears and sometimes, as in the case of *Romeo and Juliet*, by taking the inherited script and making it a hostage to the contemporary moment. That process makes the script "relevant" but only by ignoring much of what the original contains. That simplification or falsification, however, is typical of much of contemporary Shakespeare in any format.

Where useful, as in essays that deal with more than one play, I have included act/scene/line citations in accordance with David Bevington's *The Complete Works of Shakespeare*. Third Edition. Glenview: Scott, Foresman, 1980.

I

❧

Local Habitations: Scripts Familiar and Strange

When the editors of *Shakespeare Bulletin* decided to eliminate reviews from the Theater at Monmouth, they determined that a company that had been producing excellent versions of the plays for over thirty-five years was no longer worthy of notice. I was unhappy, as a member of the editorial board who had not been consulted about the decision, but delighted to discover that my local newspaper actually paid $85 for each review I wrote. In times like these when I can afford to travel only to Monmouth for live Shakespeare, what a boon! I still believe, though, that local Shakespeare has its place, however humble in the eyes of the establishment, and that it continues to teach us how the scripts work in performance, even if the performance occurs in the remotest nook of a rural state in a town that can no longer support its single restaurant. It is Shakespeare on a shoestring, forced to invent and to improvise. But it does not cut corners. And, crucially, Monmouth has educated its audience over the years as surely as did Shakespeare's theaters over the briefer span of his own career. And so here I will look at some of Monmouth's conventional mountings of the scripts, some successful, some not as successful, as I responded to them at the time. Each teaches us some things about the script as it moves forward in time.

Production is an immediate experience. At the same time, however, I advocate the archival aspect of the critic's work, as conducted for so many years by Jim Lusardi and June Schlueter, who assumed the obligation in *Shakespeare Bulletin* when *Shakespeare Quarterly* ceased, without warning and without warrant, to publish intriguing and valuable reviews from around the world. Productions in smaller venues and isolated locations have as much to teach us as those from the great theatrical companies—sometimes more, because they can embody the innovation that, a few years later, may show up in those grander places. Too often, in the provinces, however, the clichés of contemporary production turn up as "bright ideas." For better or sometimes for worse, these productions are shaping the Shakespearean experience of the many who cannot go to London,

New York, Washington or one of several Stratfords.

Love's Labour's Lost is a difficult play. Monmouth has never done it, and I've only seen it a couple of times on stage—a dreary RSC version and a very good production at Stratford, Ontario. The script demands superb ensemble work and, since it is "about" language, precise diction. Monmouth's presentation was relatively successful.

The advantage of this script lies in its unfamiliarity. Along with *Richard II*, it is among Shakespeare's least-produced plays. Therefore, as Kenneth Branagh's often spritely musical version demonstrated, it can accept treatments that better-known plays tend to resist. Branagh killed his film with a huge and irrelevant production number of "There's No Business like Show Business" that obliterated even the film's thin musical comedy plot. At Monmouth (2007), actors wandered around the auditorium and talked with audience members before the performance began. They did their "pre-game" clasping of hands and then drew the names of their characters from a hat. So—it was all impromptu and a matter of chance and suspended our disbelief with more suspension than usual. The approach allowed Director Bill Van Horn to cast across genders—Berowne was played by Sally Wood, the French Princess by Nick Gallegos (who towered over 'her' suitor), Don Adriano and Boyet by Janis Stevens, and Dumaine and Costard by Mark S. Cartier. Once the production 'style' was established, the audience had no trouble accepting it. It involved only one awkward moment—Dumaine's upstaging entrance during the final scene, after exiting as Costard. We watched Stevens negotiate the "law of reentry" between Acts 2 and 3, and in the final scene, for example, simply by applying or removing Adriano's moustache and beard.

The production was enhanced by a set that incorporated tall panels against a black background. The panels showed a stylized forest, so that they doubled as elegant tapestries or formal paintings in a room of state and as the woodland surrounding the park in which the French ladies are pavilioned. They also permitted the Gentlemen of Navarre to hide and eavesdrop and confront their fellows during the "infant play" that exposes their infatuations. The production was played with the houselights up so as not to separate the fiction from those participating in it. The issue of "race" in the play, which post-modernist critics raise, was dealt with by "race-blind" casting, which found both the Princess and Maria played by African-American actors (Gallegos and Henry Bazemore). This approach was pioneered by Ray Rutan (Virgil Logan as Duncan) in the late 1960s, Joseph Papp (James Earl Jones as Lear) in the 1970s, David Chambers' *Cymbeline* at the Arena, in DC (with Peter Francis James as Posthumus) in the 1980s, and by Robert Egan on the other coast in the early 1990s (with Robert Jason as Bolingbroke in a production that starred Kelsey Grammer as Richard) and it has become accepted practice. And that is good—it opens roles up for the best actors, regardless of race or, as in the case of Monmouth's production, gender.

Sally Wood's Berowne carried the play—as this character must. Berowne has more than twice as many lines as the next two most voluble characters combined (the King and the Princess). During Berowne's soliloquy ("And I, forsooth, in love..."), Wood mimed being hit by the arrows of the Cupid in the old mural above Monmouth's auditorium. The speech was beautifully spoken, making clear the meaning of "But being watched that it may still go right'—that is, a woman is only true if closely monitored. The gender payoff came in having the French Princess explain to the King that the men have, in modern psychological terms, merely projected their self-love upon the "sign of she"—that is, engaged in the classic process of infatuation. That shallowness is signaled in the play by the King's continuation of his suit even when it has become unmannerly in the face of the Princess-Queen's grief. Gallegos played a softly-spoken Princess, a technique that was particularly moving in "her" incomprehension of the King's protestations: "My griefs are double."

The production reached for its "serious" moment when Adriano insisted on respect for Hector: "When he breathed he was a man." The background music for the "Play of the Worthies" ceased, as Adriano lectured the inner audience. This on-stage breaking of dramatic convention—it happens in "Pyramus and Thisbe," "The Murder of Gonzago," and Prospero's Wedding Masque—reminded us that we were *also* watching a play and that we were involved in the construction of that fiction. I felt that the moment somewhat undercut Mercade's entrance, which can be shocking if the messenger is "discovered" within the play-within-the-play. Here it was a conventional entrance, down left.

The production did have its problems. The King's opening speech was a garble, so that one of the premises of the comedy—that he is basing his plan on false assumptions—only became clear when Berowne interrogated the agenda. And thank heavens for Sally Wood's Berowne! At the end, Rosaline's demand that he "enforce the pained impotent to smile" was a mumble, so that the impossibility of the task she assigned was to be understood only in Berowne's "To move wild laughter in the throat of death? It cannot be, it is impossible. Mirth cannot move a soul in agony." With a female Holofernes, the amusing (or to the politically correct, offensive) suggestions about how women have learned under "him" were lost.

In Adriano's disquisition on Hector, Mercade's entrance, and Rosaline's charge to Berowne, the play moves beyond and challenges the agendas of comedy. Shakespeare almost invariably issues that challenge, but usually through a character like Egeus, Shylock, Jacques, Malvolio and Sir Andrew, Parolles, or *The Tempest's* Antonio, characters who refuse to join hands in the "dancing measures" of the endings, or who are ineligible due to their religion or their class or their sheer incapacity. The final song of *Love's Labour's Lost* distinguishes between folly and wisdom, which is the argument of comedy, and separates actors and audience. It was wonderfully delivered by Stevens but was upstaged by an attendant who collected props from the actors. That reacquisition of company property signaled that the game was over, of course, but anyone who has taken Directing 101 knows you don't do that while one of your actors is speaking. Stevens, who delivered a flamboyant Spaniard and a clever and cynical Boyet, deserved better at the hands of her director.

Still, in spite of some reservations, I applaud Monmouth's willingness to bring this rarely heard script forward. The blending of genders and races made it eminently worthwhile. This script, along with *Shrew* and *As You Like It*, interrogates stereotypes and exposes the assumptions made on their basis. *Love's Labour's Lost* questions the premises of its own genre by deferring, if not canceling, the "comic ending." What better way to suggest what the play is all about than by undermining an audience's inherited assumptions about race and gender through "non-traditional" casting decisions?

Production values can challenge what Robert Weimann calls the "locus" of a script—its hierarchical and conservative values—with "platea"—that is, theatrical techniques that transform the script into a medium that speaks to us and to our ways of understanding it, that thus make the production much more than an intriguing visit to a culture that is no longer ours, a visit that must be accompanied by notes from a college professor. (Weimann 1988) Furthermore, the performances of Sally Wood and Janis Stevens made this production sparkle during the moments when they were in charge.

Sally Wood's *Othello* (2006) was an awkward affair.

The problem lay in the leads who dominate the play. Of First Folio's 3572 lines, Iago has 1098, while Othello has 891. Unfortunately, Adam Heffernan's Iago was often incomprehensible. We must grasp Iago's every syllable to recognize that his explanations don't explain a thing, except to suggest that he cannot articulate his anger. Most actors these days suggest a racial-sexual rage which the rationalist Iago cannot access. He doesn't have a complex. The complex has him. We sense the "controller" being controlled by some power prior to his assumption of rationality. It is as if a serpent has learned to think and to speak. Iago's downstage center soliloquies were spotlighted, with the stage behind him darkened, so that his musings were part of *our* universe of meanings. This technique worked brilliantly for his first soliloquy ("Thus do I ever make my fool my purse"). The effect was augmented by the bright red robe he wore. But we needed a calm, understated approach framed for this small, shallow auditorium. That would have forced us to provide the power, the subtext for the words. Heffernan sometimes rushed past the signals. "You are a senator"—an insult in any culture—emerged without attitude. When Heffernan spoke about Cassio's wiping his beard with Desdemona's handkerchief, he gave the line none of its concupiscent suggestiveness. Charles Waters' Othello was at times clearly spoken, at other times all aroar, so that we understood a fury in the words but not the words. Underplaying is almost invariably the way to go in smaller spaces, as it is on film and TV. At moments, as in Othello's "This fellow's of exceeding honesty" soliloquy, I did not get the sense that Waters understood what Othello was saying. A soliloquy is invariable a "figuring out," an expression of what the character believes to be true. It should never resemble a recitation. Othello and Iago made a great moment of their discussion of how to kill Desdemona. Iago's "do it not with poison" did indeed suggest that he does not want Othello to employ Iago's methods. While the pace of the production was blessedly brisk, it might have slowed just a bit to let us experience Othello treading the fatal carpet of his own rhetoric as he lands on Cyprus. We understand his ecstasy, but we should also grasp the lethal hyperbole he unleashes. I was not, then, convinced of

the process whereby Iago ensnared Othello. Nor did I believe Othello's sol-
diership. His "put up your bright swords" should convince us of who he
claims to be, as should his final reassumption of command. The speech, in
which Othello mourns his "occupation gone," then, carried no sense of a
fabulous past departing like a dream. Lawrence Fishburne, though robbed of
many of Othello's lines in the Parker film (1995) had just portrayed a fighter
pilot in *The Tuskegee Airmen* (1995), and it was a good east-running runway for
a depiction of Shakespeare's warrior.

An index of the production's awkwardness was Othello's crouching
downstage while Iago and Cassio, upstage, discussed Bianca (4.1.110 ff). The
lines suggest that Othello observes them: "Look how he laughs already!" And
I question the editing. Of course, cut Iago's misogyny on the wharf as all
await Othello's arrival and Desdemona's banter with the Clown as she seeks
Cassio. But Iago lost "Divesting them for bed" (2.3.193), after "like bride and
groom," a seemingly innocent simile, but a telling initial thrust at Othello's
sexuality and a description of what he and Desdemona have just been doing.
For some reason, Othello's interrogation of Desdemona about the handkerchief and his subsequent description of its supernatural origins were gone.
This omission was unfortunate because Lindsay Torrey effectively expressed
Desdemona's endearing naiveté and thus captured the difference in ages that
the script (but not Shakespeare's source) defines. Also gone was Othello's
powerful comment to Desdemona about her upbraiding look "when we shall
meet at compt." He stabbed himself after his "base Indian" (Quarto's dull
choice) "threw a pearl away richer than all his tribe." Why delete the lines that
demonstrate that Othello is executing an enemy of the state who happens
to be himself and that validate his heroic self-conception? Surely some of
the 17 or so lines describing confessions found and uttered can be sacrificed
for the sake of speeding up the second half of the play without denying us
some of the play's greatest poetry—although Roderigo's almost posthumous
confession eerily parallels Desdemona's dying lie. Othello killed Desdemona
with a suffocating kiss, borrowing Ronald Colman's technique with Signe
Hasso in *A Double Life* ((1947), but arousing some unfortunate laughter from
the audience.

Othello is a tricky script. Olivier's Othello was powerful on the Old Vic
stage, but Frank Finlay's lithe and clever Iago stole the film version from an

Olivier who imported his stage performance to the camera. At the Winter Garden in 1980, Christopher Plummer had so demoralized James Earl Jones in rehearsals that the latter merely went through the motions as Othello and became an empty suit of armor. But Trevor Nunn at the Other Place in 1989, with Ian McKellen, Willard White, Imogen Stubbs, and Zoe Wanamaker, showed how to deliver the play quietly but powerfully within a limited space. The subsequent TV version (1990) continues to demonstrate to actors and directors how the script can work. The value of the Monmouth production was that it showed the difficulties that the play presents to those who would perform it but not the solving of them.

A Midsummer Night's Dream may have been presented as part of an aristocratic wedding in the 1590s. The script does not employ some of the structural elements usually available to Shakespeare, like an "above" (for Juliet's balcony) or a "discovery space." The action seems to occur in the "available space" of a great hall in a palace or mansion. Oberon has merely to say "I am invisible" and so he is for the characters on stage. Some scholars speculate that Queen Elizabeth attended. Oberon's reference to "the imperial vot'ress" is taken as a graceful allusion to the Virgin Queen. (Bevington, 236)

Elizabeth's possible presence helps us understand the play. It is all about rule, a mirror for a Christian queen. The rational Theseus must try to control the passions of the younger generation, particularly when a father (Egeus) wishes to marry daughter Hermia to Demetrius. She prefers Lysander. This gets sorted out when Theseus, at the end, comes out in favor of romantic love. Oberon, King of the Fairies, tries to bring his consort, Titania, under control. He uses chemicals on her and on the lovers who have escaped to the woods. His manipulations consume most of this short play. Peter Quince attempts to shape a drama out of a radically unpromising script, whose short rhymed lines conflict with its tragic content, and from a company that has no understanding of how drama works. Quince, like Shakespeare, through Puck at the end, is also hoping that his royal audience will approve his play. If anyone doubts that a playwright wrote these plays, incidentally, let him look to Quince, who is Shakespeare asking his audience—you think this is easy, this production of plays? The question is launched in the midst of Shakespeare's first masterpiece, a kind of "control" within the superb poetry and the dazzling complications of the rest.

Although always a very popular play, *Dream* challenges a company. It demands a depth of acting talent and a skillful balancing of several ongoing narratives. It must move quickly, but it cannot confuse us as it goes.

Sally Wood's *Dream* (2007) reached for a "dark" version of the script. And that is legitimate. The play explores the shadows cast by patriarchy and rationality and the sexual tension lurking beneath propriety. Wood's was fast-paced, usually clear, and often violent. The set was spare, with only a large Japanese lantern standing in for the moon. Puck controlled its illumination with a flick of his fingers, thus lending an appropriate metadramatic touch to the proceedings. The production got a standing ovation on the night I attended.

But for me, it was not as good as the 1971 production of *Dream* at Monmouth, directed by Robert Joyce, with Lee McClelland and William Meisle at their height of their considerable powers, or as Richard Sewell's 1982 version with the magnificent Maryann Plunkett as an ethereal Titania. Sewell created a Victorian world, with Lysander as a young Tennyson and Demetrius a subaltern in a good regiment.

I am not a fan of doubling Theseus and Hippolyta with Oberon and Titania. Yes, Peter Brook did it in his famous 1970 production, suggesting that the characters in the court are as consciousness to their unconscious counterparts in Fairyland, but the technique tends to merge the zones of court and forest. R. Chris Reeder's Theseus seemed to be warming up for his Oberon. The later Theseus, though, was much calmer and really did contrast with his woodland counterpart. Melissa Graves' Hippolyta was at best ambivalent at the outset, in chains, attracted to Theseus, but angry at his edict on Hermia. She was reconciled at the end, but seemingly *before* Theseus had acceded to the pairings that had been established. As Titania she was angry. The production's pace permitted her to slow down for her big speech on the seasons, but she rushed angrily through it. We may not know what "the nine men's morris" is, but the actor must, and "rheumatic" must be pronounced as the line renders it, not as we would say it today. I could not discern much conviction in Graves' Titania as she described the vicarious pregnancy that has so upset Oberon. Anna Soloway's Helena also tended to overpower her early soliloquy, so that her later vulnerability was not anticipated. She simply went further over the top. If we take the young lovers as "real people," they are very unfunny, as Michael

Hoffman's recent film showed us. If they are trying to "be themselves" within a situation of which they are unaware, they are very funny, as was Christine Baranski's Helena in a Joseph Papp production of years ago, trying to reestablish her dignity as she pulled on her long gloves after having had some of her clothes ripped off. Monmouth's young women were powerhouses, capable of tossing their men around like mannequins. I felt that they too easily reconciled with their men and each other after waking up. In Liviu Ciulei's production some years ago in DC, some residual sting from their nightmare remained as they wandered out of the woods. I did appreciate Will Harrell's slightly thuggish Demetrius.

The doubling that worked was that of the mechanicals and the fairies. When Bottom arrived at Titania's bower, he was greeted by people he knew, as he seemed vaguely to grasp. It was a "Wizard of Oz" effect and a good one. Wood achieved a particularly dazzling transition when Molly Schrieber's Starveling suddenly became Moth and encountered Michael Anthony's Puck. Quince & Company did a fine job—too too solid fairies perhaps but skillfully inept as actors in 'Pyramus and Thisbe' The latter were led by an engaging Dustin Tucker. Mike Anthony's Puck and R. Chris Reeder's Oberon were amusing as they watched the antics of the young lovers, popcorn boxes in hand, as if the lovers were performing in a Mickey and Judy flick.

Monmouth could use a dramaturge. It is simply not true as a note told us that this play has no sources. It has many, including Plutarch, Chaucer, Ovid, Scott, and probably Apuleius and Caesare Ripa. For some reason, Director Wood cut Oberon's lovely aubade ("But we are spirits of another sort") and almost all of the debate between Theseus and Hippolyta in which Theseus' case for rationality is trumped by her insistence on the congruity of the stories of the night. He is delighted to be interrupted by the approach of the lovers. The oscillation between reality and dream and the primacy of the latter is central to this play. Spectators may not notice the absence of some superb poetry, but they will appreciate its presence if well presented. It makes no sense for Hermia to say something like "yet sat smiling at his cruel prey" when she means to indicate Lysander. And Shakespeare's choice of an accented or unaccented "ed" was consistently unobserved. It gives Shakespeare flexibility in his use of the iambic line and is essential to the rhythm of that line, as in "Lamenting some enforc*ed* chastity." The final song, blessedly not Mendelssohn, took time away not just from the script but also from the actors, who delivered the microhone to each other with superb technique but who did not always deliver the play with the same facility. I would trade "Dream Lover" anytime to get back some Shakespeare.

Measure for Measure is one of Shakespeare's least-produced plays, though it has become more popular recently.

The heroine, Isabella, is not a powerful Katharine, resisting her father's marriage auction, a resourceful Rosalind, educating her lover out of his infatuation, or a lovelorn Viola, trapped in her disguise even as she presses Orsino's suit to Olivia. Isabella is a severe young woman seeking a place in the restrictive order of St. Clare but pulled from her novitiate by her brother Claudio's plight. He is about to be beheaded for impregnating his girlfriend just a bit short of all legal ceremony.

Claudio is in jeopardy because the easy-going Duke, Vincentio, has apparently left Vienna and placed a strict Deputy in charge. Angelo, the Deputy, dusts off the old laws and applies them rigorously. He, like many present-day hypocrites, is particularly obsessed with sexual offenses.

Isabella makes a powerful appeal to Angelo, invoking the Sermon on the Mount: "ask your heart what it doth know That's like my brother's fault. If it confess A natural guiltiness such as is his Let it not sound a thought upon your tongue Against my brother's life." And as she makes this plea—Zap! Angelo is smitten: "She speaks and 'tis Such sense as my sense breeds with it." The guilt that Nature confers on all is suddenly his.

Isabella communicates, as Claudio says, with "a prone and speechless dialect." We would call that "sex appeal" nowadays, and the once impervious Angelo falls within its spell. He promises to save Claudio if Isabella will yield to him, a perverse version of measure for measure. She, having no one to complain to, lashes out at poor Claudio, who, after all, hopes that she can save him from an imminent beheading. Angelo, believing he has consummated his relationship with Isabella, via a shadowy liaison with the Mariana he has rejected, reneges on his promise to spare Claudio. The "absent" Duke, in disguise as a friar, must exercise his ingenuity to make things come out right.

At the end, in pleading for Angelo, Isabella makes a legalistic defense: "I partly think A due sincerity govern'd his deeds Till he did look on me." That is not exactly St. Matthew.

Isabella, then, is at best a problematic heroine and the play is not a comedy but a "problem play" that raises deeper problems than comedy can resolve. Angelo has closed Vienna's brothels, and that underworld provides a subplot that suggests that some aspects of society are absolutely resistant to any efforts at imposing order.

If it is "about" something, the play deals with justice. It is the only play in Shakespeare's canon that takes its title from the Bible, the passage in the Sermon on the Mount that tells us to judge not lest we be judged.

The Duke disguised as a friar—in the old "once upon a time the king made himself up like a common man and went out among his people" motif that Shakespeare also uses in *Henry V*—has been there all along, of course. He returns as Duke to expose Angelo and responds to Isabella's "prone and speechless dialect"—that subtext of sexuality—by proposing to her. Does she accept? She did until John Barton's Estelle Kohler in 1970 refused Sebastian Shaw's Duke and got herself to the nunnery.

Monmouth mounted an excellent version of this play in 1971 with Lee McClelland and Peter Michael Webster as Novitiate and Deputy. The major problem with Richard Sewell's production was that it did not integrate the role of the Duke (Gary Filsinger), who remained outside the action, a kind of unmoved mover.

Jeri Pitcher's 2006 version incorporated R. Chris Reeder's Duke within the wide compass of judgment. Once he exposed Angelo, this Duke exercised ruthless control over everyone. At the end, Reeder and his character showed us what he has been all about all along. Anna Soloway's Isabella lent a radiant centrality to this production. Her passionate defense of her chastity awakened what juices remained in Mark S Cartier's dry prune Angelo and, just as perversely, roused the desire of the moralistic Duke. Soloway lit up the stage, communicating as the script suggests, the opposite of what she intends. This production knew, as Shakespeare anticipated, that the action takes place in Sigmund Freud's hometown and subtly probed the psyches of the major characters. Chris O'Carroll delivered a conscientious Escalus, way over his head in an out of control Vienna, Dustin Tucker's Claudio was trapped by his having already lived a little too much and his understandable desire to live longer. He delivered the "Aye, but to die" speech, a chilling disquisition on the after-death, with the power it deserves. Patrick Pope achieved a self-amused and amusing

Pompey. Marcy Amell was a convincing Mariana, asserting her love for the sainted/tainted Angelo in spite of all of his radically unlovable qualities and actions. Dennis Price's Lucio lacked nuance, but the character came into his own in his witty interruptions in the final scene. The production emphasized that Lucio, who has mercilessly berated the absent Duke to the disguised Duke, is the only one punished at the end of the play. The shifting finger of judgment finally pointed at the Duke. A reluctant Isabella yielded to his control at the end, suggesting in her bewildered silence that she had no choice.

Chez Cherry's gothic set incorporated stained-glass windows and iron bars that neatly enclosed convent, prison and city. Clinton O'Dell's opulent costumes—conservative but elegant for the rulers, flamboyant for Lucio—embodied the tug-of-war in Vienna between rigidity and license. Isabella's white gown was a site on which this conflict was inscribed. Lynne Chase's subtle and constantly shifting lighting was superb.

Congratulations to Monmouth for giving us a splendid version of a rarely produced and difficult script.

II

❧

Local Shakespeare and Anachronism

Davis Robinson's *Measure for Measure* at Bowdoin College in November 2008 featured a chain link fence against which prisoners in orange jump suits were slumped. This, I take it, was Guantanamo. But the prison in Shakespeare's play is neither a reflex of tyranny nor a byproduct of a war against terror. It is, like most prisons, a home for the guilty and for the refuse of society that has neither a place to live nor to hide. It is the most prison-like of Shakespeare's prison, worthy of a Foucaultian analysis. In *I Henry VI*, the prison is irrelevant. It is necessary, however, so that the dying Mortimer can chronicle the past to Plantangenet. The prison in *Richard III* incorporates Clarence s detailed nightmare and Richard's delectation at being the villain within it. Richard II's prison provides time for his solitary contemplation. Malvolio's imprisonment represents a symbolic, Dantean punishment in self-inflicted darkness. In *Cymbeline*, Posthumous is visited by a reassuring dream. The prison in *Measure for Measure* shows the workings of a prison—the presentation of warrants, the preparations for execution. Although its Provost is a good person, he is the functionary of authority, good or bad. The prison has sucked in all of the diseases that float in the surrounding cesspool of Vienna. It is therefore very modern but does not make a convincing metaphor with Guantanamo. As we consider that half of the metaphor, we are distracted from the prison that Shakespeare presents.

A more dynamic approach, as Robert Smallwood reports, was to stage the opening as a coup, with the Duke euphemizing the event, then going underground to affect a counter-coup. Michael Boyd's RSC production of *Measure for Measure* (1998) found "Robert Glenister's Duke alone and in apparent collapse... his dukedom (somewhere in the Balkans in the early twentieth century...) on the verge of... destruction... ready for the *coup* that was soon made manifest by the smashing down of the door in Laertes-like rebellion... [T]he Duke just preserved the fiction of having voluntarily abdicating power before it was taken from him perforce [by Angelo]." (Smallwood, 1999) Such an approach renders the play very modern and the script very dynamic. Predictably, "It divided the critics in the national press, the left largely in favor, the right very hostile." (241) Modernized Shakespeare usually seems subversive to the status quo, with *Henry V* sometimes a jingoistic exception. David Thacker 's police state 1995 Vienna was a culture of surveillance, full of hidden cameras and listening devices, precursor of George Bush's Amerika. (Coursen 2002, 59-66) It was also an example of Foucault's description of society's emulation of the modern prison's constant eye on its inhabitants. (1975)

When I heard that Monmouth's *Shrew* (2006) was a Wild West version, I thought, Oh No! Having seen the wit and bandying of *Much Ado* trampled by that concept, and the aristocratic concerns of *Twelfth Night* completely massacred by it (Olivia as Miss Kitty, presiding over her bordello), I was prepared to dismiss Monmouth's *Shrew* automatically. It would be a "don't try to understand 'em, just ride and rope and brand 'em" interpretation, another bright idea that casts the script into outer darkness.

I was wrong. The concept was lightly employed, at times merely a placing of the script in an American frontier setting. Michael Anthony's Grumio was inept with his pistol and carbine, and very funny—though an ex-military type like me cannot totally relax when witnessing a careless use of firearms. Accents—Bianca's southern, Gremio's Slim Pickens—were somewhat distracting, but Director David Greenham's approach gave Sally Wood's Kate a "through line." She could be strong and assertive early on, and, as a girl of the golden west, quite understandably admiring of masculine qualities at the end, as she showed when she put her arm around her father in her final speech. Although that final speech was unironic, it did *not* signal a surrender. Rather, Kate was saying, "This is who I am, too!—for all my femininity." Firearms were not deployed in the second half of the production. Kate had proved that she was "quick on the draw." We accepted her ability to go along with (and better) Petruchio's game with Vincentio and her accurate appraisal of the scenario that Petruchio had constructed in the final scene. One of the strongest performances was that of Nick Gallegos as Hortensio, often just a nonentity in any *Shrew* production. Gallegos carried himself like a great black crow, or perhaps a character out of Dickens (Bradley Headstone) and was very amusing—almost (but not quite) an upstage crow. Frank Omar was wonderful as Baptista—obviously liking Petruchio and finding his antics very funny, even as they enraged Kate. Omar created an anticipatory sense of welcome to the Minola family to which Kate finally acceded.

The production rushed along (as it should) and only Timothy Davis-Reed as Petruchio seemed to be rushing himself. Some of the hilarious and also profound elements of the "road to Padua" scene at the end of Act IV were lost in Davis-Reed's hasty delivery. Another problem was that Vincentio was a young man, so that Petruchio's "old, wrinkled, faded, wither'd" seemed as wildly inaccurate as his "Fair lovely maid" had been moments earlier. The scene anticipates Henry V's wooing of another Kate ("or rather the sun and not the moon"), but it was a muddle here. Too bad. It is perhaps Shakespeare's greatest early scene, a precursor of so many that will follow. Having an energetic, female "Biondella" (Tracie Merrill) may have been a casting necessity, but the change in gender argued favorably for Petruchio as someone much more than just a male "tamer." In the script Biondello is a "reflector" of Petruchio, in a Jamesian sense, which is a version of the more rounded, major character. That Biondella, a *woman*, already understood Petruchio signaled Kate's coming to awareness of who this crazy suitor really is.

Interestingly, in a Wild West context, Biondella's disquisition about equine ailments was excised—"lampass, windgalls, staggers, bots," etc. A more logical but unfortunate victim of the editing was Tranio's upping Gremio's "argosy" with "three great argosies, besides two galliases, And twelve tight galleys." Argosies are hard to float in the dust of Dodge, but Tranio's expanded fantasy is great fun for the actor and audience and a reinforcement of the "dream" theme of the play. As so often in Shakespeare's early comedies, roles are reversed so that "proper" societal relationships can be established. Tranio fulfills this function, and in one production I recall, his wooing of Bianca was so successful that it argued a subversion of established patterns beyond the end of the play. That was Bill Alexander's 1992 version for the Royal Shakespeare Company, wherein Bill McCabe's Tranio became Jonson's Mosca—man become master—and was obviously planning something with Rebecca Saire's Bianca at play's end. As in *Much Ado*, it was proxy wooing run amuck but not contained by comic closure. McCabe and Saire challenged the "containment" of Kate by Petruchio. We got none of that dangerous undertone here, in spite of the "lawless" territory in which the script was placed.

I did hear some strange words. Grumio calls Gremio a "stripling," not a "stripeling," which is a fish. Petruchio says "politicly," not "politically," a word Shakespeare does not use. And the word is "froward," not "forward," a word in early Shakespeare that appears almost exclusively in *Shrew*.

But I quibble. The myth explored by Greenham's production was the coming of order to the West, as in Crane's "The Bride Comes to Yellow Sky" and in films like *Broken Lance* and *Shane*. Monmouth's *Shrew* demonstrated why people go to Shakespeare. It was rapid, wittily sketched, clearly spoken for the most part, and entertaining—without ignoring the inevitable truth that the play 'means' something. Here it meant that a "bright idea" need not render Shakespeare's script the depressed aspect of bi-polarity, but can be a vehicle for showing us how the script works when challenged by chaps and spurs as opposed to merely settling into doublet and hose. This version ended neatly with a sleeping Petruchio-Sly completing the frame by waking up just as Kate wandered by. He pursued her to what we assumed was to be a happy ending in the waking world as it had been in the extended dream he had enjoyed as master while wrapped in his serapé. And we spectators came out into the waking stars, savoring the happy dream that Monmouth had delivered to us.

Monmouth's *Merchant of Venice* (2008), directed by Jeri Pitcher, was an effective take on the play. The production left its audience somewhat puzzled, still responding to the questions it raises. And that is good. *Merchant* is a "problem play," probing at issues that can't be resolved by the "happily-ever-after" comic ending.

The problem is more than Shylock. He is an outsider, a consciously alienated being who recognizes the irrational and inexpressible qualities that can underlie human motivation. His comedy ended when his wife Leah died, probably in childbirth (though that is not said in the play). Suffice it that Shylock would not embrace "Christian culture," even if asked. And he isn't asked. His forced conversion is a punishment and, if he does not willingly accept Christianity, he is, as the Reformation theology tells us, damned.

The problem, though, is also Portia, trapped in a lottery by her father's will, with a bunch of unsuitable men vying for the golden fleece. We hear of some of them—princes, counts, and ducal nephews, who frown, or drink, or shoe their horses—and we see the florid Morocco and the fatuous Aragon in action.

But here, the men of Venice seemed hardly better. Bassanio (Dustin Tucker) was a pint-sized fortune hunter. Antonio (Dan Olmstead) was dark, handsome, and clothed in bespoke suits, but it seemed he didn't "like girls." The only men in Venice with any vitality were Dennis A. Price's fat slob anti-Semite, Gratiano—and Shylock (Bill Van Horn).

So, within this production, Portia must become a man. Within the script, she did so, literally, with a vengeance. She drove Shylock into his own trap. The revenger inevitably falls into the trap he has constructed for others, from the Old Testament, to Marlowe's Barabas, to Shakespeare's Claudius and Laertes. And then, Portia gets that Freudian ring back so that she can reconfer it upon Bassanio. In control at last, she dictates the ending. In this production, the ending was uneasy. Portia and Bassanio looked at each other, he saying, in effect, I still don't know you, but I am just a bit afraid of you, and she saying, in effect, I know you and so far I don't like what I know.

Those women in Shakespeare—boy actors, of course—who assume male disguise define their attitudes toward men and thus their own self-perceptions by what they say about the male role they assume. Of all those characters— Julia, Portia and Jessica, Rosalind, Viola, and Imogen—Portia is the harshest toward "these bragging jacks" that she is about to imitate. And that is understandable. Furthermore, the script does not suggest that Portia, like Rosalind and Viola, readily reassumes her feminine role and thus accepts the reestablishment of balanced gender relations at the end of the play.

Anna Soloway's lissome Portia was not helped by the modernization of the script. A lawyer's robes and hat permit us to suspend our disbelief as we watch the play. Portia's suit and feminine voice encouraged doubt in what we witnessed and suggested a lesbian's effort to pass as a man. This production is set in 1961, the year after Bill Mazeroski's famous home run off Ralph Terry over the left field wall at Forbes Field on 13 October, 1960. Shylock had a tattoo from Buchenwald on his left arm and the ladies wore Jackie O, fanny-hugging dresses. Miranda Libkin's disguise as the Clerk was wonderful. She looked like a teenage Al Capone.

This production, though, needed a more powerful Portia to offset Shylock's energy and to convince us that, given the chance, Portia can dominate the male world that has victimized her. A very effective custodian of her beautiful mountain, this Portia did not accompany her descent to Venice with the pent up power that has been latent until she is free of the paralysis her father has imposed upon her.

One wonderful moment occurred when Ian Austin's Morocco was drowning his disappointment with a couple of Peronis at a Venetian bar. Shylock walked over to him and asked "And if you prick us, do we not bleed?" Morocco had already claimed that his blood was as red as that of Portia's other suitors, and here, the two outsiders were nicely linked.

At the end, Jessica read the letter describing her father's dispossession. She had fled him. Now she mourned him by singing a Jewish hymn. She had escaped neither her own identity nor her complicity in her father's fall. She lives, as Arnold says, "between two worlds, one dead, the other powerless to be born." This ending borrowed from Jonathan Miller's production which closed with Jessica listening to the off-stage voice of Laurence Olivier's Shylock singing The Kaddish, the Jewish prayer for the dead.

Neither of the two value systems in the play—Shylock's "eye for eye" from Exodus or Portia's "quality of mercy" from Matthew—prevailed. Greed was the basis of human motive until Shylock abandoned it for pure hatred. At the end of the play, we were left with no basis for ethical behavior, or for love.

The reason for pulling the script toward our own times, of course, was to suggest that it still applies. It does, and the production made that point powerfully. But it did not need a modernization to do so.

Having described a variety of irrational responses to such things as pigs and cats and bagpipes, Shylock says "So can I give no reason" for such reactions. "Are you answered?" he asks the Duke. "This is no answer," Bassanio responds. Indeed it is not. And, to this production's credit, it did not try to give an answer.

The Winter's Tale (circa 1610) reflects the trend of the first decade of the seventeenth century away from tragedy and toward a mixed genre in which seeming tragedy swings at the end to reconciliation and reunion. Shakespeare himself originates the tragi-comedy in *Antony and Cleopatra*. After Antony's fall—a tragedy of world-shaking proportions—Cleopatra creates an alternative ending, in which she and Antony will live free of Caesar's interference: "I am again for Cydus," she says, dying, "to meet Marc Antony."

Such endings rule out inconveniences like gravity, politics or the finality of death. They exist in the world of glimmering shape and shadow that Hawthorne describes as the locale of the romance. The god Jupiter appears in thunder and lightning perched upon an eagle. Prospero summons up a wedding masque from spirits dwelling on a magic island. *The Winter's Tale* glides past sixteen years in thirty-two lines to waft us to an idyllic zone wherein a prince woos a lovely shepherd maid, Perdita. She is, of course, a princess, in this version of the Cinderella story, and her identity is finally revealed. Her mother, Hermione, comes to life at last and all is happily-ever-after—though the joys of the ending are muted by the time it has taken and by the long-ago deaths of Antigonus ("pursued [and consumed] by a bear") and of the young prince, Mamillius. But the boy actor who had played Mamillius would also have played his sister, Perdita, so Shakespeare's audience would have sensed that time itself had a restorative finale in mind. (Mahood 1992) This play really does incorporate a tragedy—that of Leontes—and is the only one I know where Shakespeare intentionally deceives us, in the case of the "death" of Hermione. He usually lets us in on things—as when the Chorus and characters in the play inform us about the traitors in *Henry V*, or when Hamlet tells us in soliloquy (and then informs Horatio) about the play he is planning for Claudius, or when Imogen comes across a headless corpse of Cloten and believes it to be Posthumus. We enjoy the privileged position known as dramatic irony.

Bill Van Horn's version for The Theater at Monmouth only partially succeeded in moving us into the strange and unpredictable world of the play. Strong performances like that of Janis Stevens as the vehement Paulina, Dan Olmstead as the brooding madman, Leontes, who falsely accuses Hermione of adultery with Polixenes, Dennis A. Price as the foolish Clown, and Miranda Libkin as Perdita were undercut by concept and intrusive music. When music competes with language the language loses. Thus was Leontes' "Too hot, too hot" aside wiped out by a mournful accordion. Antigonus's magnificent transitional soliloquy was obliterated by music and approaching storm. From where I sat I could see no bear—though I am told that a shadowy shape with a bear's head did appear on stage and was visible from the first couple of rows—and Zach Greenham's subsequent description of Antigonus's fate was incomprehensible. Unless we knew the play, we did not know what has happened to him.

The concept was—for no useful reason—nineteenth century Maine. That eliminated Hermione's significant line about her father having been emperor of

Russia, as she (Jeri Pitcher) asserted her identity and implicated Leontes in the terrible future he is inflicting on himself and—since he is king—on everyone else. Ladies from Christmas Cove tend not to have Russian monarchs as parents. And I doubt that many people in Boothbay Harbor in 1830 were awaiting word from the Oracle at Delphi. The very-nice-clambake problem was less apparent in the Bohemia scenes, simply because the concept was dropped. There, some judicious editing would have kept Autolocus (Dustin Tucker) from becoming tedious in his repetitious interplay with the rustics. Why Leontes lost his "What fine chisel could ever yet cut breath?" though, was inexplicable. The line reiterates the play's consistent concern with the difference between nature and art and its exploration of Shakespeare's grand theme of appearance versus reality. (I am told that the line was in the performance script. It must have been dropped on the night I attended).

One excellent directorial touch, however, in the second to last scene, found the narrative of discovery and reunion artfully distributed among members of the cast. And Jeri Pitcher's statue neatly recaptured her earlier assertion of stoical resolve.

In Shakespeare, the spoken line is the bottom line. Here, the words tended to compete against sound and concept and, as must happen, the words lost out.

Julius Caesar is always seeking contemporary relevance. In 1937, as fascism threatened Europe, Orson Welles and the Mercury Theater produced a version in which Welles vastly oversimplified the issues by making Caesar a fascist. Antony's oration played out against long red banners and klieg lights. Whatever he is, Caesar is the person in charge. Remove him and anarchy must result. A few slogans that anticipate the sentiments of Locke's "Second Treatise on Government" are no substitute for a power vacuum. The neo-cons who conned us into the invasion of Iraq had forgotten their 10th grade reading.

John Houseman tells us that during one performance of the Welles' production, a New York city fireman in uniform stood in the background of the assassination scene. Another time, a delivery boy delivered one of Welles's suits across the stage during a performance and took another one out to be cleaned, without disturbing the funeral orations. (Houseman 303) This was an intensely "modernist" episode, as Auden's "Musee des Beaux Arts" would remind us. Even amid the violence of anarchy turning to chaos there must always be some who require a well-pressed pinstripe. Modern dress versions do have their advantages, but they seldom deliver the complexity of the Shakespearean script.

But Welles's *Julius Caesar* may have been an exception to my objection to updating productions. As Houseman says, "The decision to use modern dress was not an economic decision and it was not conceived as a stunt. It was an essential element in Orson's conception of *Julius Caesar* as a political melodrama with clear contemporary parallels. All over the Western world sophisticated democratic structures were breaking down. First in Italy and then in Germany, dictatorships had taken over; the issues of political violence and the moral duty of the individual in the face of tyranny had become urgent and inescapable. To emphasize the similarity between the last days of the Roman republic and the political climate of Europe in the mid-thirties, our Roman aristocrats wore military uniforms with black belts that suggested but did not exactly reproduce the current fashion of the Fascist ruling class; our crowd wore the dark, nondescript street clothes of the big-city proletariat." (298-99) The question remains, though, whether Brutus's response to Caesar's *potential* tyranny, a possibility that, as Brutus admits, runs counter to his knowledge of Caesar, is justified. Tyranny seems a *result* of Caesar's assassination.

Welles made one decision that, for me, would be crucial to modern dress adaptations of any play. He "eliminated all formal battle scenes and, with them, all need for armor and weaponry. The only arms seen on our stage were the daggers of the assassins and short, bayonet-like blades for the final suicides." (Houseman, 299) Plays like *I Henry IV* and *Richard III*, if modernized, inevitably suffer a collision between language and visualization. One cannot eliminate Shrewsbury or Bosworth Field. Philippi involves parley and reports of battle and occurs, according to Welles's stage direction on "The Plains of Philippi."

The toga-clad Mankiewicz film of 1953 sought parallels with Mussolini in its use of monuments and spectacle; but, for its audience, it was all about McCarthyism. (Crowl 1994, 149-150) Since Louis Calhern was Caesar in the production, it was filled with busts of Calhern. I wonder whether he snared any for his mantlepiece. The film betrays its plastic premises by making Philippi an ambush at Drygulch—Antony and his wild Indians lurking in the hills as Brutus and the cavalry march confidently into a trap. The film is worth watching for Gielgud's assertive Cassius as he overwhelms passive, soft-voiced James Mason's Brutus, and for Brando's powerful combination of passion and cynicism in his oration. Had the film given us a late 1930s fascist setting, a la Welles, it would, ironically, have failed to link itself with its contemporary moment. As it is, its black-and-white photography has a powerful documentary effect, particularly in the oration scenes—the crowd swarming below the dangerously steep steps of the Capitol.

The version at Portland Stage attempted to draw energy from the upcoming U.S. 2008 election. The characters wore suits and skirts, communicated via cell phone, and, if Caesar, had Secret Service types prowling the edges of events. One of them betrayed Caesar by failing to intervene in the assassination. A giant TV screen above the marble playing space gave us images of storm and mob. This production looked very much like David Thacker's 1993 production for the Royal Shakespeare Company at The Other Place in Stratford. Thacker's production included a gurney for Caesar's body, bemedalled aristocrats and other contemporary trappings.

Julius Caesar has its anachronisms—doublets and striking clocks in Rome, for example. And some scripts will work in generalized modern contexts: *Richard II* and *Much Ado about Nothing*, for example. But productions often collide with modern weaponry. Luhrman's *Romeo and Juliet* had to rename its pistols "Swords." Almereyda's contemporary *Hamlet* reintroduced in Laertes' hand the gun that had killed Polonius. How had it gotten from the NYPD evidence locker to the final "duel"? Loncraine's late-30s Richard III (Ian McKellen) forgot to include an air force within his modern army (Hitler did not) and thus lost at Bosworth Field. His rival Stanley had the only B-25 extant. It had sprung fullblown from Kitty Hawk, North Carolina.

Here, Octavius (a woman) fought the Battle of Philippi in a skirt and brandished a .45 in her hand, calling it a sword. Such women are dangerous. No need here for anyone to hold a sword for another to run upon when pistols were so prevalent. We could only conclude that suicide by sword emerged from some old tradition that had migrated from the Orient. While machine gun fire punctuated the background of Philippi, we heard no aircraft. I wondered how and where Marc Antony had won his Purple Heart and whether the National Defense Service Medal was really Cassius's highest decoration. A detailed "modern" treatment, unfortunately, invites such questions. The effect is a schizophrenic contest between what we see and what we hear.

Gender issues were a more basic problem here, however. Shakespeare's histories tend to show women as victims of male politicians—Margaret of *Henry VI*, Lady Macbeth and Cleopatra being exceptions. While Elizabeth was Queen in the 1590s, the women in the history plays are marginalized and complain, as does Kate Hotspur, or curse, as does Richard III's mother, the Duchess of York. The women in *Julius Caesar* are victims. But here, Cassius, driver of the conspiracy was a woman. Rebecca Watson's biting and dynamic Cassius would not, *as woman*, be jealous of Caesar, as he says she is. And she must say "we petty men," even when the script is otherwise edited toward her gender. That Octavius—Rome's first emperor—became a woman (Sally Wood) was even more ludicrous. To tamper thus with the script for the purpose of bringing us a Golda Meier or a Margaret Thatcher is to tamper with history. It is impossible to believe that the Octavius of *Antony and Cleopatra* could be depicted as a woman.

Perhaps because of the basic changes made in the roles of Cassius and Octavius, the two great parallel scenes with the women and their men were all wrong. In other words, with gender issues so confused in the assigning of parts, the areas were gender *is* considered were incoherent. The Portland Stage bibliography listed Mary Hamer's article on Portia and Calpurnia, but the production did not suggest than anyone had read it. Natalie Rose Liberace's fetching Calpurnia seemed to be saying, subtextually, to Caesar, you are being a fool. What she should be saying is, I am sorry that you are being a fool. The latter sense conveys love, not scarcely-concealed contempt. Sally Wood's Portia shrieked at Brutus. No. Portia creates an understated zone of love for him to enter. He does so, but only with his cramped concepts and Roman vocabulary. This Portia's high-decibel shrillness would have driven even the most confirmed of stoics away from her.

Thus one of the profound issues that this script raises—the depth of the woman's understanding vs. the superficiality of the men's posturing and rationalizing—was lost here.

This production edited out the "second revelation" of Portia's death. It permits Brutus to pose as philosopher and thus win Messala's support for the decision to confront Antony and Octavius at Philippi. The BBC-TV version showed how effective that interpretation can be. Messala, still dumbfounded by Brutus's apparently instant acceptance of Portia's death, nods when Brutus overrules Cassius.

The high points of this production were the assassination and the oration sequence. The former was violent and vividly choreographed. Caesar defended himself (as Plutarch suggests he did), in this instance by wresting Casca's dagger from him and lashing back at his circling murderers. The moment validated the courage that Kevin Kelly's suave Caesar attributed to himself. The speeches came at us via microphone. Don Domingues's Brutus had not conveyed any "interiority" up to his point. As muddled as Brutus is, he attempts to think. Domingues was "acting" all the time, paying more attention to hitting consonants than working on the rhythms that would make the lines mean something. But his straightforward oration set Antony's demagoguery—his motion, his specificity, his use of props, his pose of plainness—up nicely. The effect would have been more potent had live voices responded from within the auditorium, as opposed to recordings. Years ago, the Theater at Monmouth infiltrated the audience with respondents who rushed up to view Caesar's body. Then, all exited before the intermission, thereby reframing the action and pulling the emotion away, lest we rush out and put the ticket booth to the torch. Here, the intermission occurred after the assassination of Caesar. All that red vegetable dye had to be sponged up.

Obviously, the production used doubling. But what point did it make by doubling the parts of Portia and Octavius? The great Terry Hands production of *Henry V* in the mid-1970s doubled traitors with soldiers, thereby raising the question of treason and loyalty. What issues did the technique illuminate here? Director Lucy Smith Conroy said in her interview, included in the opulent booklet Portland State produced, "I'm understanding Cassius in a totally different way in this production than I ever did just reading the play." Of course. The script provides speeches—an outline that an actor completes with voice, body, subtext and interaction with the energy field created by the other actors and the audience. Watson's Cassius might have worked had she played the role as a man, a la Garbo in *Queen Christina* or Whoopi Goldberg in *The Associate*. But that would have required a more traditional design, either Elizabethan or "Roman." To understand Cassius as woman is to understand something that is not there. *He* is cut off even from his feminine psyche, or anima, and blames his temper on his mother.

The links between the assassination of Caesar and our own election are murky at best. The death of Caesar brought civil war and then empire. Once he defeated Antony, Augustus reigned for decades. Our own imperial assumptions are being challenged as I write in the late summer of 2008 and whoever wins the presidency had better follow George Bush's advice in 2000—that is, to conduct foreign policy "with humility." We now have no choice.

It was Caesar who stood in for Strato and held Brutus's sword. Thus the production fulfilled Plutarch's suggestion about Caesar's immortality. The gods, Plutarch tells us, were upset with the assassination of Caesar.

In spite of that nice final choice, this production put us in a modern world where the gods have little to do with anything. Thus it lost the much of the play's spectacle and its emphasis on the unseen forces working through the politics of mere mortals. Those are some of the values that we seek in Shakespeare. The play is haunted—not just by Caesar's ghost, but by storms that reflect cosmic outrage, omens uncovered in the entrails of birds and portents that persuade even Cassius to abandon his epicurean premises. This production gave us what so much modern media provide—savagery with no meaning beyond domestic fury and fierce civil strife. That we have in abundance in the world beyond the stage. Director Conroy says of this production that "It is the type of thing you might see in a movie house." Yes, but we go to theater for something that movies do not provide. When we go to a live performance, we are in a space where the action *is* occurring, where we suspend our disbelief and invite our imagination forward. As soon as theater becomes film, we are better off with that version of reality. Film does itself better than theater can. But film can never do what theater can when the latter medium is free to display its power to that breathing audience out there and to invite that audience to respond.

For all of my objections, the production was clearly spoken—except for the Flavius, Marullus, Cobbler opening. And the comments of the elderly audience as it left the auditorium were uniformly positive.

The production was aimed at high school students who came from distant towns in this geographically large state. NEA gave Portland Stage $25,000 to permit 2,500 students to come. (Keyes 2008) I would wish that the students had seen a more conventional production, as opposed to one that presented "the world they know." But this production and the ones in the summer at Monmouth are the interface between live production and people who live in this isolated province. When the productions pull the imaginations of their audiences forward into the construct that the actors are creating the results are worthwhile. It can be an experience that young people will never forget. Too often, though, they are asked to remember the wrong thing.

Derek Marsh writes of a *Richard II* in Perth in 1978:

> *Richard II* is a play set for study in high school in [Perth], and many of the audience were high school pupils, probably being introduced to Shakespeare on the stage for the first time. It was a great pity, then, that... the cast spoke the verse so badly, mutilating both rhythms and sense, and therefore not holding the ear of the audience. On the night I attended, many laughed aloud at... the wrong places... I could only agree with their responses. (1979, 272)

How many of us, veterans of many performances, good, bad, and in between, have cringed as we recognized that this bad performance, with so many young people attending, will be their criterion of "Shakespeare?" I recall saying to students after we had watched the BBC *Antony and Cleopatra*, "Believe it or not, it's a great play!" I don't think that I achieved even a willing suspense of disbelief among them. But then, I muse that Perth chose *Richard II* as its set play.

III

❧

Richard II as Script

i

To understand *Richard II* one must listen not just to what the characters say, but probe for what they don't say. The opening scene obscures more truth than it reveals, and we must wait for the second scene to tell us what the first scene was all about. That is no problem when we attend a performance, but it can be puzzling if we go back to re-read that first scene to try to figure it out. It is in those intentionally concealed meanings and motives, though, that we see politics at work, as opposed to good government. And by exploring the murkiness that underlies the rhetoric of this play, we can grasp the issues of the three plays that emerge from this one.

A production of *Richard II* must dramatize a paradigm shift. A dramaturge should suggest to a director that the play depicts a movement away from a stately, ceremonial world in which time transmits understood relationships, as exemplified by the spondaic opening line: "Old John of Gaunt, time-honoured Lancaster." This world is profoundly traditional, and its inhabitants are responsible for maintaining a continuum between man and God. By the end of the play we are in a "modern" world, in which allegiances are changeable and military power is the criterion for political control. In this brisk dispensation, a subject omits to call Richard by his title "Only to be brief." (III.3.10) The problem with the new paradigm is that all it takes is a larger army to wrest the crown from those in power. The two principal figures, Richard and Bolingbroke, cooperate in a sequence in which one dies and the other triumphs. But Bolingbroke becomes king only to realize that Richard has destroyed the sanctions and continuities whereby kingship is sustained. The means whereby Bolingbroke has gained the crown will confront him in the shape of civil wars. "God" is now a word, no longer the energizing reality that gave England its sacred qualities.

The old dispensation, in fact, is already fading as the play begins, but it is vividly recalled by John of Gaunt. His is a timeless zone that constantly regenerates within itself the dynamics of the grace of God. England is an "other Eden, demi-paradise," (II.1.42) a projector of chivalric combat and of crusades to "the sepulcher in stubborn Jewry Of the world's ransom, blessed Mary's son." (II.1.55-6) England is a sacramental entity, a visible manifestation of the invisible grace of God. But the land has been debased from inestimable quality to merely commercial quantity. It "is now leas'd out... Like to a tenement [a tenant farm] or pelting [paltry] farm," Gaunt says. (II.i.59-60) His is an elegy for an England that is no more. It may go without saying that the qualifications that we would apply to the Crusades from our vantage point today do not apply to Gaunt's description.

Richard has denied sacred meaning to England. He has cut off the exchange of positive energy between his kingdom and God by spilling Gloucester's "sacred blood" (I.2.12 & 17) and by reducing "this blessed plot" (II.1.50) to "rotten parchment bonds." (II.1.64) Ritual, or God-contacting activity, cannot occur in Richard's kingdom. "God's substitute, His deputy anointed in His sight" (I.2.37-8) has committed sacrilegious acts that prevent him from being a channel through which God's positive energy can flow into England. Richard has debased his land and his office. The royal plurality—whereby a king says "we" and speaks for his whole kingdom—no longer includes the divine sanction created when a king is anointed in God's name, as God's representative on earth. Gaunt argues, however, that only God can resolve the issue of England's alienation from His benevolence. For man to attempt to do so will only compound the problem. We never learn, of course, whether God would have intervened in some way. That option included within Gaunt's passive obedience has probably been canceled already. Bolingbroke's revolution renders it irrelevant. As Donna Hamilton points out (1984), Richard's use of kingship for his own advantage violates the concept of commonwealth, where, regardless of hierarchical arrangements, all elements within the body politic cooperate toward the common good. The kingship and the kingdom represent a mystical incorporation. This is hardly the relationship involved in being merely a "Landlord," the word Gaunt uses in accusing Richard. (II.1.113) The landlord-tenant situation is intrinsically antagonistic.

A production should help us to sense that England is in a position similar to that of Denmark as *Hamlet* begins. A secret murder rides under the surface of things, poisoning all efforts to contact God and thus undercutting the king's effort to rule effectively. In *Hamlet*, a coronation is shadowed by a too-recent royal funeral, a royal marriage is conditioned by the same immediately prior event, a former king complains of his being denied last rites, a current king cannot pray, a prime minister is buried without ceremony, his son leads a brief revolution protesting that hasty interment, the prime minister's daughter drowns in a reverse-baptism, her spare funeral reminds us that she might have been Hamlet's wife and is broken up by a brawl between Hamlet and her brother, and a dying prince forces wine down the throat of a dying king in a perverse parody of the mass. In *Richard II*, as in *Hamlet*, the secret murderer is also the king.

And that fact lurks under the opening scene of *Richard II*.

Richard can only preside over *ceremonies* (as opposed to rituals). Katherine Maus says that "the assumption that God intervenes continuously in human affairs in order to guarantee just outcomes underlies the ritual of trial by combat." (1997, 947) The combat between Mowbray and Bolingbroke does not occur, of course, but even if it had, it could not have reflected God's judgment. Richard, after all, is presiding over the adjudication of his own crime. He can only cancel the trial with makeshift and self-serving rhetoric:

> And for we think the eagle-winged pride
> Of sky-aspiring and ambitious thoughts,
> With rival-hating envy set on you
> To wake our peace, which in our country's cradle
> Draws the sweet infant breath of gentle sleep;
> Which so rous'd up with boist'rous untun'd drums,
> With harsh resounding trumpets' dreadful bray,
> And grating shock of wrathful iron arms,
> Might from our quiet confines fright fair peace
> And make us wade even in our kindreds' blood.
>
> (I.3.129-139)

Here, peace frightens peace. (Goddard, 1951, 151-52) Richard is like Neville Chamberlain, waving "a rotten parchment bond" with Hitler's signature upon it, speaking of "peace in our time" after the Munich Agreements in 1938.

Richard is correct, of course, at some unconscious level. His compromise will fright fair peace from England for generations to come. But then, he is already compromised.

Later, drawing on his self-selected role of martyr—"the expressive opportunities provided only by misery," as Maus says (948)—Richard will dictate a devastating anti-ceremony calculated to show Bolingbroke and England that the all-important intangibilities of kingship are now as meaningless as images in a mirror, indeed lie "crack'd in an hundred shivers" (IV.1.290) like the mirror Richard shatters. "God save King Henry, unking'd Richard says" (IV.1.182), using an almost ubiquitous negative prefix. Richard forces Bolingbroke into a mime that captures the latter's rise to power: "Here, cousin, seize the crown." (IV.1.182) He tells everyone what that crown is worth: "God pardon all oaths that are broke to me! God keep all oaths unbroke are made to thee!" That is an invocation to anarchy. But Richard's was the prior disruption of continuity, and he suggests as much in finding himself "a traitor with the rest." (IV.1.249) Later, Pistol will reiterate the loss of intrinsic value in the kingdom in a line that also glances at the emptiness of sacramental value: "For oaths are straws, and men's faith are wafer cakes." (*Henry V*: II.2.50) The political economy of these plays will dictate "seizure" as a dominant activity—from the Gad's Hill robbery to the seizure of the French crown. Bolingbroke introduces the theme for the Lancastrian reign when he asks about his "unthrifty son," (*I Henry*: IV.1.1) who, is reported to "stand in narrow lanes, And beat our watch, and rob our passengers." (IV.1.8-9)

> When Richard hears of Gaunt's illness, he engages in an anti-prayer:
> Now, put it God in the physician's mind
> To help him to his grave immediately!
> The lining of his coffers shall make coats
> To deck our soldiers for these Irish wars.
> Come, gentlemen, let's all go visit him.
> Pray God me may make haste and come too late.
>
> (I.4.59-64)

Richard's followers, Aumerle, Bushy, Bagot, and Green cry "Amen!" (I.4.65)

One could argue that Richard himself is infected by the poison he himself has introduced to the kingdom. His frivolous response to Gaunt's illness, however, seems to emerge from his character. As far as I can tell, Shakespeare makes nothing of the historical fact that Richard became King at age ten. His wish to gain real power was one of the motives for his dispatch of the troublesome Duke of Gloucester. But the play does not introduce that motive. Shakespeare uses Richard's history as a subtext for Richard's character. Even as an adult, he behaves like a spoiled child. Like Lear, Richard has never had to learn any other mode of behavior.

Bolingbroke, an ambitious young man, scion of a virtual principality within the kingdom, poses first as justicer, usurping the king's abandoned role, claiming to hear the blood of Gloucester crying to him "like sacrificing Abel's." (I.1.104) Bolingbroke knows what he is doing, even if his immediate goal is to create fissures of unrest within which he can maneuver. He has discussed all of this with his father, as we learn at the outset, and Gaunt knows the facts: Richard, "God's substitute… Hath caus'd [Gloucester's] death." (II.1.37-9) We learn that after the opening scene, of course, where Shakespeare forces us to share the confusion that troubles much of the kingdom. Richard must feign impartiality, and Bolingbroke is careful never to reveal his motive until his goals have been achieved. And, by then, any definition of motive has become unnecessary. He is a victim of injustice, of course, but on his return to England, he engages in legalisms, elevating himself in a world where other names and titles are reduced or erased: "As I was banish'd, I was banish'd Hereford. But as I come, I come for Lancaster." (II.3.112-113) He quickly takes retribution for the erasures he has suffered and reassumes his role as judge, and now, executioner, telling Bushy and Green that they have

> From my own windows torn my household coat,
> Rais'd out my imprese, leaving me no sign
> Save men's opinions and my living blood
> To show the world I am a gentleman.
>
> (III.1.24-27)

Bolingbroke's response to injustice, however, does not obscure his goal. Maus claims that it is "unclear whether he initially realizes that his return from exile commits him not merely to regaining the Lancastrian estates but to a more thorough attack on Richard's sovereignty." (947) Not so. Bolingbroke articulates his goals only when they are within his grasp, responding even to the cues that Richard provides:

Set on toward London, cousin is it so?
Yea, my good lord.

(III.3.208-209)

York admonishes him: "Take not, good cousin, further than you should
Lest you mistake. The heavens are over our heads." (III.3.16-17) In responding,
Bolingbroke hardly claims to be an instrument of God. He poses as an almost
passive element in a larger design. "I know it, uncle, and oppose not myself
Against their will. "(III.3.18-19) But he breaks off before his need for instant
intelligence: "But who comes here?" (III.3.19)

Bolingbroke knows that, if power no longer derives from above, it must
emerge from below. We find him deploying his yet unattained wealth like a
character in *Vanity Fair* issuing promissory notes, as when Ross and Willoughby
offer their services to him:

Evermore thanks, the exchequer of the poor,
Which, till my infant fortune comes to years,
Stands for my bounty.

(II.3.65-67)

The feudal contract was hardly a new concept in the early fifteenth century, but it is the only model available to Bolingbroke. When Henry Percy,
Northumberland's son, tenders Bolingbroke his service, Bolingbroke says that
he will remember "his good friends,"

And as my fortune ripens with thy love,
It shall be still thy true love's recompense.

(II.3.47-49)

Geographical considerations alone would argue that the linkage of Lancaster
and Northumberland is more than a merely local arrangement.

A conservative defender of the ancient rights of property and inheritance,
Bolingbroke finds himself falling into the trap of which York warned Richard:

Take Hereford's rights away, and take from Time
His charters and his customary rights;
Let not tomorrow then ensue today.

(II.1.195-197)

To interfere with the sequence of lawful inheritance is to disrupt the rhythm of Time itself. If Gaunt argued England's cooperation with positive supernatural powers, York asserts an equally valid, if diminished, principle. "How art thou a king," York asks, "But by fair sequence and succession?" (II.1.198-99) Time is a manifestation of a nature prior to and superior to any action that even a king might take. Man's law is an effort to codify natural law. Richard "wasted time" (V.5.48) in an essential sense of the word. And even mere ceremony suffers as a result. "Only to be brief Left I his title out," says Northumberland (III.3.10-11). In a deep sense, the word *king* has been erased. The concept no longer participates in a sacramental essentialism. The redemption of "time" that Prince Hal will promise (*I Henry IV*: I.2.211) must needs be only temporary. The final chorus of *Henry V* confirms as much. Henry V's "time" may have been "great..." but it was also "Small." (Epilogue, 5)

Richard has fomented an anarchy within which basic principles no longer cooperate. They collide. Aumerle and his party take the sacrament to seal their conspiracy to kill the king at Oxford. (V.2.97-9) The most sacred of rituals sanctifies the most heinous of crimes. The Duchess of Gloucester has argued family values against allegiance to a king. The Duchess of York does the same later, although England now has a different king. Word as *logos* is set against itself. The Duchess of York accuses her husband of "set[ting] the word itself against the word" (V.3.121) and Richard himself will complain that scripture sets "the word itself Against the word." (V.1.13-14) As Richard parts from his queen he cries,

> Doubly divorc'd! Bad men, you violate
> A twofold marriage; 'twixt my crown and me,
> And then betwixt me and my married wife.
>
> (V.1.71-73)

Richard defines the divisions that have occurred and will occur within families and the alienation that has developed between the crown as a sacred plurality and he who wears it. The "mystical incorporation betwixt Christ and his church" is the archetype here. Now, the crown is merely physical, a prop, as in the play of the tavern (*I Henry IV*: II.4. 375), or a consumer of life, as in Hal's apostrophe to it. (*II Henry IV*: IV.5.20-36) Richard captures the sudden negation of the crown in his metaphor of the buckets. One is empty, the other "down and full of tears." (IV.186-89) Crowns are objects to be seized.

And crowns become mere coins.

Bolingbroke discovers that his effort to behave as king merely elicits a sequence of rebellions. In "this new world," as Fitzwater calls it (IV.1.79), Bolingbroke cannot enjoy the sacred continuities that Richard inherited and destroyed. Henry IV's crown becomes the focal point of a "common 'larum bell (*II Henry IV*: III.1.17), and all that he can do is to confront "necessities" (*2 Henry IV*: III.1.93) in the sleepless middle of his nights.

Mowbray, accused by Bolingbroke at the outset, is banished by Richard as part of the King's effort to cover up his crime. Mowbray believes that the confession he has made to Gaunt, "ere [Mowbray] last receiv'd the sacrament" (I.1.139) has cleared him. Mowbray has followed the formula outlined by the rubrics for the order of Holy Communion, as found in the Queen Elizabeth prayer book (1558):

> The sinner must "openly declare... his selfe to have truely repented, and amended his former naughty life."

The curate will "not suffer [that is, permit]... those, betwixt whome he perceyveith malice and hatred to reign... to be partakers of the Lordes table, untyll he know them to be reconciled."

If one of the parties refuses reconciliation, "The minister, in that case, ought to admit the penitent person to the holy Communyon."

A director can cut Mowbray's lines, of course, but to do so is to rip out part of the fabric of a prior world in which some of the characters still believe. One of the underlying realities of the script is that the world does *not* function the way it did only recently. Mowbray and, apparently, Gaunt—who issues no denial—have met the conditions outlined in the Communion rubrics. But ritual no longer works in England. Bolingbroke's indictment cancels any healing of old wounds. Mowbray takes the sacramental possibilities with him into exile, and lives out England's crusading past as an existential sliver of Gaunt's embracing vision of what all of England once was:

> Many a time hath banish'd [Mowbray] fought
> For Jesu Christ in glorious Christian field,
> Streaming the ensign of the Christian cross
> Against black pagans, Turks, and Saracens;
> And toil'd with works of war, retir'd himself

To Italy, and there at Venice gave
His body to that pleasant country's earth,
And his pure soul unto his captain Christ,
Under whose colors he had fought so long.

(IV.1.92-100)

Carlisle describes a solitary warrior whose entire career is played out during a few brief and brutal months of English history. He lives in a different time, in the zone described by Gaunt. Like Mowbray, it has been banished from England, whose time is dictated by a politics no longer marching under the "ensign of the Christian cross."

Bolingbroke might wish to return himself and his nation to the world that Gaunt described, and lead a crusade:

As far as the sepulcher of Christ—
Whose soldier now, under whose blessed cross
We are impressed and engag'd to fight.

(*I Henry IV*: I.1.19-21)

But even as he speaks, he knows that "Therefore we meet not now." (*I Henry IV*: I.1.30) His piety is merely political. News of rebellion that he has *already* received as he begins the first of the plays that bears his name means that he "must neglect Our holy purpose to Jerusalem." (*I Henry IV*: I.1.100-101) Richard lies "breathless" (V.6.31), and "fighted peace" has found no "time… to pant" in the year since his death. (*I Henry IV*: I.1.2) Mowbray has already achieved—within a different conceptual framework that includes a different concept of time—the goal that for Bolingbroke becomes increasingly unattainable. Bolingbroke will die in "Jerusalem"—a room in Westminster—his grand scheme reduced to four physical walls. (*II Henry IV*: IV.5.233-240) Bolingbroke's hope "To wash [Richard's] blood from off my guilty hand" (V.6.49) devolves as it must to a purely political "purpose now To lead out many to the Holy Land, Lest rest and lying still might make them look Too near unto my state." (*II Henry IV*: IV.5.209-212) The projected crusade becomes, in the hands of Henry V, merely a "foreign quarrel" (*II Henry IV*: IV.5.214) with no sacred goal in mind—only a power grab intended to change the subject of how the Lancastrians achieved their crown.

Carlisle delays Bolingbroke's ascent to the throne with grim predictions of crucifixion that play against the career of Mowbray that he has just described:

> The blood of English shall manure the ground,
> And future ages groan for this foul act.
> Peace shall go sleep with Turks and infidels…
> Disorder, horror, fear, and mutiny
> Shall here inhabit and this land be call'd
> The field of Golgotha and dead men's skulls.
> O, if you raise this house against this house,
> It will the woefullest division prove
> That ever fell upon this cursed earth.
>
>   (IV.1.138-148)

I would argue that the "religious" element of the play—its former positive function and the negative history that will result from its abandonment—is part of what Robert Weimann calls *locus* (1988), that is, the thing represented. That is always the fall of Richard II and the ascent of Bolingbroke. *Locus*, Weimann argues is never subversive. It is conservative. It represents authority. (1988, 409-10) It is *platea*—company, space, audience, editing, Zeitgeist—that represents a potential subversive element. In other words, basic aspects of the world of the play can be altered, but only at the expense of how the script meant when produced and how it can still mean now. A *platea* that modernizes the inherited script can deny us those meanings and thus can deny us the opportunity to arc between those unlike things—the play by Shakespeare and our own moment in time.

Richard himself is hardly to be trusted as close reader of the Bible. In setting word against word, he neglects to notice in his prison soliloquy at the beginning of Act V that it is the "rich man" (in Matthew, Mark and Luke) who is denied the Kingdom of Heaven. Richard, of course, has yet to shake off the thought that he "was better when a king." (V.1.35) He cannot be "a prophet new inspir'd" like Gaunt (II.1.31) or a prophet "Stirr'd up by God," like Carlisle. (IV.1.134) He does, however, predict the future accurately in his admonishment of Northumberland:

> The time shall not be many hours of age
> More than it is, ere foul sin gathering head
> Shall break into corruption. Thou shall think,

Though he divide the realm and give thee half,
It is too little, helping him to all.
He shall think that thou, which knowest the way
To plant unrightful kings, wilt know again,
Being ne'er so little urg'd, another way
To pluck him headlong from the usurped throne.
The love of wicked men converts to fear,
That fear to hate, and hate turns one or both
To worthy danger and deserved death.

(V.1.57-68)

One of the corollaries of Shakespeare's sense of history seems to be that only the powerless, like the dethroned Richard or the workers in the Queen's garden, can predict that results of any action that power dictates. Power blinds those who wield it to the consequences of their actions.

Bolingbroke's calculated magnanimity in pardoning Carlisle at the end (V.6.24-29) is smashed by Exton's entrance with Richard's corpse. (V.6.30-33) Bolingbroke can make a "Cain" of Exton, (V.6.43) as he would have done to the killer of Abel (I.1.105), but the new King knows that the blood is on his hands, and it is not the blood of a ducal uncle but that of a king. The murder by proxy of Richard will haunt the Lancastrian dynasty even unto the eve of Agincourt, as Bolinbroke's son, Henry V, prays

Not today, O lord,
O, not today, think not upon the fault
My father made in compassing the crown.

(*Henry V*: IV.1.289-91)

We are in "this new world," (IV.1.78) where one looks back not at a glorious past that forever reflected the same truth, but at a past that contains one terrible truth that cannot be rationalized, and also a past that has been loosened from its fundamental premises and thus can be reshaped by expedient and selective memory. Bolingbroke, for example, revises Richard's indictment of Northumberland, erasing ambition and emphasizing kinship. What Richard said was "Northumberland, thou ladder where-withal The mounting Bolingbroke ascends my throne." (V.1.55-56) What Bolingbroke recalls is "Northumberland, thou ladder by the which My cousin Bolingbroke ascends my throne." (*II Henry IV*: III.1.70-71) And Pistol, pondering his cudgeling by Fluellen, says, "patches will I get unto these cudgel'd scars, And swear I got them in the Gallia wars." (*Henry V*: V.1.86-87) In a world where history itself can be rewritten, Pistol will quote Henry V and say, "These wounds I had on Crispin's day!" (*Henry V*: IV.3.48)

Carlisle's prophecy is more far-reaching than is Richard's self-serving comparison of himself with Christ. Carlisle foresees a "cursed earth" covered with skulls, where Gaunt had looked back upon an "other Eden, demi-paradise" (II.1.43). Carlisle incorporates both the Wars of the Roses—which Shakespeare has already dramatized in the *Henry VI—Richard III* sequence—and the warning of the New Testament: "For if a kingdome be devided against it self, that kingdome can not stand. Or if a house be devided against it self, that house cannot continue." (Mark 3.24-25, Geneva Version) The Geneva gloss to this passage warns that "when a man fighteth against his own conscience, & striveth against the trueth that is revealed unto him: for such one is in a reprobate sense and can not come to repentance." Nor, of course, can a kingdom. If Gaunt's vision of history was sacramental, Carlisle's is biblical and negatively dynamic. Unlike the fall of Adam and Eve, which opens into the bloodbath of human history but leads ultimately to "New Heav'n, new Earth, Ages of endless day Founded in righteousness and peace and love, To bring forth fruits, Joy and eternal Bliss," (*Paradise Lost*: XII.548-550), the fall Carlisle describes is not fortunate, not redeemed by Christian teleology. Perhaps the master-metaphor of *Richard II* is the exile from Eden. But the gates open only into a "modern" world, devoid of basic, sustaining premises. The myth of Eden reflects basic change. It incorporates both phylogenic and ontogenetic development—a coming to consciousness of both species and individual—and, for "this England," it predicts a movement to some zone "east of Eden."

ii

Richard II, then, makes remarkable demands on those who present it and on its audience as well. Some productions mime the murder of Woodstock— the Duke of Gloucester—to explain what the opening scene is all about. Unless we know the history, the opening scene is bewildering until we get to the second scene, where Gaunt explains that Richard is really the guilty party, and that his attempt to adjudicate the matter of Gloucester's murder is really the kind of cover-up that recent politics have made too familiar to us. When we get to that second scene, we say, "Oh, I see! That's what all of those charges and counter-charges were all about." The history plays force us to rethink what we have already witnessed in light of subsequent revelations and of the results of a previous decision. But history forces that multiple vision upon us as well. We are not just witnessing a linear event, but a layered set of meanings within which the past comes alive in ways that disturb the present and dictate a future, which, in the case of this play, is profoundly negative. In these plays, as in history, the past must constantly be revised to account for the ways it continues to reach forward to influence the present. The removal of Richard from the throne permits the Lancastrian party to take over. When it does, the murder of Richard becomes necessary. It will haunt the new regime, elicit civil wars and encourage Henry V to launch an unjustified war on France. He wins. The next generation, however, will lose France and find England imploding in a long sequence of terrible battles known as the War of the Roses. As Shakespeare says at the end of *Henry V*, his stage has "oft shown" the *Henry VI—Richard III* plays. That sequence ends with the Battle of Bosworth Field in 1485, which ushers in the Tudor dynasty. Elizabeth Tudor, daughter of Henry VIII and Anne Boleyn, is, of course, Queen of England when Shakespeare writes his histories.

The play begins "in media res," with an ambiguous dispute that is never resolved. (History itself has never answered the question of who murdered the Duke of Gloucester.). Thomas Mowbray, Duke of Norfolk, is Richard's surrogate, as Richard tries to control a tricky agenda that, if not skillfully managed, would reveal his own involvement in Gloucester's murder. And what is the accuser's motive? Bolingbroke claims to want justice for his uncle Gloucester. But at some point we recognize that his own ambition is the driving force behind his accusations. The play begins with an event that it never explains and demands that we reinterpret what we have already experienced in light of our subsequent insights.

The play involves an unsympathetic main character and, in Bolingbroke, an unengaging opponent to Richard, even if Bolingbroke is wronged by Richard in several significant ways. I don't think that Bolingbroke ever enlists our sympathies as "underdog." I also believe that Richard's subsequent exercises in self-pity deflect our sympathy for him. But those assertions are debatable, depending as they do, on what a production may show us.

The play is heavy with rhetoric—some of which is designed to confuse its on-stage audience. It is often "political" language and at other times, it is ornate poetry, deeply embedded with metaphor. The language is, quite simply, difficult to understand.

The events are profoundly implicated in concepts that require an understanding of medieval political theory. A grasp of these underlying ideas permits an audience to discern the paradigm shift that occurs within the play, from one mode of kingship to another. An audience's understanding cannot, however, depend upon the explanations delivered by "background notes" in a program. A good production must show that we move into "this new world," as Fitzwater calls it, (IV.1.69) and that the "England" that John of Gaunt celebrated has become a distant and unattainable memory, as it is even as Gaunt speaks. The loss is incalculable and yet the process is inevitable, even before Bolingbroke launches his attack against Mowbray. Some of this should be familiar to a contemporary audience, as it witnesses "conservative" values translate to radical alterations of the moral and political landscape, but much of it would seem to be more appropriately treated in a scholarly monograph or a treatise on unintended consequences. It is weighty material for a play to carry.

When I read Anne Barton's brilliant program note to the early '70s RSC production, I thought, Wonderful—she understands the play! Her husband's production undermined that grasp. But Adrian Daumas, in his program note for the 1998 *Richard II* in Spain talks of the transition from "the rigid, ceremonial and hereditary structure of the Middle Ages to a pragmatic, Machiavellianism based on convenience, normative control and efficiency, the genesis of modern structures of power." (Gregor, 214) Exactly. The production appealed to its audience, Gregor suggests, because of the "inevitable referent [of] Spain's own recent transition from the dark days of Francoism to the more liberal, but at the same time more 'Machiavellian' system based on pragmatism as well as an, at times, bewildering compromise coupled with technocratic 'efficiency.'" (Gregor, 216) But, as Gregor's detailed analysis suggests, Daumas did not force the analogy. If the content of the play sparked across the arc from stage to recent history, it did so in the spectator's imagination.

iii

For Shakespeare, "modern" England begins with the fall of Richard II.

As I suggested earlier, to understand what that fall represents we have to know what the world was like before Richard participated in the murder of his uncle, Gloucester.

Gregor tells us that Richard signaled the diminution that England has suffered by holding a glassless mirror frame up in the deposition scene, so that it held Bolingbroke's face as Richard looked through it. (Gregor, 215) Both kings stared at emptiness. The means whereby Bolingbroke has gained the crown will confront him in the mirroring of his action—civil wars. Time itself becomes negative—an interval in which bad news travels and in which enemies can gather and in which civil wars must be fought, not a zone charged and recharged with sacred energy, a place that participates in an imaging of the grace of God.

iv

It is a static England that Shakespeare as dramatist has no wish to sustain. It exists on the upper level. People below the aristocracy are invisible. No taverns exist in it. Usurpation opens up that underworld. Suddenly, Bolingbroke is complaining about the rumors that his son inhabits that world. Very soon we are there.

In a recent essay, Stephen Greenblatt argues for Shakespeare's consistency of world view: "There is no position outside the world or outside history from which Shakespeare's characters can authenticate their actions or secure an abstract, ethically adequate object for their ambitions." (2007, 77) Not so. In some of Shakespeare's worlds—and they vary—ambition itself is ethically wrong. It must be accompanied by an "illness," as Lady Macbeth says. Greenblatt is talking about *Macbeth*, but he immediately uses *King Lear* to make his case for an equivocal and unknowable universe. Yes, *King Lear* will work. But *Macbeth* will not. Shakespeare clearly employs the concept of the chain-of-being in that play to show that the murder of a king has not merely political ramifications, but cosmic reverberations. Furthermore, both *Richard II* and *Hamlet* play out amid the wreckage of an essentialist world view. Modern "ambition" is not something that exists in John of Gaunt's world, though it does exist for Bolingbroke, Claudius and Macbeth. In each instance, the upward rise of the one involves not just the fall of a former king but the collapse of the essentialist system that that king embodied, and, in Richard II's case, cooperated in destroying. Shakespeare demonstrates the paradigm shift. Hotspur would have been a great hero in the old dispensation, not a rebel. The shift does not occur in *King Lear* since we do not know what the former dispensation was—except that it was based on the absolute "authority" of the king who abdicates at the outset. *King Lear*, like *The Tempest* is syncretic. *Richard II*, *Hamlet* and *Macbeth* are not, even though prior rituals are rendered irrelevant by the actions of characters within the plays, or in the instances of the murders of Gloucester and King Hamlet, by actions that occurred before the play itself began.

v

Shakespeare undoubtedly "doubled" the minor roles in his production of the play. In doubling, the "law of reentry" applies: An actor must be absent for a complete scene before he reenters as another character. A brilliant example of this technique was Terry Hands' *Henry V*, in which two of the actors who played the traitors, Scroop and Grey, who appear only in one scene (II.2), were later doubled as two of Henry's loyal soldiers, Williams and Bates. Hands raised the issues of treason and loyalty and the very tricky question of loyalty to a leader's dubious cause simply by reminding us of the previous scene in the later scenes. In *Richard II*, the Duchesses of Gloucester and York could be doubled, thus reinforcing the emphasis that each places on family values ("Finds brotherhood in thee no sharper spur?": I.2.9; "wilt thou pluck my fair son from my age, And rob me of a happy mother's name?": V.4.91-92). Minor roles—the Marshall, Fitzwater and the Groom could be doubled. Gaunt and the Gardener—both choric voices who bewail the loss of England's Edenic qualities—could be doubled. Mowbray and Exton could be doubled. One is accused of and one commits a murder. Both are exiled. And each is linked by Bolingbroke to the first murder of Abel by Cain. Mowbray and Carlisle could be doubled. The latter utters the former's eulogy. Mowbray and the Groom could be doubled. Each exhibits loyalty to Richard. Once the possibility of doubling is opened, many connections become apparent. We glimpse not only Shakespeare's techniques of staging, but also, his mode of composition. (T.J. King 1992) Knowing that he had a limited number of actors, he crafted his plays from that set of limitations—and possibilities.[8] (The author of these plays—whoever he or she was—was a person working in the theater).

vi

A production of *Richard II* must capture the profound change that it depicts. Part of the process will involve a contrast between the perceptions of the older men in the play—York, Gaunt, and Carlisle—and those of the younger men, particularly Bolingbroke. Richard, of course, is the transitional figure and the center of the play. He is rightful king, with a direct heritage going back to the 12th century. He is also complicit in a relative's murder and guilty of an illegal seizure of a relative's estate. In other words, he participates in his own destruction, which is also, as the political economy dictates, the destruction of a concept of governance. A production then should contrast the rhythm and pace of the older men with the brisk and efficient movements of what turns out to be the revolutionary party. Richard's rhythm is uneasy—at times he is absolutely sure of his secure position as king. At other times, he despairs. The second scene of Act 3 shows him alternating without transition from manic highs to gloomy lows until he finally discovers the role of martyr that he will play with powerful effect against Bolingbroke in the deposition scene (IV.1), in a gradual, grandly articulated suicide. He uses his own downfall to demonstrate that Bolingbroke inherits in kingship only an empty crown. It is a truism of theater that the actor playing a king achieves his effect not by some imitation of "kingliness," but through the response of the other actors to his royal character. How can a production of *Richard II* suggest that Richard and Bolingbroke are very different kings through the response that the other characters give to each? Richard's followers respond to him by supporting his self-indulgence. Bolingbroke's supporters follow his orders.

At the end, Bolingbroke assigns the guilt of "Cain" to Exton, who followed Bolingbroke's calculatedly vague command to kill Richard. At the beginning, Bolingbroke claimed that Gloucester's blood cried to him like "Abel's" for "justice." Whether Richard wielded the sword or not, he was guilty of an uncle's murder. Now, by deputation, Bolingbroke is guilty of a king's murder. He inherits the profound guilt that attaches to the first murder after the expulsion from Eden. All those images of gardens in *Richard II* reinforce the point.

And the result will be a long series of battles known as the War of the Roses, as Carlisle predicts.

vii

The most famous of any Shakespearean production happens to be of *Richard II*. In February 1601, followers of the Earl of Essex commissioned Shakespeare's company to perform the play, believing that it justified the deposition of a reigning monarch. That made them bad literary critics. Essex paid with his head for leading a rebellion against Queen Elizabeth I, but, fortunately for all of us, Shakespeare and Company were cleared of any complicity in the abortive revolt.

Since then, *Richard II*, has rarely been produced. Not only are other plays in the sequence more popular—*I Henry IV* and *Henry V*, for example—but the complexities of *Richard II* make it difficult for the stage. Its political rhetoric— "peace fright [ing] peace," as Richard breaks up the trial by combat in I.3—its master-metaphor of a ruined garden, its self-pitying hero, indeed its depiction of a bad king, and its "inextricable tangle of right and unright," as A. C. Bradley has it, (1909, 255) have all conspired to keep the play from the stage.

Nevertheless, once Edmund Kean reintroduced the script in 1815, after an absence of more than two centuries, some notable productions have occurred in recent years.

They begin with Sir John Gielgud's Richard in 1929. Gielgud's wonderful way with verse made Richard a king who would rather be a poet composing elegies to his own failures as king.

In 1972, John Barton brought his version to the Brooklyn Academy of Music. It was highly stylized and, I thought, gimmicky. Bolingbroke and Richard decided before each performance who would play which role. Richard Pascoe and Ian Richardson were, in a sense, interchangeable. One may be consciousness and the other shadow in the Jungian sense, but Barton's toss of a coin blurred distinctions. It can be said, of course, that some of the Bolingbrokean energy finally flows to Richard, as he valiantly fights off his assassins. Barton, however, made Bolingbroke the Groom who visits Richard in prison. Barton gave Bolingbroke Henry IV's speech about "uneasy lies the head." Thus Bolingbroke was guilty-in-advance of Richard's murder. The plays show that the working out of guilt is a process that extends even unto the eve of Agincourt, not a sudden insight before the fact. For the trial by combat, Barton had Mowbray and Bolingbroke encased in toy horses. The combatants looked as if they had escaped from a merry-go-round. While the trial is phony, in that Richard cannot permit it to go forward, Barton's approach trivialized the importance of the scene. At the Deposition Scene, Richard smashed that mirror over his head, making it look not like "a Christ-like halo" (Powell, 181), but an awkward albatross. Barton had Northumberland in a crow-suit on stilts— an upstage crow—and had a snowman melt behind York's description of the triumphant Bolingbroke and the defeated Richard. That visualized Richard's earlier wish to be a "mockery king of snow," but it pulled attention away from York's speech. What the hell is that snowman doing there? At the end of the production, Death wore the crown. That, of course, reiterated Richard's earlier linkage of kingship with death and it was one of the few moments that really worked here. The other was Richard's glittering descent in a robe of gold as he compared himself to "glistering Phaethon." At the time of the production, the Watergate scandal was working its way toward the deposition of another Richard. I felt that John Barton's production picked up a lot of unearned energy from events in DC.

The 1978 BBC production, with Derek Jacobi and Jon Finch, is a strong, straightforward version in which Jacobi uses self-pity to draw his followers into his game of martyrdom. This is brilliantly done. Finch plays the economical Bolingbroke with a sneer, not recognizing that his character is moving inexorably toward the destruction of the very system that he has returned to England to restore. This is a *television* production, limited in the depth that the camera can contain. It is, however, brilliantly edited. Notice for example, how the camera tracks after the arrest of Carlisle for denouncing Bolingbroke. It moves past Charles Gray's wonderful Duke of York, who stares at Carlisle in stupefied admiration. The production includes the great Sir John Gielgud as Gaunt and a wonderful Northumberland in David Swift. As Swift broaches his plot against Richard, his eyes flick back and forth to access the effect of his words on his listeners. That technique neatly mirrors Jacobi's trolling for tears from his followers. This production is, of course, available and worth watching attentively. Given television's inevitable tendency toward normalizing, the production shows the anti-Richard conspiracy beginning against the background of Gaunt's funeral. That removes the intriguing possibility that Bolingbroke returns *before* he learns of the confiscation of his estate.

Barry Kyle mounted an opulent version in 1986 for the Royal Shakespeare Company, with Jeremy Irons as Richard. The production made its points through costuming. Richard was splendid in a blue robe trimmed in gold that matched the King's long, blonde hair. And then—the prison. Was that haggard face with the black and grimy hair and the eyes staring at nothing, that man in the filthy white smock chained by the neck to the prison bars? Was that Richard? Yes. It was an effectively shocking contrast. At the end, red and white roses sprouted, suggesting that the events we have just witnessed presage the War of the Roses. That is true, of course, but the production itself had made its points less heavy-handedly than that.

Deborah Warner's *Richard II*, with Fiona Shaw, a BBC television version of a 1997 stage performance, is a spectacular production that compares favorably with the BBC version (1978). Shaw plays Richard as a homosexual male in love with his cousin Bolingbroke. It may be in the stage production, Shaw played Richard as "girl," as she says (Rutter 1997, 314), or as "woman" (Berkowitz 1996, 9). Certainly the television version argues some ambiguity as to the King's gender, but I and other observers see this Richard as a gay man. His clothes—trousers and gowns in white and gold—are unisex, similar to the garments of his male followers, "pretty youths dressed in Florentine taffetas." (Rutter, 320) When Mowbray mentions the man without honor as being merely "gilded loam or painted clay," he glances at this gaggle. The King is called "King," referred to as "he," and married, even if he obviously despises his Queen. When Richard gives Bolingbroke a lingering kiss in the opening scene, the King seems to be flaunting his sexual orientation in the open court. He turns with a smirk and resumes a white, "designer" throne surrounded by the group of male favorites. Richard takes off his crown before the trail by combat to kiss (not just "fold him in [his] arms") Bolingbroke one more time, suggesting again a doffing of the political for the personal role. When the dying Gaunt gives Richard a long kiss later on, one that disgusts the King, Gaunt seems to be revenging himself for something he does not wish to put into so many words. Bolingbroke's accusation of Bushy and Green before he has them executed mentions, of course, the "divorce" that these favorites have wrought between Richard and Isabel, but picks up further energy from the possibility that the two were Bolingbroke's rivals for Richard's affections. Bolingbroke was "near in love Till [they] did make [Richard] misinterpret [him]." (II.iv.17-18)

Bolingbroke's murder of Richard by indirection is powerfully understood here—it is not just political. It is intensely personal.

The production is splendidly scaled to its medium. The original stage version was set in the National's tiny 170-seat Cottesloe, which resembled, says Carol Rutter, an "elegant but austere antechamber to the gorgeous state rooms seemingly just beyond." (1997, 319) The television studio at Three Mills Island is a long rectangular space that can become Richard's throne room, the Duchess of York's spare chamber, a setting for a trial by combat (the only scene which fails here), a garden, and a mini House of Lords for the exchange of gage scene (which BBC cut) and the Deposition Scene that follows. When Richard lands on the stony coast after his return from Ireland, he stands against the blank wash of a seaside overcast. He receives the sacrament from Carlisle, but the elements are like the stones of Timon's banquet. Richard's effort at piety is much too late. (The later ironic sacrament the anti-Henry party take is cut here, as is the entire Aumerle subplot). Richard's "salute" of the earth cannot be a kneeling and a sifting of soil in his hands. It is instead a wave of the hand at a rocky wasteland. A "fire-escape-like balcony" (as Berkowitz describes the stage set: 1996, 9) serves Richard for his confrontation with Northumberland at Flint Castle. The prison is dark, barred and subterranean, but offers a small upward glimpse of sunshine—a chance for Richard to look backward at the time he wasted. Most of the interior scenes are washed by candlelight that sends a golden texture across most of the faces. Bolingbroke, with his wild gaze and smashed warrior's face thus seems very much out of place in this dreamlike, nocturnal space that Richard has created for himself.

The Bolingbroke of the television version is Richard Bremmer, who played Exton in the original. David Threlfall, the original Bolingbroke was unavailable. According to Rutter, Threlfall and Shaw shared an "uncanny physical resemblance." (1997, 318) I did not see the stage version, but I found the physical contrast powerful between the dreamy Shaw, hardly delicate, but dressed in flowing garments, and Bremmer, with his bulging eyes, sheer size and armor. I do not agree with those who believe that Richard and Bolingbroke are "doubles" and can be interchanged, as in the famous—or infamous—John Barton production of the 1970s. As Joseph Price said of the production at the time, "The stage devices that were used to blur the personalities of Richard [and Bolingbroke] into one personality ran counter to the psychological foils these characters are to each other."(1977, 262) The relationship between the two can be expressed through Jung's metaphor of "Shadow," which represents the personality formed by elements repressed by conscious orientation. In the *television* production, the two are physical and psychological opposites, who, taken in the aggregate, make up a whole. They love each other here. There is no doubt about Bolingbroke's reciprocity in the television production. This is a love affair cancelled by political imperative, a matter of two body naturals yearning for what their bodies politic deny, indeed a love which politics destroys. Even in the Deposition Scene, Richard seeks comfort from Bolingbroke as Northumberland urges the petition upon the ex-king. Richard's "They shall be satisfied" follows from Bolingbroke's "Urge it no more." The two lovers are doing what they can for each other even here at the eleventh hour. Never, I would wager, has that subtext been brought to that scene, or, at least, never so powerfully. The relationship—and its failure—reaches deep into human experience. As in Aristophanes' metaphor in *The Symposium*, each yearns for the completeness the other represents.

In the opening scene, Richard and his courtiers laugh and begin to move away when Bolingbroke accuses Mowbray of "all the treasons for these eighteen years complotted and contrived in this land," but turn as Bolingbroke goes on to mention Gloucester's murder. Richard's mouth trembles for an instant. Bolingbroke smiles slightly. Has that got your attention? The point of Bolingbroke's later adjudication of the same issue is not, as Rutter suggests that Richard and Bolingbroke are "doubles." (1997, 317) The later scene extends Bolingbroke's pose as "justicer" and shows us how differently he handles things. *He* will assign the "days of trial" to the contending parties, meaning that he has them under his control. If they cross him, the assignment of trial will be immediate. As it is, the trials never occur. Percy becomes Henry IV's enemy. Aumerle becomes Duke of York and dies in the van at Agincourt (though Shakespeare does nothing, as far as I can tell, with York's previous manifestations as Aumerle or Rutland). It is Northumberland's idea to arrest Carlisle here. In the BBC version, he does so only after a nod from Bolingbroke.

The trial by combat (1.3) is interrupted by Richard's apparent panic at the commotion the men are creating. The contrast between Richard's effete gay court and the brawling that "real men" want to enjoy is nicely drawn, but the scene becomes chaotic and incoherent. Furthermore, Richard's under-scoring of stereotype here—the gay man as limp-wristed, lisping and upset by violence—undercuts the political point. Richard cannot afford to have Bolingbroke win. He is usurping the King's role by posing as the bringer of justice to England. Nor can Mowbray defeat the most popular man in England. Mowbray is Richard's stand-in here, regardless of his denial (in this play and in Holinshed) of his guilt for Gloucester's death. Richard has to intervene and craft his frail compromise. His speech on "peace" is self-refuting ("peace" ends up fright [ing] "peace"), a kind of Neville Chamberlainian "peace in our time" declaration, emerging from a desperate and improvisational politics. Mere "gay fright" in no way suggests what is happening here. A basic point the script is making—that, since Richard is the guilty party, the trial by combat can deliver no true verdict—gets lost in the jumble. If Richard *is* being played as a wom-an, some of the same stereotypic baggage pertains. Carol Rutter paraphrases Richard's reaction thus: "When 'womanish' Richard threw down the warder, it was because she couldn't stand it anymore... Her gesture read as a wholesale indictment of male 'order,' male protocol." (1997, 323) Either way, the issue of gender obscures the point about Richard's precarious *political* position.

Richard's frivolous attitude toward Gaunt's illness is particularly telling. Richard kneels and crosses himself as he prays to "make haste, and come too late"—an anti-prayer that shows how far Richard is from understanding the spiritual issues the play explores. Richard arrives with a funeral wreath and a mourning band in place, a reminder of Ian McKellen, as another Richard, wearing a mourning band to the scene in which he reveals the death of Clarence. Shaw interrupts the Queen's prayer for the repose of Gaunt's soul: "So much for that!" York's complaint, splendidly delivered by the fussy Duke of Donald Sinden, is merely another old man's interruption of Richard's oblivious agenda. In the BBC production, Northumberland's revelation that Bolingbroke is at hand is delivered after Gaunt's funeral. Some time has passed. Here, the inference the scene presents—that Bolingbroke has made his move *before* Richard has given him a pretext for it, a la a Napoleon or a Franco—is possible. In the BBC version, though, David Swift's Northumberland is much more subtle and cautious as he sounds out Ross and Willoughby. In the newer production, all are in agreement from the start, so that the scene merely im-parts information as opposed to dramatizing the formation of a conspiracy.

The production belongs to Shaw. She graphs Richard's manic surges and depressed drops superbly in the seaside scene: "keeps death *his* court" suggests what the poetry is saying. A king may have a great court, but King Death surrounds and pervades it. The lines are read as if Richard is actually thinking them as he speaks. The deposition scene is this production's high point. A sudden feminine voice intrudes upon male game-playing and asks "why am I sent for?" Aumerle, who has refused to kneel to Bolingbroke, kneels to Richard. Richard sits down between an uneasy Hotspur and Northumberland. He puts the crown on the floor. Bolingbroke won't pick up it ("seize" it). Richard then insists that Bolingbroke and he "seize" it together. It is a child's game—boys playing at being king. Bolingbroke will, much later, repeat the metaphor of play-acting. (*II Henry IV*: IV.v:196-97) And, of course, that is what Richard is demonstrating to the new king. None of this is worth anything anymore. Richard removes an invisible crown from his head, suggesting that the spiritual, intangible qualities that he inherited as king are gone. "Ay, no, no, aye," as Shaw reads the line is "Yes. No. No I," and then "Therefore no, know." What Richard knows, as Rutter has Richard saying, is that Bolingbroke has "shattered the fundamental contract that keeps me king." (1997, 321) Richard's demonstration of what Bolingbroke does *not* get with the crown is devastating, of course, but Richard's has been the prior destruction of fundamental bases of kingship. Richard puts the crown on Bolingbroke's head, then prostrates himself at his feet. He rises to embrace Bolingbroke for his "mockery king of snow" speech, a brilliant physical reinforcement of the destructive interaction they have experienced.

The garden scene ends with the Gardener (John McEnery) wishing that his "skill were subject to [the Queen's] curse." The earth, though leased out, though wounded with traitor's hooves, though devoid of its sacramental resonance, will continue to be fruitful. The BBC version of 1978 ended with the Queen's curse ("Pray God the plants though graft'st may never grow!"). That is illegitimate. It suggests that she has power within a play where women are subject to the decisions that men make. Even the Duchess of York's appeal for Aumerle is granted only because Bolingbroke, on top of the fragile feudal system he has set up, needs friends. This is not a play where the curses of queens have efficacy—even unwittingly, as in the case of Lady Anne's curse of whoever becomes Richard Gloucester's wife.

The moment at which Richard capitulates would seem to come after

Salisbury tells him that the Welshmen have defected to Bolingbroke: "they are fled," Richard says. It is an acceptance of fact and of relief—I don't have to fight. Richard's aversion to combat has been established. Jacobi makes the statement a question "And they are fled?" He is still incredulous as he absorbs the totality of his abandonment. Here, as Berkowitz says of the stage production, "Bolingbroke himself turned out to be the last person to realize the full implications of his insurrection." (1996, 9) Bolingbroke is a legalist who returns under a different name than that he carried into banishment, in this play about the loss and the gaining of names and what they represent. Bolingbroke never states an objective beyond gaining his inheritance. York sees "the issue of these arms," as Richard does. We infer that Richard's resistance to a coup would merely create a conflict that this Richard would avoid at all costs. To play Bolingbroke as unaware of the end result of his return, however, is to ignore the careful formula he provides for Percy, Ross and Willoughby in 2.3, where he pleads present poverty but promises future largesse. His words and the response to them constitute a feudal contract—the only available basis of power left to Bolingbroke. He cannily shows that he knows as much. The distance between Lancashire and Northumbria, after all, argues a dynastic arrangement. The play renders some interpretations simplistic. This production tends not to understand the politics of the play.

One of the strengths of the production is that Sian Thomas's stalwart words as Queen to the deposed Richard ("The lion dying thrustest forth his paw") emerge from a woman who would have opposed Bolingbroke regardless of the consequences. This production emphasizes the Queen's piety, suggesting that she represents that dead or dying sacramental set of values that Gaunt describes that might have resisted Bolingbroke's incursion. That this despised Queen adores Richard makes her words even more poignant here. She would have been Richard's natural ally had he not abandoned her for the male favorites who helped bring him down.

This production cuts the moment after the execution of Bushy and Green, as Bolingbroke politicly asks York to send "kind commends" to the Queen. It was very strong in the BBC production—Jon Finch's Bolingbroke effortlessly switching gears, Charles Gray's York shocked and heartbroken, scarcely listening to his nephew. Both productions cut Carlisle's description of Norfolk's career—he has fulfilled England's chivalric tradition as a banished man during a long lifetime that has somehow occurred during a few short and brutal months in England. The speech belongs in any production. It brings back an important character from early in the play and informs us powerfully about what Richard and Bolingbroke have conspired to exile from their country. It works particularly well if Mowbray and Carlisle are doubled.

The finale is a possibly confusing conflation of Richard's prison soliloquy and his assassination. "Music" is the splashing of Exton and his accomplices through the sewer that opens into Richard's cell. As Richard struggles on an existential level with his killers, the words argue that he is more than "half in love with easeful death." In an "all-hating world," Richard can love only death. He falls face down into the water and the scene shifts. Bolingbroke takes *his* crown off and leans into the Richard's coffin to kiss the corpse, expressing a final reflex of body natural beneath the trappings of recent kingship.

The framing allusions "like sacrificing Abel's" and "With Cain go wander" are gone. In the first, Bolingbroke is a biblical avenger. In the last, though he assigns the guilt to Exton, he is the one who is guilty (as Richard was of Gloucester's murder) and who will pay a price for his role in regicide. The murder of Gloucester is now irrelevant. Bolingbroke has rushed headlong into the guilty world he claimed he would redeem at the outset. The editing here, toward the love of former King and new King, excludes some of the deeper resonances of this superb script.

As we engage a millenium of mumbles, one must pause to remark that this production is beautifully spoken. It should be made commercially available. This is a wonderful play and deserves to have two splendid productions representing it. The new television production emphasizes *personal* relationships, as befits the scale of the medium. The triangular conflict—Richard passionate about Bolingbroke but entangled in a political marriage—is movingly depicted. The death of Richard ends this version. No further history is to unfold. No wars will spin into time from these events. No further plays are to be performed. This treatment of *Richard II* differs radically from the BBC, which knew, as Shakespeare did, that more was to come. The Warner-Shaw production serves then as a generic contrast to the 1978 version and helps us see it—as it helps us see the newer one—as a separate work of art emerging from this neglected script.

In 2006, Brian Kulick directed Michael Cumsty in a Classic Stage Company

(New York) production. Cumsty, who had played Hamlet for the same company the previous year, won praise for his moving discovery of "the hollow, provisional nature of worldly stature, the lie inherent in all life's promise." (Isherwood, 19 Sept. 06) Although critic Hilton Als found "the first half of the play... unrealized... as if the text had been sewn together from two separate plays entirely—a somewhat dull court drama and an early take on the existential themes that Shakespeare parlayed with unquestionable brilliance... in *Hamlet*," Als suggested that Cumsty "manages to knit together the two halves of Shakespeare's discordant, ultimately minor work." (2 Oct 06, 94) This was a modern dress production—a mode to which this script lends itself nicely, as long as the period is not overly specified—in which Richard's decadent court sniffed cocaine and chased it with champagne. Suggestions about Richard's homosexuality were suppressed.

I would suggest that the play is not as disjointed as Als claims. If Bolingbroke at the end is standing in the same position as is Richard in the beginning, the parallel between the two will be visually reinforced. Richard at the outset is guilty of a kinsman's murder. For all of his assumed superiority ("not to sue, but to command") he is in an uneasy position between two antagonists, one of whom is a stand-in for the guilty King. At the end, Bolingbroke receives a series of crown-confirming reports and burnishes his kingly image by pardoning Carlisle. Then Exton appears with the body of Richard. Bolingbroke, too, has commissioned a murder. But this one is regicide.

IV

꧁꧂

Henry V in Performance

i

I remain stunned at how much Shakespeare expected of his audience, and how much he expects of us and of those who present his scripts to us. The "rhythm" of *II Henry IV*, for example, involves a movement and counter-movement in almost every scene. After rumors of Hotspur's success at Shrewsbury, Northumberland learns that "Hotspur" is "Coldspur." He throws away his crafty crutch and vows to fight. He is dissuaded by Kate Hotspur. And then we meet Feeble, who, of all people, is the last character we expect to sound like Hotspur. The Archbishop and his cohort anticipate their own pardon at Gaultree Forest, but are summarily beheaded. Hal believes that the King is dead. But the King awakens. This scene leads to reconciliation and Henry IV's almost joyful embrace of death ("Laud be to God!") and his acceptance of the shrinking of his projected crusade to the four walls of a chamber in Westminster. A good production must instill this ebb and flow of expectation and result in us. And thus we are prepared for the "second father-son scene"— the rejection of Falstaff. Audience and production work together, beneath the surface of the words, to create an imaginative context and a rhythm that allows us to respond to "I know thee not old man…" as possibly shocking but absolutely inevitable. We are expected to recall "I know you all…" and to say, Yes, now I see where all of this has been leading. We are also expected to remember, I think, even smaller moments. Bolingbroke says to Warwick,

> But which of you was by—
> You cousin Neville, as I may remember
> When Richard… Did speak these words…
> 'Northumberland, thou ladder by the which
> My cousin Bolingbroke ascends my throne…'

But what Richard said was:

> Northumberland, thou ladder where withal
> The mounting Bolingbroke ascends my throne…

Bolingbroke revises history to suggest, not overwhelming ambition, but family ties. And, of course, there remains the enticing possibility that Warwick may have edited Richard's words for Bolingbroke's consumption. That possibility, of course, is too subtle to suggest in performance.

We must hold everything that has gone before in mind as we encounter Henry V. He can despise his "dream," "being awake," but he imposes upon himself the radical consciousness—the insomnia—that is a Lancastrian malady. And he cannot forget the event that made him king—his father's usurpation.

ii

Some doubling is merely functional. A minor character like Francisco in *Hamlet*, who appears and disappears early in the play could fill one or two small roles later on. Polonius and First Gravedigger are sometimes doubled. Shakespeare wrote with this process in mind. His minor actors were "hired men," as opposed to permanent members of his company. Major roles would not be doubled. I disagree with the tendency, for example, to double Theseus/Oberon, Hippolyta/Titania in *A Midsummer Night's Dream*, even if they are psychological opposites of each other as Peter Brook argued when he doubled Alan Howard and Sara Kestleman in the roles. And I doubt that Cordelia and the Fool were doubled, regardless of their linkage in *King Lear*. Robert Armin was a singer and musician who even repeats a version of one of Feste's songs in *Twelfth Night* during the storm in *King Lear*. Armin was not about to surrender that position to the boy actor playing Cordelia. Nor would Shakespeare write the Fool's songs for someone other than Armin. I have always believed that at least one of Macbeth's Murderers—the Third—should be the boy actor who played one of the Weird Sisters, though I have never seen that done. It may violate the law of reentry. I have also never seen Hermione and Time doubled in *The Winter's Tale*, as a way of hinting at something that we will learn. Hermione lives! Certainly Mamillius and Perdita would have been doubled, the young sister suggesting something to us about "the triumph of time."

Shakespeare created great secondary roles as foils for his great actor, Richard Burbage. Bolingbroke has 399 lines to Richard II's 749, Claudius has 529 lines to Hamlet's 1240, Octavius has 403 lines to Antony's 839 and Cleopatra's 693. None of those big parts would be doubled. In *Henry V*, the title character has most of the lines. The King has 1056 lines in First Folio compared to 281 for Fluellen. Another play where one character dominates, of course, is *Richard III*, which Richard begins with a long soliloquy and in which he has 1116 lines. Buckingham is next with 388 lines. Henry and Richard bestride their history and dominate their plays as few other characters do.

A brilliant example of "thematic" doubling in *Henry V* occurred in Terry Hands' production in the mid-1970s, when he doubled two traitors and two soldiers. With only Henry V incapable of being doubled, here are some possibilities: Merely functional doubling might have the actor who plays the French Ambassador early also play Montjoy at Agincourt. Grandpré has only one speech—but it is significant, in that it describes something that should not even be there: the English army (IV.2.38ff). Since his speech has a "choric" function, he could be doubled with Chorus. You could double the cowardly soldiers, Bardolph and Nym, with two of the stalwart group around the campfire. You could double Canterbury, who encourages Henry into war, with Burgundy, who details the evils that war brings. You could double "second fiddles" like Ely and the Dauphin. Doubling helps the director make connections—comparisons and contrasts—and permits the director to bring his creativity forward to coincide with Shakespeare's. When we look at the possibilities for doubling we also experience Shakespeare's creative process. He was doing the same thing when he wrote the plays. The Boy and Princess Katherine could be doubled, for example. Each is, in a different way, subjected to the vicissitudes of Henry's war. And each is vaguely bilingual and is involved in a scene in which the play's two languages interact. Suffice it that when a director takes on a script by Shakespeare, the director becomes a collaborator with the playwright.

iii

I confess that I did not realize what a great play *Henry V* is until I saw Terry Hands' production at Stratford, with Alan Howard, in 1975.

I had appreciated Henry's bloodcurdling threats and his inspiriting orations, the play's subtle depiction of collusion between king and church, its exploration of the corrupt underside of Henry's military adventure, as well as its demonstration of the courage that resides within some soldiers, its analysis of politics, particularly of the human price the successful politician must pay to maintain his façade, the vividness of Henry's guilt about the duplicity and murder whereby his father gained the crown. I had also watched Henry's failed game with Williams, where it seems the King would like to revert for a moment to his days with Falstaff, but finds he cannot. I had recognized the ways in which Henry, privately, arrives at insights Falstaff had had long before. "Canst thou [ceremony] when thou command's the beggar's knee, command the health of it? No." (IV.1.253-54). "Can honor set to a leg?" Falstaff asks at Shrewsbury. "No. Or an arm? No. Or take away the grief of a wound? No. Honor hath no skill in surgery, then? No." (*I Henry IV*: V.1.131-133). Both Falstaff and Henry V convey the contempt for the abstractions that Hemingway's Frederick Henry would share much later in *A Farewell to Arms*. I had appreciated Shakespeare's giving a face to statistics—in a 20th century so overcome with numbers that mere human beings got lost in the zeros. We do not meet Davy Gam, Esquire, but we do meet the Boy and Le Fer. Each becomes one of many in the killing of boys and prisoners, and each gives poignancy to those general slaughters. I had marveled at Henry's virtuosity—his deployment of the skills he acquired from constant combat with Falstaff, even as he posed as playboy prince. And I had recognized the play's reminder that political skill is not genetically transferable to the next generation. Shakespeare implies that the most devastating of historical cycles are repeated. Edward the Black Prince, hero of the victory against the French at Crécy, dies young and leaves a child-king on the throne. Henry of Agincourt dies young and leaves another child-king on the throne.

I had enjoyed Olivier's brilliant film version, of course, but that was achieved by overwhelming all the limitations that the Chorus says pertain to stage. "Can this cockpit hold The vasty fields of France? Or may we cram Within this wooden O the very casques That did affright the air at Agincourt?" (11-14). No. But Olivier's camera could do so, assuming that it could discover in 1944 a field free of burned-out Me 110s. While Olivier reminded us first and last of Shakespeare's stage, he took us to Agincourt, a place where we did not have to suspend our disbelief. The charge of the French must be the longest tracking shot in the history of film.

But then, I had seldom seen the play as play. Michael Kahn's Stratford, Connecticut, production of 1969, where the dead of Agincourt became the citizens who cheered Henry back to London, had used the script as an anti-war vehicle, and I, at least, was willing to take it that way during the dark days after Nixon's election. Hands and Howard went *into* the play, exploring the script for what it might mean rather than using it for either jingoistic or anti-war propaganda. (See for example, Derrick 1999) When Howard, for example, first spoke to the conspirators in II.2, he said, "My lord of Cambridge, and my kind lord of Masham, And you...," Howard's Henry paused. He had forgotten Grey's name, but continued, with "my gentle knight." That might have signaled some nervousness on Henry's part, but a little later, he said "Cambridge, Scroop, and"—he paused smiled, and pointed at Grey—"Grey!" You thought I had forgotten your name? This was a delicious moment, particularly since Henry was just about to spring his trap. As he chatted, Henry held Grey by the hand, as the latter looked helplessly at his soon-to-be-indicted co-conspirators. The drunken soldier against whom the conspirators had argued was visibly set free just before Henry handed the three traitors their "commissions."

Hands also used doubling—traitors (Scroop and Gray in II.2.) became soldiers (Williams and Bates in IV.1). I glimpsed something Shakespeare had probably done. The doubling subtly raised the issues of treason and loyalty in the play simply by reminding us of the earlier scene through the latter.

Norman Rabkin describes the response to *Henry V* as a Rorschach test—one person may see a rabbit there, another a duck. (1977, 279-96) And that is certainly true. The Hands' production kept holding the play up to us at slightly tilted angles—having the King share a sense of humor with us that he could not share with his on-stage audience after his excoriation of the Dauphin, for example—so that we knew that we were experiencing something more complex than just a black-and-white image that could only suggest one thing. We, the audience, were given the ultimate compliment of having to respond intensely with mind and imagination to this production. Shakespeare asked the same of his spectators.[1]

Olivier's camera had boomed upward and outward during Henry's magnificent "band of brothers" speech, showing us the army that his rhetoric was incorporating and uniting. It was what film can do—begin with a single point and pull outward to all that that point includes. And, of course, the film encouraged the unity that World War II demanded of its allies. Howard moved among his soldiers, extending brotherhood with a handshake. It was what stage can do—pull us into its imitation of an action, letting us sense as individuals what each of Henry's soldiers was feeling in the moments before battle. And film, of course, can close in, as it did on Kenneth Branagh's Henry, showing the young king struggling with the forces he has unleashed and cannot now control. (On these and other productions, see Loehlin, 1997.)

iv

It has seldom been remarked that Henry turns down at the outset the vast funds that would add to England and to his reign a greatly enhanced feudal system. How much?

> As much as would maintain, to the King's honor,
> Full fifteen earls and fifteen hundred knights,
> Six thousand and two hundred good esquires,
> …A hundred almshouses right well supplied;
> And to the coffers of the King beside,
> A thousand pounds by th' year.
>
> (I.1.12-19)

Henry, of course, chooses war, but we should be aware of the option he discards. James Black suggests that Canterbury's disquisition reminds Henry "of both usurpation and glorious conquest. Henry is being offered, as it were, a choice of heritages: If he wishes to clear his title of the dubiety associated with his father's accession, then he had better show himself clearly and by deed in the line of his more respectable forebears." (1975, 15) Henry, of course, has made his mind up. All of the argumentation in the face of his seeming passivity is designed to convince his followers into *being* followers. The motivation—to "busy giddy minds With foreign quarrels" (*II Henry IV*: IV.5.213-14) in the abstract—is for the mature leader, Olivier's Henry, a chance to add warrior to his list of accomplishments. For the youthful monarch, Branagh's Henry, it is an opportunity to test himself in one of the crucibles of medieval kingship. The Branagh narrative is a *Bildungsroman*, as Peter Donaldson astutely notes. (1991, 60-70) Regardless of the personal motive behind the political, however, the prolix first scene demonstrates Henry's ability to let others convince themselves by seeming to urge him on to his own foregone conclusion.

History does not tell us, of course, what might have happened had Henry chosen the alternative of that bill in Parliament that would have added so much land (and wealth) to the crown. It is one of those enticing roads not taken.

Productions that delete the Archbishop's catalogue, as many do, rob the spectator of the chance to consider the option presented to the King before he chooses war. We lose, then, our sense of how the drama emerges from decisions that characters make. Those decisions made, the characters often become helpless before the consequences they have set in motion.

Canterbury's discourse on the Salic Law has recently been accompanied by "multiple, detailed display charts." (Rosenbaum 2003, AR 5) Director Mark Wing Davey explains: "Its function is to persuade, so just as Colin Powell addressed the United Nations, there will certainly be an echo of the seriousness with which Henry takes at least the appearance of going into war with 'right and conscience.'" (qdt in Rosenbaum, AR 6) Davey's explanation may be an example of the production's being too close to the historical event—as, I suggest, Barton's *Richard II* was to Watergate. Yet the historical analogy turns out to be prophetic. Powell's speech of February 2003 was seen by many at the time as persuasive. In retrospect, it seems clear that the administration used the only person on their roster who had a shred of credibility and, of course, squandered him. Powell now calls that moment his greatest regret. Powell called information obtained by torture and later debunked "the story of a senior terrorist... telling how Iraq provided training in [chemical and biological] weapons to al-Queda." Iraq was a war of choice that continues to damage us. By now, the rationale for the invasion has been definitively discredited. The analogy, in retrospect, makes *Henry V* "a slyly subversive critique of an unnecessary war," and the justification scene "a corrupt, blood-for-tax abatement excuse for an unnecessary war... [a] cover-up for an exercise of imperial power and self-promotion that will leave ten thousand dead for one man's glory." (Rosenbaum, AR 5) Curiously, Rosenbaum claims that the scene with Canterbury is "the very first time we see Henry." (AR 5) We have seen him as King at the end of *II Henry IV*, as he accepts the Chief Justice and, vividly, as he rejects Falstaff.

The BBC-TV production (1979, dir. David Giles) left no doubt about the hypocrisy underlying the trade-off. It opened with Canterbury (Trevor Baxter) and Ely (John Abineri) apparently at their devotions in front of a crucifix. Actually, they were discussing the threatening bill in Parliament and Canterbury's scheme for avoiding it. This was a tightly focused scene ideally suited for the limited field of TV.

What tends to be ignored in the Salic Law scene is that Henry, already having decided on his "foreign quarrel" elicits enthusiastic responses from the assembled nobles who will fight the war. He pretends to be ultimately persuaded by the incitements to arms of his followers. It is a superbly calculated, brilliantly orchestrated, tactic on his part and very Machiavellian—as Shakespeare came to understand Machiavelli after the publication in English of *The Prince* in 1596. The historical parallel may be to the ease with which Bush and company persuaded a credulous Senate to support his Use of Force Resolution.

v

Any Shakespeare play imposes many decisions on its director, small and big.

A Shakespearean script is made up of small units—what Stanislavsky would call "beats." A good production will account for those beats, without rushing past. Even a pause can be significant. Consider, for example, the end of the Grandpré speech that I mentioned above:

Description cannot suit itself in words
To demonstrate the life of such a battle
In life so lifeless as it shows itself.

(IV.2.53-55)

He is not merely reiterating the French over-confidence here. He is saying that there's something strange about the presence of the English, something that doesn't add up. His words should create a brief moment of doubt that passes across the faces of the French nobles. And then the Constable says, briskly, "They have said their prayers and they stay for death." (IV.2.56) The pause permits an instant of premonition to invade a scene that is otherwise full of bluster and bravado.

A larger choice a director of *Henry V* must make is what to do with the Chorus. Clearly, the Chorus misleads us about the scene with the soldiers. (IV.1.85ff) The "presentational" mode tells us that we are about to witness Henry's "cheerful" and "comfort[ing]" (40,42) presence. The "representational" mode gives us a bitter quarrel between the disguised King and Williams. Is the Chorus "the official spokesman for the Ministry of Defence" as Ralph Berry says (1993, 29), a version of Donald Rumsfeld? Is the play, then, "a great war play embedded in a greater anti-war play?" as Berry goes on to say. (30) An examination of the Chorus leads to the issue of what the play itself "means." Can it both glorify and expose Henry's war in France and his victory at Agincourt? What does the final Chorus—a sonnet—say about the process of history itself?

vi

With the traitors—Cambridge, Scroop and Gray (II.2)—Henry shows what he learned from Falstaff. This is a brilliant scene, and it makes tremendous demands upon an audience, insisting that they know their English history and the background provided by previous plays, even as they hear it reshaped in Shakespeare's new play. The director must have that background and impart it, where it will prove helpful, to his actors. Henry now applies his tutorial "with terrifying efficiency to coldly political ends" as Hugh Richmond says. (1967. 67) The world may believe that this new king has sprung full blown from a heedless Hal, but we have been in the taverns and have watched and listened as Hal tried time and time again to trap Falstaff. We saw Falstaff run into the ultimate trap, in which he is denied his weapon, language, with which to transform reality into a convincing construction of his ready imagination. "Reply not to me with a fool-born jest," the brand new King commands. (*II Henry IV*: V.5.55) We heard Hal say early on "I know you all." (*I Henry IV*: I.2.189) We—and the world of the play—hear him say, "I know thee not, old man." (*II Henry IV*: V.5.47)

The traitors, too, run into a trap, this one not extemporaneous but carefully crafted by Henry. His management is magnificent here. The rationale for the Cambridge Conspiracy is to replace Henry with Mortimer—the heir to the throne Richard II and Parliament had named years before. The story would be well known to Shakespeare's audience by dint of its narration by the dying Mortimer in *I Henry VI* (II.5). Henry V, then, is confronting a challenge to his own throne even as he ships off to fight for the French crown. He suppresses the former and emphasizes the latter, indeed pulls God into the equation, as he does so often:

> We doubt not of a fair and lucky war,
> Since God so graciously hath brought to light
> This dangerous treason lurking in our way
> To hinder our beginnings.
>
> (II.2.184-87)

His handing of written "commissions" to the conspirators permits him to detail their complicity while generalizing about the heinousness of their crime:

you would have sold your king to slaughter,
His princes and his peers to servitude,
His subjects to oppression and contempt,
And his whole kingdom into desolation.
(II.2.170-73)

The conspiracy, according to Henry has been at the service of an incomprehensible nihilism. Cambridge—who might have been the beneficiary of the assassination, since Mortimer was childless—comes the closest of anyone to revealing the political motive. Henry could deliver a warning glance to Cambridge after his first line:

For me, the gold of France did not seduce,
Although I admit it as a motive
The sooner to effect what I intended.
(II.2.155-57)

Henry's rhetoric would have the traitors turning England into the desert place Henry's father predicted for Henry's kingship:

O, thou wilt be a wilderness again,
Peopled with wolves, thy old inhabitants.
(*II Henry IV*: IV.5.136-37)

Henry IV does not know, of course, that Henry V and not Hal will become king. "King Hal" is an oxymoron, and the last person to call him "Hal" is Falstaff (V.5.41). But Henry V cannot know that the England he so piously protects here will be plunged into desolation when the heirs of Mortimer overthrow the Lancastrian Henry VI in favor of the Yorkist claim. As in so many scenes in these plays, the historical ironies ride outward out to adumbrate the War of the Roses, already dramatized in detail by Shakespeare. History is a gray sea closing over a bright bubble.

vii

Olivier incorporates the death of Falstaff, who lies in bed listening over and over again to the new King's "I know thee not, old man" rejection in *II*

Henry IV (V.5.47). It is a World War II film, designed to coincide with the Normandy invasion (although the film came out some four months later) and it suggests that all sinews must be placed against the great wheel of the war. Olivier cuts the scene with the traitors, one that he would have delivered brilliantly, apparently because treason is not to be bruited in 1944. But Olivier includes the campfire scene and some of Williams' objection to "battle," though that speech is shifted to Court. Olivier recognizes that Shakespeare has invented the night-before-battle-foxhole scene to be replicated so often in World War II flicks, including this one. The narrative, after all, goes on to the next day and triumph at Agincourt.

Nothing in the play suggests that Henry doubts his cause, regardless of the specious rhetoric that he and others use to "sell the war." Therefore, for him, the war's premises are not debatable. Indeed, since the war is merely an extension of national policy by other means, as Carl von Clausewitz would say, Henry's response to Williams is not as "poor, muddled, and irrelevant" as John Palmer says it is. (1961, 228)

Williams does not believe that many men "can die well that die in a battle." (IV.1.141) He goes on to suggest that "if these men do not die well, it will be a black matter for the king that led them to it." (IV.1.145) It is to the question of the King's accountability that Henry responds: "So, if a son that is by his father sent about merchandise do sinfully miscarry upon the sea, the imputation of this wickedness by your rule should be imposed upon the father that sent him." (IV.1.147-50) Williams has argued the sinfulness of battle *per se*. But that is to utter "the thing that is not." War and commerce are interchangeable for Henry. The quest for a crown and a voyage for "merchandise" are the same thing. Henry's response does, of course, remind us of the "fault [his] father made in compassing the crown" (IV.1.290-91) and also of his father's dying advice about "foreign quarrels." (*II Henry IV*: IV.5.214) Henry is about his father's business, trapped in a Lancastrian point of view that he dare not see beyond. The analogy with the current war of choice in Iraq seems about as strong as such analogies can be. If it is there, let it be there. Don't force it upon us.

vii

The wooing of Katherine, so often objectionable when merely *read*, usually comes off as amusing and even moving in performance. It is a great actors' scene—as are so many in a canon that is not to be read silently like a novel, but to be experienced communally in a theater as we respond to actors interpreting the script for us and *with* us. I don't think that the source of some of the scene's humor has been noticed—that is, Petruchio's wooing of another Katherine in an earlier play. Each male instructs the woman about behavior that must not merely conform to convention. Both women are told, in effect, that they are exceptions to the stereotypes, whether those of Padua or the "fashion for the maids in France" (V.2.267) or "a country's fashion." (V.2.272) They each relent and kiss their insistent lovers. Henry claims that "a good heart, Kate, is the sun and the moon—or rather the sun and not the moon, for it shines bright and never changes, but keeps his course truly." (V.2.163-66) And this, of course, finds its echo in the earlier Kate's "And be it moon, or sun, or what you please... Henceforth I vow it shall be so for me... But sun it is not when you say it is not, And the moon changes even with your mind." (V.5. 13-20) Hortensio uses a metaphor from battle for Petruchio's triumph: "the field is won." (V.5.23) Henry's reach of conquest includes Kate as his "capital demand." (V.2.96)

But unlike *Shrew*, this comedy is surrounded by the processes of history. Henry excuses his clumsy wooing by blaming his "father's ambition. He was thinking of civil wars when he got me." (V.2.226-27) For Henry IV, insurrection was an encompassing preoccupation. What could Henry V have been thinking when he got Henry VI? The civil wars are yet to come.

Perhaps Pistol has the last word on the glory of Agincourt. Having been beaten by Fluellen, Pistol says "patches will I get for these cudgel'd scars And swear I got them in the Gallia wars" (V.1.86-87). Back in London, Pistol will claim over another pint of bitter in his lower-class pub, with the other scarred veterans of the French campaign, "These wounds I had on Crispin's day." (IV.3.46)

ix

Patricia Tatspaugh speaks of "Nicholas Hytner's highly acclaimed modern-dress *Henry V* [which] alluded negatively to the British government's involvement in the Iraq war." (2006, 325) But it's been done and done, and done. Justin Shaltz, for example, writes of Jeannette Lambermont's version for Stratford, Canada, in 2001: It was staged "with a huge upstage projection screen that looms over the action. Photographic slides, artistic images, video clips, and live hand-held camera footage—all in stark black and white—fill the screen, which is almost constantly in use." (2002, 33) Does an upstaging device like this amplify and illuminate the action? Doubtful. Television tends to reduce meanings, not expand them. A director's reliance on television argues his or her insecurity with the ways that the stage works. True, we get *our* news via TV and Internet, but it is almost invariably after the fact. The simultaneous action of actors and their images can only be distracting. Director Lambermont says that the "The video... addressed the role of the camera in our contemporary world and the ability to get information back home through videos and journalists." (Shaltz, 39) But what does that have to do with the play? And how does it coincide with Henry's carefully stage-managed return to London, as depicted by the Chorus? Shakespeare's plays, like Hardy's novels, often trade on the tardiness of the dissemination of information and on its unreliability, as at the beginning of *II Henry IV*. If television is used as part of the texture of production, as in David Thacker's police-state *Measure for Measure* (1995), then, at least, the modernization is cooperating with the text, not fighting it. What I am suggesting here, however, is that modernizations of *Henry V* are legion, thus passé, thus cliché. Why not leave in Canterbury's speech to Ely about the remarkable trade-off—a ready-made feudal system—that Henry is relinquishing for his "war of choice"? That makes the French invasion current (and on-going as of 2009) without falsifying the script or flattening it to our Zeitgeist. The play itself tells us that this kind of thing is still going on. And, if it does not, a production should implicate us in its issues, not merely remind us of our own.

The Hytner production of 2003 incorporated a real Jeep, a Fluellen who suffered a breakdown at killing prisoners, who were hooded Iraqis, and a French princess who listened to Henry's hair-raising speech before the gates of Harfluer on TV and decided that she needed a crash course in English. But we have seen this before—in Ron Daniels's wildly anachronistic production at Cambridge (Mass.) in 1995. (Coursen 1996, 239-245) If the play relates to a contemporary historical moment—and it must—let it do so on its terms and not as a product of the director's cleverness. Of course the director hates the war in Iraq and his nation's complicity in it. So do I. But let the play mirror larger historical moments by neutralizing its latent content. Olivier's film does that. The invasion of France that had occurred a few months before the film was released in 1944 was designed to liberate and not to subjugate France. Olivier's placement—in a Book of Hours influenced by Disney within a 1600 London—permitted the production to *blur* its historical moment the better to emphasize its relationship to World War II and the necessary push to topple fascism.

But here is Michael Billington on the topic:

> The real debate lies with the histories. I used to believe that since the plays deal, however freely, with actual events, it was sensible to set them in their historical periods. When Michael Bogdanov updated the whole cycle for the English Shakespeare Company, I felt one lost sight of the fact these plays hinged on a crucial act of deposition and involved an internecine battle for the crown. But, with time, I've come to modify my views. The late Stephen Pimlott, for instance, directed a brilliant *Richard II* for the RSC that muddied periods and reminded us that the play is much more than a study of the divine right of kings.
>
> It is actually a highly contemporary work in which an incipient tyrant (Richard) is confronted by a master of presentational politics (Bolingbroke) who comes to learn that populist manipulation is not enough.
>
> My suspicion is that [Michael] Boyd is generalizing from his own current experience. He is deep into rehearsals for *Henry V*, the final installment of his Stratford history cycle. In his Cheltenham talk, he took a sideswipe at Nicholas Hytner's recent National Theatre production, suggesting that this wasn't simply a play about Iraq. But *Henry V* is an extraordinary shape-shifting play that easily bears the impress of current events. And what Hytner did, dazzlingly well, I thought, was to highlight the topicality of a play in which a charismatic leader takes a reluctant country to war by appealing to religious sanctions and patriotic sentiment. There was an unforgettable moment when the Chorus announced "Now all the youth of England are on fire"—only for Hytner to show us Pistol sitting in a pub and switching TV channels from the leader's jingoistic rhetoric to the snooker. That caught precisely the cynicism of the times.

But Pistol expresses the cynicism of his times and ours without the telly.

Let the shape-shifting occur in our recognition and imagination. Even a brilliant production like Hytner's occurs only within *our* Zeitgeist. He takes away our ability to make metaphors.

Justin Shaltz in describing Stratford, Canada's, 2001 *Henry V* says "The battlefield scenes and military costuming have an early twentieth-century feel, with blighted soldiers wearing World War I era helmets, boots, and long olive-colored coats, and carrying carbine rifles and heavy packs. Yet the play begins like a 1990s telecast, with microphones, wiring, and television lighting-standards visible onstage and with an unseen director issuing amplified commands... The Chorus [is] a television documentary host." All this, says Shaltz "provide[s] a sense of timelessness." (2002), 33) Perhaps. But such a mishmash might lead a spectator to ask: When is all of this occurring? It can't be in "non-time." I think that our own suspension of disbelief might be challenged by such a production, as in absurdist theater.

But, of course, Billington, one of the most astute observers of Shakespeare on stage for many years, is right, within limits. *Richard II* and *Hamlet* can be effective in modern settings. The former does not encompass military action and can, conceptually, be configured as an "old world" vs. "new world" conflict, with the new world suddenly taking a wistful glance backward to where the old world has just been. Trials by combat and duels can be incorporated into this conception. *Hamlet* has found a home in the modern world—often uneasily—since Barry Jackson's production of 1925. And, of course, Freud's Vienna becomes an inevitable locale for *Measure for Measure*. But as soon as you have actors running around the stage with AK-47s, when the long bow is the historical weapon of choice (though virtually unmentioned by Shakespeare), you have lost me. I have seen enough of that in real life and on TV. I go to Shakespeare not for some quality known as "universality" but for the arc of the metaphor that permits me to return imaginatively to that time and to see it as like our own, or *un*like, as the script dictates its meanings to the spectator.

V

꧁꧂

Hamlet, and the Question of Ophelia

i

Why does *Hamlet* continue to interest us today?

One of the great detective stories is that of Oedipus, as rendered by Sophocles. We, the audience, know that Oedipus himself is the guilty person he seeks—the one who has killed his father, married his mother, and brought a plague to the city of Thebes, of which he has become king. We watch in helpless fascination as Oedipus discovers the truth. Shakespeare goes Sophocles one better in *Hamlet*. Here, we have *two* detective stories on a collision course. Hamlet wants to find out whether the king, Claudius, really did kill Hamlet's father, the former king. Claudius is intent on discovering what is wrong with the crown prince, his nephew Hamlet, who has been acting very strangely.

Furthermore, *Hamlet* is a story of revenge. This basic story goes back to the Old Testament and Homer. In the Elizabethan configuration, the revenger is usually less powerful than his adversary, often feigns madness, and invariably achieves his revenge through a situation that the evil person sets up—a banquet or a play—or agrees to. Claudius, in *Hamlet*, encourages the play-within-the-play, "The Murder of Gonzago," and arranges the final duel scene with Laertes. The evil person inevitably falls into his own trap. (Gardner 1963) This is "poetic justice," as when Macbeth believes that the prophecies of the Weird Sisters predict good things for him. We as audience members tend to associate with the revenger and thus enjoy the "wild justice" of his vengeance. It takes five acts, of course, before the revenge does take place. *Hamlet* is an unusual revenge play in many ways, including a) that Hamlet seldom raises the moral issue of revenge for his own consideration, and b) that the Ghost does *not* ask Hamlet specifically to kill Claudius. That is Hamlet's inference.

The revenge play is a special sub-category of tragedy. If *Hamlet* is a tragedy, the hero, Hamlet, makes it so. But when? He must revenge, as the Ghost asks him to do, and set "the time…right," as he says of his mission. That means more than adjusting a clock. It means that he must restore Denmark to health. We notice that no rituals go right in Denmark. Until the murder of the former king is solved and the political situation set right, Denmark suffers from a version of Theban plague in which normal rhythms and the sacraments themselves go awry or cannot function. The opening changing of the guard is confused—the wrong person issues the challenge. The marriage of the new king and the former queen is haunted by a funeral. The former king has been killed without receiving last rites, as he complains. Claudius cannot pray. Polonius is denied a funeral. Ophelia dies as a result of a reverse baptism, sinking to "muddy death" rather than rising cleansed into newness of life. She receives a "maimed" funeral, further disrupted by a brawl between her brother and her former lover. Rosencrantz and Guildenstern are denied "shriving time" before their execution. A ceremonial duel is a death trap for both participants. Hamlet forces poisoned wine down the throat of a dying man. Finally, a new king comes in and orders a new funeral. That last sequence is appropriate in a sense, in that it is the "King (and Prince) are dead, long live the King" formula, but we notice that, in this Christian climate of Denmark, none of the efforts to contact God succeed. By the end the royal line of Denmark is extirpated. (Coursen 2005 and 2007)

How can Hamlet set the time right? How can Hamlet return Denmark to the healthy oneness with God's universe that it enjoyed before the murder of the former king? How can Hamlet restore Denmark's sacramental premises? His only opportunity is in the play he presents before Claudius. It is his idea. It has the potentiality, as he suggests, of striking a guilty party "so to the soul" that that person "presently"—meaning at once—"proclaim[s]" his guilt. The allusion ("guilty creatures sitting at a play") is to a woman in Lynn, England, who confessed to her husband's murder during a play that depicted a similar episode. Drama—the imitation of an action, in this case a version of "This is *Your* Life"—can have a powerful effect upon the guilty conscience. (Goddard 1951, Hardison 1969) The play fails, of course, but is that because Claudius flees? Look at the text. It appears that Hamlet, not Claudius, breaks up the play. If so, this is that act that dooms Hamlet, just at the point when it might have saved him. One cannot argue what does *not* happen in a play, except when the character himself has suggested what might happen. We go into the play scene believing that Claudius may confess. He has already demonstrated a tortured soul ("How smart a lash that speech doth give my conscience!"). If Claudius confesses, Hamlet becomes king as a result of a bloodless coup and Denmark returns to its positive relationship with the surrounding super-nature. Claudius would face appropriate punishment, of course, but he might manage to save his soul. The potential confession does not occur, of course. If the play is a tragedy in the formal sense of the word, the positive ending does not happen because Hamlet interferes with his potentially redemptive play-within-the play, and, in so doing, dictates the final scene, in which almost everyone dies.

Such a reading makes *Hamlet* a coherent and well-constructed drama which builds, as a good narrative should, toward the explosive moment of "Gonzago," where the two detective stories collide in midair. Hamlet determines that Claudius is guilty of the former king's murder. Claudius realizes that that murder is what has been on Hamlet's mind. But as an immediate result of the play-within, Claudius cannot pray, and Hamlet, thinking the voice behind Gertrude's curtain (arras) may be that of the king, kills Polonius. Nothing good comes of "Gonzago." The Players leave Elsinore wondering what *that* was all about. Suffice it that a good production of the play can follow the curve up-ward to the moment of confrontation as the play-within breaks up and then pursue the denouement, which is made up of the events after the climax. After "Gonzago," the fate of almost everyone we see—physically and perhaps eter-nally (since the play is set in a Christian world)—is sealed. (See Pennington's analysis [1996, p. 90] and Shurgot's [1994, p. 7] which correct the standard mis-reading of the Play Scene).

A director editing the script for performance would be wise to ask—how is this play put together? Is the climax Hamlet's unwillingness to kill the apparently praying Claudius? Is the climax Hamlet's sudden killing of Polonius—as if the sword Hamlet has just put up very reluctantly has leaped through the curtain almost of its own accord? These are the candi-dates that critics tend to nominate as the action that determines Hamlet's fate. Each, however, is a result of the "Gonzago" scene and (regardless of what Hamlet says about it) its failure. The later scenes are moments played out amid the wreckage.

The "thematic" approach to the play, though thoroughly discredited by post-modernist critics, can be useful to a director trying to sense the rhythms of the play and attempting to edit the script toward that rhythmic imperative. This approach suggests one method whereby Shakespeare organizes his play. This assumes that the play *is* organized and that Shakespeare intended that it be. The opening line is, "Who's there?" The question gets repeated throughout the play in various ways. Hamlet asks it of the Ghost—is it an "honest ghost"? Hamlet asks it of Claudius—is he guilty of the former king's murder? Claudius asks it of Hamlet—what is wrong with him? Hamlet asks it of the Polonius he has just stabbed—"Is it the king?" Hamlet asks it of Ophelia—"Are you honest?" and later, "Who is this they follow?" "The Murder of Gonzago" interrogates both Hamlet *and* Claudius. Hamlet forgets that the power of drama may affect him as well as the king. The questions about identity are ubiquitous. That is intentional, of course. The play asks us who *we* are—who *I* am—as we respond to it. Anything we say about *Hamlet* or Hamlet is likely to be also about ourselves. Who's there? A director, editing the play for performance, might wish to keep that question riding through the production, probing at the characters inside the play as it probes at us out there in the audience.

Two approaches that can be useful with this play in dictating the emphasis of performance are the psychological and the feminist. The Freudian approach suggests that Hamlet delays because Claudius has taken his (Hamlet's) place with his mother, Gertrude. Hamlet suffers from "an Oedipus complex"—the desire to kill his father and possess his mother. Since Claudius is Hamlet's alter ego, Hamlet cannot move against him. Notice that Hamlet's intervention in his play, "The Murder of Gonzago," occurs *after* the sleeping duke is killed but *before* the murderer "gets the love of Gonzago's wife." That represents a fulfillment of the Oedipal dream. The problems with this approach is that a) it tends to see Hamlet as paralyzed and b) it tends to treat Hamlet as a "real" person. No reason exists, however, for Shakespeare's not to have characterized Hamlet as unconsciously in love with his mother and therefore disgusted at her sexuality. (Coursen, in Kliman 2001)

An intriguing approach to the oedipal issue occurred in the Smetana Theatre production in Prague in 1982, as described by Zdenek Stribrny:

...human relations in the players' company are meant to foreshadow the play they perform...—*The Mousetrap*, ...which [reflects] the chief conflicts of *Hamlet*. Evidently, the boy player is the son of the First Player [and] the Actress. However, she becomes infatuated with the other Player... Lucianus, the poisoner... the poisoning of the Player King by Lucianus parallels the poisoning of the union of the First Player and the Actress and the ...frustration of their little son, who [reflects] the fate of young Hamlet. (1984, 213)

The mirroring effect that Stribrny describes creates smaller contexts within a production that permit a spectator to grasp surrounding contexts without the imposition of heavy-handed directorial pressure. As we experience one moment of the play we learn how to experience other moments. It is up to the actors and directors to discover and perform these moments so that we can glimpse the subtle relationships latent in the script.

The feminist approach looks at marginalized characters in the scripts, particularly at women who tend to be victims of a male dominated environment. Gertrude, for example, is the woman who acquires power by dint of her husband's position. All kings look alike in the dark. In the play, Gertrude is a considerable figure. Her position, however, is compromised by Claudius's guilt. Hamlet gives her the choice to side with him or to continue at the side of Claudius. The actor playing Gertrude has to make that choice without indicating it in words. In the Franco Zeffirelli version, we notice that Glenn Close begins to wear a cross toward the end of the film. It is far too late for that. She is implicated in the guilt of Elsinore, whether consciously or not, so that the object becomes an ironic icon, an emblem of her "cleft... in twain" being. Ophelia is an obvious victim of the political power games, an object to be sold to the highest bidder. Love is a luxury that cannot be indulged in this poisonous atmosphere. No wonder she kills herself in self-defense, as the Gravedigger makes clear. Feminist criticism is extremely valuable in isolating the victims of male power games and in examining the usually futile defenses these characters throw up against the patriarchal demands of the dominant culture.

Hamlet as full-length film goes back to 1920, when the great Danish star, Asta Nielsen, played Hamlet as a woman disguised as a man for political reasons. She, of course, falls in love with Horatio, who falls in love with Ophelia. It is a moving and superbly photographed film. The Olivier version of 1949 is "the story of a man who could not make up his mind," as the voiceover tells us. It eliminates Rosencrantz and Guildenstern, and Fortinbras. Hamlet is king, very briefly, at the end. It is a black-and-white film with deep field camera work, featuring parapets and twisting staircases. Although a "Hamlet-centric" film (Olivier stars and directs), it includes the lovely blonde Jean Simmons as Ophelia and the scene borrowed from the painter Millais of Ophelia cruising down the river to muddy death. The camera watches her float by, pauses on the surface of the water, then pans downstream. She has disappeared. At one point, Hamlet puts a blonde wig on a boy actor (Tony Tarver). With the wig, he looks just like Ophelia. The Olivier is an intense and powerful film. The Richardson (1969) gives us a quirky Hamlet in Nichol Williamson and a brilliant Ophelia in Marianne Faithfull, who is played as a subversive force undermining the smooth regime of Anthony Hopkins's Claudius. Clearly, this Ophelia and Laertes (Michael Pennington) have been having an incestuous affair—an outgrowth of the incest occurring between Claudius and his brother's wife, Gertrude.

Rodney Bennett's BBC-TV production of 1980 gives us a bitingly ironic Hamlet in Derek Jacobi and Patrick Stewart's suave Claudius. It is a television production and thus lacks little sense of space or distance, except when it constructs an inner stage for "Gonzago." It makes of Denmark a claustrophobic place, as television does when a script calls for dimensions beyond those of a mere room. The Lyth (1984) has as Hamlet the great Swedish star, Stellan Skarsgard, who plays Hamlet like a spoiled rock or tennis star. Here, Hamlet makes a puppet of Yorick's skull in the most powerful graveyard scene ever filmed. Pernilla Wallgren's Ophelia is also a political danger and breaks in on an official reception, destroying the function with her search for "the beauteous majesty of Denmark." "Beauteous majesty" has become an oxymoron. The Zeffirelli (1990) gives us an active and attractive Hamlet in Mel Gibson and another superb graveyard scene, in which Hamlet loses himself for a moment in the past as he gazes at Yorick's skull. This film contrasts delicate human flesh against granite structures and is a bright and energetic contrast to the Olivier version. Kenneth Branagh's complete version gets all the words in, often via long tracking shots, and should be viewed for the wonderful Claudius and Gertrude of Derek Jacobi and Julie Christie. It has too many Hollywood hijinks and a lugubrious musical score, but it includes lines that even the long

BBC-TV version edits out, and is therefore fascinating in that we get to see and hear, for the first time, how these lines fit into production and how they are spoken by actors trying to make them mean something. The Almereyda production (2000) suffers from its low budget. It is a tawdry affair, based on the ubiquitous surveillance one encounters in the big city. It was very favorably reviewed, however.

Placing the play in a very specific modern context—as opposed to a generalized aristocratic setting—is a mistake. And it has become a cliché. Michael Collins describes a 2001 RSC production that featured "a huge television screen... Elsinore [was] a world much like our own resembling the nerve center of a police state, or, more often, the executive suite of some Western government. Hamlet drew a pistol from his jacket during his first soliloquy and later shot Polonius with it... He instructed Polonius to videotape the King and Queen from the runway during *The Mousetrap*, and their faces appeared on the huge television screen during the performance... [Hamlet] shared a joint with [Rosencrantz and Guildenstern]." (2002, 11-12) Such an approach sucks all the air into one plane of the metaphor. *Hamlet* becomes all about our contemporary world, which it is and (if we believe in metaphor) is not. Furthermore, the emphasis of such productions is on what we *see*. Hearing a play is passé, but it is mostly what we *hear* that activates our imaginative response to the script. It is what we hear that overcomes our disbelief. That had to be true for Shakespeare, after all, and a good production can still make it true for us.

Two "offshoots" that are likely to be neglected are Stoppard's *Rosencrantz and Guildenstern Are Dead* (1990, with Gary Oldman and Tim Roth) and Branagh's *A Midwinter's Tale* (1996)—both very enjoyable commentaries on their "host" *Hamlet.* (Coursen 2005, 78-81, Coursen 1999, 162 173)

Hamlet is still very much alive in our culture, as the repeated productions on film suggest. It does speak to our humanity, asking "Who's there?" A specific 'who's there?' is a production's approach to Ophelia.

ii

Until recently, Ophelia has been more popular with artists than with actors. That is not to say that, after the Restoration allowed women on the stage, great actors did not essay the role—Peg Woffington, Sarah Siddons, Mrs. Charles

Kean, Helen Faucit, Harriet Smithson, Helena Mojeski, Ellen Terry and Julia
Marlowe are just a few who played Ophelia up to the 20th century. Most of
them are noted for other roles, however—Siddons for her Lady Macbeth, Terry
for her Portia in *The Merchant of Venice*. Faucit thought that the role of Ophelia
was too small for her.

Things begin to change with the psychoanalytic approach to the play in the
early 20th century. The focus on Hamlet as character on Freud's couch did not
keep some observers from noticing that, while Hamlet may or may not be mad,
Ophelia really is. As Sidney Thomas suggests, the play shows in Hamlet an
"ambiguity of personality, the conscious assumption of different roles"—including the conventional madness assumed by the revenger within the revenge
tradition—and in Ophelia "the disintegration of personality, which is madness." (Thomas 1943, 6) In Prince Hamlet we see discontinuity of character.
He says to Rosencrantz and Guildenstern that he "has foregone all custom of
exercise" and later to Horatio that he "has been in continual practice" with
his sword. Ophelia's disintegration serves as a context against which to chart
Hamlet's frantic dashes in and out of bipolarity.

Feminist criticism, beginning with Rebecca West's *The Court and the Castle*
(1947) sees Ophelia as a victim of patriarchy and thus make of her a standin
for the victimized women of 20th century consciousness. Elaine Showalter
(1985, 77-94) shows that the victimization goes back into the 19th century,
making of Ophelia a prototypical mad woman. Even the tubercular Miss Siddal
was a victim. She posed in a pan of warm water for the famous Millais painting of Ophelia in the river. Romantic fascination with aberration and mental
disease—Coleridge's Ancient Mariner, Shelley's Cenci, Byron's Manfred, Mary
Shelley's Frankenstein—found a focal point in Ophelia. She developed in the
Victorian age into clinical madwoman.

Ophelia is always being deconstructed—why? Because the part is written
that way. It is full of options for the actor playing the role, choices. It insists on
interpretation, and so we get as many Ophelias as there are actors to play her.
Cultures change, of course, and different Ophelias emerge as a new Zeitgeist
or episteme comes into contact with the ongoing archetype of a script. The
meanings are there but are not decipherable until cultural vision can see them.
My use of the notion of deconstruction in regard to Ophelia illustrates the
point. The text, says Robert Hapgood, becomes, when productions in time are

added to the equation, "more a kaleidoscope than a single dramatic vision." (1986, 124)

Words in a script are a surface awaiting the completion of interpretation— or subtext. The words provide cues to character, but, on the page, there is no tonality, no inflection toward personality, no timber, and the pace of the words is only hinted in the vowels. Not until one reads the line aloud does one hear the options and alternatives for meaning and emphasis in the line— and then, one glimpses Shakespeare's intention, which is to insist that actors make decisions. Marlon Brando, as Antony, facing a mob that is denigrating Caesar tries to placate them. "You gentle Romans," he calls to them. Charlton Heston, listening to the same bad-mouthing, says "You gentle Romans," cynically to himself. One is beginning an appeal. The other is suggesting the subtext, the discrepancy between words and meaning he will develop in his oration. Ophelia was on stage when Jim Helsinger at Orlando in 1994 delightedly asked Polonius, "Have you a daughter?" Hamlet was playing the part of an old friend who had not seen Polonius in twenty years. That was an option that Helsinger had selected as part of Hamlet's antic disposition.

The Ophelia Shakespeare wrote is much more than Laertes's "rose of May." Directors can cut Rosencrantz and Guildenstern, as Olivier does in his film, and can eliminate Fortinbras, as Zeffirelli does in his film. Who, after all, is going to take over for Mel Gibson? They can cut the Graveyard scene, as did F. Curtis Canfield at Amherst in 1951 and Liviu Ciulei at Arena Stage in 1978. But if Ophelia is, as the early 20th century critic Levin Schucking claims "a beautiful dramatic luxury… superfluous" to Shakespeare's design (1922, 172), try editing her out of the play. Schucking had never edited the script for performance.

In the psychic structure of the play, Ophelia is a compensatory energy in the world of Claudius—as his own conscience becomes, of course. She is Gertrude's conscience: "I will not speak with her," says Gertrude. Then, reluctantly, "Let her come in." Ophelia represents the subversive feminine that Hamlet rejects within himself. When Horatio suggests that the duel be cancelled because of Hamlet's premonition—"something ill all's about [his] heart"—Hamlet shakes him off with a sneer: "It is such a kind of gaingiving as would perhaps trouble a woman." Ophelia exemplifies the conflicting agendas of many of the inhabitants of Elsinore. Of the woman in Ophelia's St.

Valentine's Day song, Anna Nardo says, "If she refuses his sexual encounter, she will jeopardize [the] marriage proposal; but because she accepts the offer, he withdraws the offer. Like Ophelia, the lass is simultaneously treated like a whore and told to be a virgin." (1983, 186)

Robert Kole provides a nice example of Ophelia as compensatory energy, even in memoriam: "Though Ophelia and the Queen show little liking for each other, the Queen tries to make amends to Ophelia in death. She makes the girl's drowning sound as pretty as she can. We even see Laertes smile at the words 'mermaid-like.' The speech seems to praise Ophelia's beauty and style, so that Laertes' confusion makes sense when he asks, 'Alas, then she is drowned?'" (2001, 12)

Ophelia is, however unwillingly, a central player in Elsinore's game of espionage. Once Hamlet is off on his sea adventure, she takes on his role as Denmark's jester, a singer of songs, a teller of truths, a respondent to the repressed system Claudius has established. Since she is unlicensed, she represents a danger to the kingdom, a palpable manifestation of the sickness raging around this usurped throne, that incestuous bed. Her role as jester is signaled to us, in case we missed it, by her interment in Yorick's grave. We learn there, at grave's edge, that she might have become Queen of Denmark had events turned out differently. She signals, then, the happy ending with which Shakespeare's tragedy always entices us.

Furthermore, Ophelia fulfills one of the depth structures of the play—that of the corrupted ritual: from the changing of the guard at the outset, which goes awry —the wrong soldier issues the challenge—to a marriage tinged with memories of a different rite of passage—"Thrift, thrift, Horatio, the funeral bak'd meats did coldly furnish forth the marriage tables"—to a ghost claiming he was murdered before he could enjoy the benefits of last rites, to Hamlet's failed effort to elicit public confession from Claudius, to Claudius's inability to pray, to the hugger-mugger interment of Polonius, to the denial of absolution to Rosencrantz and Guildenstern, to the use of a poisoned chalice to confer damnation on a dying man—"Here, thou incestuous, murd'rous, damned Dane"—to a new reign that begins, as so many new reigns do, with a funeral, where a dead prince's body confers validity to the body politic of a new king. Ophelia's death—as she sings hymns on down the river ("old lauds," Q2)—is a reverse baptism. She sinks to muddy death and possible damnation, instead of rising cleansed to newness of life and the promise of salvation. Her funeral rites are themselves "maim'd" and marred by Laertes's quarrel with the Priest and then by one of those brawls that most of us try to avoid at weddings, funerals and other solemn events. Suffice it that Denmark is cut off by regicide from the encompassing and positive powers of the grace of God. That is an old-fashioned interpretation, of course, but Shakespeare was not writing to conform to post-modernists tenets. Ophelia, who might have been a medium though which positive energies could become available to Denmark, becomes just another victim. Her story reflects the tragedy of Hamlet. I say, tragedy, because Hamlet has choices and makes them. Ophelia, like the rest of Elsinore, is subject to the errors in judgement that the Prince commits. While the range of her performance is limited—she has only 169 lines (Hamlet has almost 1500)—that range is wide. Showalter (1985) suggests a cubist Ophelia—a vibrating set of possibilities emerging from the center line—the lines in the play—but taking on many shapes as she descends the staircase of time and of imagination.

The great film director, Grigori Kozintsev, emerging from Stalinist Russia, gives political weight to Ophelia: Her "madness is a social event. People… look for a secret meaning in [her gibberish]. The government reels. The mad woman is a sign of disaster." (1967, 218) According to this reading, she, like the Ghost "bodes some strange eruption to [the] state." "Her madness has a narrative meaning, and its subject is Claudius's court," says Michael Pennington. (1996, 116) Furthermore, as Karin S. Coddon suggests, "in the ambiguous space where reason and madness intersect lies treason," (1994, 390) and treason lies in word as well as action. "My brother shall know of it," Ophelia says. She, too, "is a kind of revenger," says Michael Cohen. (1989, 123) Ophelia's songs are hardly irrelevant snatches. Women in early modern times, says Diane Purkiss, are beginning to be seen "as the bearers of a subversive popular culture which challenged the high." (1996, 202) Bert O. States suggests that Ophelia manifests a dangerous, if latent sexuality that must be controlled. (1992, 129-146) Kathleen McLuskie, speaking of *Measure for Measure*, says that women are "objects of exchange within [a] system of sexuality." (1985, 97) And that is certainly true of Elsinore. "Set your entreatments at a higher rate Than a command to parley," says Polonius to Ophelia. It would seem that Gertrude moves easily within this system of exchange. Some Gertrudes suggest that Claudius is preferable to the militaristic former king, who wore his armor to bed. The contrast between the two men is drawn by John Updike in his *Gertrude and Claudius*. (1998) Whatever Gertrude learns, she learns late what Ophelia learns too soon.

It is worth defining the moment in which Ophelia is trapped and from which she will not escape. Her madness more than hints at violation and betrayal—whether her relationship with Hamlet has been consummated or not—but it does not incorporate jealousy. In other words, Ophelia sings of first love, and loss of love, but not of one of the usual reasons for that loss—its interception by another person. The instant of loss is precisely defined and it is the more painful for its having no reason. Jealousy is a terrible emotion, of course, but what Ophelia is responding to is an inexplicable death of love.

Ophelia is a victim in the play, and she has to be played that way. Some strategies, though, keep her from being merely a product of what male critics of the play and male characters within the play say of her. Response to victimization after all varies, and that variable is built into the role. She must go mad, of course, but it is up to the actor to chart the course to that madness. I think that the script suggests that her so-called "suicide" is an assertive act on her part. As the Gravedigger says, she "willfully seeks her own salvation." The Norton editor, Stephen Greenblatt says that is "probably a mistake" (1997, 1740, note 1 to 5.1). No. The Gravedigger has always been right. She kills herself in self-defense.

I hope to suggest some of the variations within the quivering dimensions of the cubist Ophelia.

One of the most victimized Ophelias ever has to be Lilly Jacobssen in the Svend Gade silent film of 1920. Hamlet is a woman disguised as a man (Asta Nielsen) and she, of course, falls in love with Horatio (Heinz Stieda). Horatio falls in love with Ophelia. That is an unusual triangle—for this script, at least. To compete for Horatio, Hamlet must woo Ophelia. It is only at the end, after Hamlet has died, that Horatio realizes that the Prince had been a woman all along. Horatio kisses the dead lips, an ex post facto recognition of the nature of Hamlet's love for him and his for this sudden and belated she. In that the throne of Denmark requires a king, as this film interprets the election, this Ophelia *and* this Hamlet can be said to be victims of patriarchal attitudes.

The first Freudian Ophelias were, almost simultaneously, Rosalinde Fuller in New York in 1922 in the Barrymore production and Muriel Hewitt opposite Colin Keith-Johnston in the Barry Jackson's modern dress production in 1925.

Fuller was perhaps the first Ophelia to zero in on Claudius with "Young men will do it, if they come to it," as many Ophelias have done since. Hewitt played her mad scenes erotically in a flimsy gown. In each instance, the bawdiness of the lines was retained, instead of decorously edited out to suggest the finer-than-Elizabethan Victorian sensibilities.

The conventional Ophelia is exemplified by Jean Simmons in the Olivier film of the late 1940s. It is worth noting, however, that she is the only character in the film who has a contact with Nature. She lives in a flowered chamber suffused with light, in contrast to the stony shadows of the castle. Her death under trees and amid flowers is grimly appropriate. When Hamlet puts a blonde wig on the boy actor, who looks exactly like Ophelia. Hamlet knows what he is seeing, but rejects it, perhaps hinting at a drowning of his own androgyny as he shakes off the image presented so innocently to him.

The feminist approach appears on stage as early as Glenda Jackson's angry Ophelia opposite David Warner in 1965. She was loud and defiant, and her suicide was seen by critics as a rebellious gesture. Gertrude's description of it became, then, an effort to enclose it within conventional pastoral and religious conventions. Since Ophelia had often been a stereotypic "rose of May," a projection of male attitudes, when male critics had gone to school and read *Hamlet*, the critics could not deal with Glenda's version. She was "shrewish," "strong-willed," "tough," and "frigidly spinsterish." This was not Dr. Johnson's Ophelia, "the young, the beautiful, the harmless, and the pious," whose "mournful distraction… fills the heart with tenderness. (Bronson 1952, 302-303) Glenda came on with a guitar and sang her songs as if at a protest rally. The only woman who reviewed Jackson, Penelope Gilliat, thought she should have played Hamlet. (Dawson 1995, 144-45) She was asked to do so, later, but made the film *House Calls* instead. In the Ciulei production of 1978 at the Arena in Washington, Christine Estabrook's Ophelia smashed in on a state dinner party. Ophelia must interact imaginatively with the script and with the world of her production. She is not a reverent reader of the lines or a wan off-key singer, a la Lalla Ward for BBC in 1980 or Kate Winslet for Branagh in 1996.

Such Ophelias stop the outer play cold and it sometimes does not recover. Ragnar Lyth's superb Ophelia (Pernilla Wallgren) interrupts a state reception, demanding "Where is the beauteous majesty of Denmark?" and has to be hustled away, as Gertrude (Mona Malm) smiles as if to say, don't mind her. Later, as Laertes and Hamlet grapple, her body tumbles out of its coffin into the mud of her grave. Even in death, she is victimized by the games the boys are playing. In the Almereyda film of 2000, Julia Stiles plays the rebellious Ophelia powerfully. Her scream replicates the circular walkway of the Guggenheim and rattles around in the atrium below, a version of her descent into a psychic malestrom. She dies in a pool under a fountain, Hamlet's letter scattered around her. Samuel Crowl quotes Keats' epitaph in the Protestant Cemetery in Rome: "Here lies one whose name was writ in water."(2001, 42) The words on the letters themselves have melted into the recycled system of the fountain. Since they represented to Ophelia "almost all the holy vows of heaven," their erasure here hints at the anti-baptismal moment that Ophelia's drowning represents. Truth has become a liar.

Ophelia is sometimes imaged as ghost, as is Ciaran Madden in the 1970 TV version with Richard Chamberlain. Wrapped in a sheet, she resembles John Gielgud's wispy King Hamlet. In her mad scenes in the Tony Richardson film of 1969, Marianne Faithfull's pale face brings a ghostly presence to a production that doesn't have a visible Ghost. Faithfull's songs are words from the dead. A young maid's wits are as mortal, after all, as an old man's life. According to Robert Brustein, Ingmar Bergman's Ophelia, Pernilla Ostergren, "appears at the rainy funeral ceremony that follows her death. [She] materializes at the back, in bare feet, blue slip and flowered crown—now a ghost haunting her own burial service." (1988, 24) Kenneth Branagh describes the drowned Ophelia as "a beautiful ghostly corpse." (1996, 142)

Ophelias on film who reward attention are Anastasia Vertinskaya, Faithfull and Helena Bonham-Carter.

In Kozintsev's great 1964 film, the striking Ophelia is, in sanity, tightly bound and rigidly choreographed. In madness her hair is down, her gown is loose, and she is eerily ecstatic. Kozintsev says that "madness is happiness for Ophelia." (1967) 101) She also moves like an old woman, as if arthritis has settled into the limbs so robotized earlier. Yet she does move, weaving in and out of the static soldiers of Laertes's rebellion, suggesting that she has gained an ironic mobility within a rigid, militaristic world.

As Laertes lectures Faithfull's Ophelia about Hamlet in the Richardson film, she begins to laugh at his priggish lines. They are having an incestuous affair, and he is saying in a man's usual awkward way, "Save it for Me." The subtext of her response is—"Oh—you want me to keep my legs crossed? Then don't pull a double standard on me!" It is a wonderful moment, but it renders her relationship with Hamlet a kind of dalliance in the midst of a long-term affair with her brother.

In the Zeffirelli film of 1990, Bonham-Carter is an intelligent Ophelia, Hamlet's intellectual soul mate. You know that she can keep up with him in debate. In a magnificent moment in this film, which so effectively places faces in front of architecture, Bonham-Carter calls for her coach and exits. She pauses for a moment, her swollen eyes surrounded by the inside of the keep of the castle. It forms a giant crown over her head. She becomes for a moment, Queen Ophelia of Denmark.

Kenneth Branagh's film of 1996 suggests Ophelia's danger to the state. Kate Winslet is excruciating, a victim of a director who gives her nothing but her lines. When Derek Jacobi's Claudius appears, however, he recognizes that the scene is about *him* and that any effort he makes in the direction of humanity compromises his fragile political position. The production misses a magnificent opportunity by not having Ophelia die of the cold water treatments to which she is subjected in what the script for the film calls "The Wash Down Cell." (1998, 133) Gertrude's pretty speech would become the "official" version that Laertes would be forced to accept. Instead, this Ophelia has secreted a key in her mouth so that she can get to the miniature icebergs floating through the winter outside the gates. I am surprised that no director has ever had Claudius signal the dispatch of Ophelia, perhaps even giving Gertrude her "willow" speech to read to Laertes.

Valerie Von Volz's magnificent Ophelia at Monmouth in 1979 was beginning to go mad at the outset. The atmosphere of Elsinore was already affecting one of its more sensitive citizens. Her first appearance—tall, dark, eyes edging into wildness, a gauntness closing in on her beauty, a kind of Madeline Usher—made the audience gasp. This Ophelia permitted one to understand why some critics suggest that Hamlet's interruption of her sewing, as she reports it to Polonius, never really occurred. (Coursen, 2001)

Frances Barber, who played Ophelia opposite Roger Rees for the Royal Shakespeare Company in 1984 sees "Ophelia as a female counterpart to the Prince" driven mad by "her powerlessness to prevent what she sees." (1988, 145) The prose and songs of her mad scenes are a way of breaking free of the controlled beat of Claudius's court—"Though yet of Hamlet, our dear brother's death, The memory be green." A good moment occurred in that RSC production as a disconsolate Ophelia wandered off after the Nunnery Scene (3.1). The Boy Actor entered and stared at her, as if recognizing another person forced to play a role that proclaimed against identity. The moment made a thematic transition between scenes and brought together two characters seldom linked. It also reminded us that all the women in the plays had once been played by boys.

In a 1994 production at Stratford, Ontario, the older generation, Claudius and Gertrude, went about things happily, as if the kingdom had suffered only minor tremors. The element of feeling had flowed into the younger generation. The production developed the distinction between generations that Zeffirelli's late '60s film of *Romeo and Juliet* depicts so brilliantly. Hamlet (Stephen Ouimette) lashed out at Ophelia (Sabrina Grdevich) with his anger at Gertrude. Ophelia became the stereotypic "my lady" who paints an inch thick. The Nunnery Scene was an extension of the scene that Ophelia had described earlier for Polonius, but it was not an effort by Hamlet to broadcast his "antic disposition." It was blind rage. Hamlet lacerated the person most like him in the play—Ophelia. His excoriation signaled his own doom, coming as it did from a repressed self, from a denial of something in himself that he might have recognized and loved, an energy his anger toward his mother had distorted. Ophelia needed that recognition and love for her own completion. Central to Hamlet's tragedy is his inability to maintain his relationship with Ophelia. Here, that failure was not a function of Elsinore's poisonous atmosphere. That he did not recognize his natural ally in that world was Hamlet's fault.

The independent Ophelia was exemplified by Dawn Lissell in the Ashland Oregon production of 1994. In the Nunnery Scene, she made a desperate attempt to communicate with Richard Howard's Hamlet, saying the lines but trying to refute them with gestures. "There, my lord" was supposed to suggest to the eavesdroppers that she was returning gifts. Actually, she pointed to where Claudius and Polonius were hiding. Hamlet, however, instead of being grateful for her confiding in him, grew angry when he realized they were being spied upon. Ophelia's "At home, my lord" was a line in a play that she was agreeing to play since they had an audience. Lissell let out an agonized cry when she realized that her efforts to communicate with Hamlet had failed. Her soliloquy at the end of the scene became a powerful expression of her own loss. Later, in her madness, her "we must be patient" imitated her gruff father's advice. Resentment had flowed in to replace hope. She played the past in her madness, and the scenes had an eerie sense of Lady Macbeth at the beginning of Act Five of that play.

An equally assertive Ophelia was that of Asch Gregory in Portland, Maine in 1994. Her report to Polonius implicated her in a political plot of which she wanted no part. She could establish "body natural"—that is the person beneath the politics—only in madness. Her identity and grasp of reality had been driven inward so that her songs and distribution of flowers emerged from an inviolable core of being. She moved intently into her role, insisting that others play the roles she assigned. Both who she was and how Elsinore had denied that self a role were powerfully expressed. Her death was the ultimate expression of her singularity as well as an indictment of Elsinore. And of course, these motives—one personal and one political—express the cancellation that Ophelia suffers in the script.

Lissell developed roles for herself from the fragments of her psyche. Gregory assigned roles to others from those same fragments.

Julia Stiles, in the Almereyda *Hamlet* (2000) is also an assertive Ophelia, trying to carve out an independent life within the stultifying corporate structure in which her father is implicated. Her extended scream ratchets around the spirals of the Guggenheim. Diane Venura's Gertrude, smiling at her guests as she hustles Ophelia out of the way, is an apologist for a social disaster and a failed regime.

In the 2000 Odyssey production, the African-American Ophelia, Lisa Gay Hamilton, is superb in her mad scene. A lonely "other" in a white world, she actually comforts Gertrude: "We must be patient." She emphasizes Gertrude's own isolation from the killing politics swirling around the women of the court. But she is not plausible earlier in the late 19th early 20th century setting. The relationship between Ophelia and Hamlet is doubtful, particularly for a debonair and shallow prince very unlikely to find value beneath appearances. Hamlet's attraction to her cannot be written off as an act of rebellion, since she is the daughter of Prime Minister Polonius.

In the 1995 Shenandoah Shakespeare Express production, Michelle Powers was also African-American. It was stage, though, not film or TV and it asked us to suspend disbelief, and we are likely, with an unadorned stage and no specific time assigned to the script, to yield to individual performance rather than to absorb historical context and make judgements from there. In her mad scene, Powers did a brief Billie Holiday imitation. Powers' inspiration was "God Bless the Chile." It was chilling in its fusion of divergent traditions into one role.

Two brilliant Ophelias on stage were Joanne Pearce and Cathryn Bradshaw. Pearce, in the Adrian Noble version (1992) with Kenneth Branagh, was on the brink of yielding to Hamlet's importunity and would have done so in the nunnery scene, played in her bedroom, had not the King and her father been lurking in her wardrobe. Her transition from Narnia to womanhood thwarted, she played a polonaise on her upright piano. Polonius (David Bradley) closed the lid. She was not permitted her escape from childhood after what her father viewed as her failure with the Crown Prince. Madness became her future, the only place where she could find music. She lost her virginity there, rolling on her back and pulling her clothes tight between her legs. That the nunnery scene occurred in her room meant that she had "remembrances" handy and thus overcame the awkward suggestion that she had been lugging them around hoping for a chance encounter with Hamlet. She was *not* lying when she said that Polonius was "at home."

Later, in her madness, she wore the formal clothes in which Polonius had been killed, blood bright on the white shirt as a displacement for the virginity she could now lose only in mime. She was a Chaplinesque clown in floppy clothes, a "fool" bringing shallow truths to this shallow court. Her face was white, predicting the Golgotha of the graveyard and her taking over of Yorick's restless grave. We observed her in that bony light once her funeral train wended into view. She was pulled "bare-fac'd [from] the bier" twice, once by Laertes and then by Hamlet, in death as in life a puppet in a game of male posturing.

Her madness seemed a direct result of Polonius's insistence that she "think [herself] a child" when she was ready to move beyond that condition. She could only express herself in the bawdy songs that she had learned, but that had been pulled forward only because the experience was denied her. In other words, sexual repression expressed itself in sexually charged words that should have dropped from memory as her sexuality developed. The interrupted recitation piece on her piano was the sound of the interruption of her progress toward womanhood.

Bradshaw in the John Caird production (2001), with Simon Russell Beale used Claudius's (Peter McEnery) arm as the "door" that swung open to admit the "maid" of her song. It was delivered as an imitation of the voice of the roguish male who lets the maid in—"And thou hadst not come to my bed." This was the voice of her repressed *animus*, the male component of her female psyche, but an element not integrated into a healthy consciousness. That aspect could not now countervail the destructive pressures of the masculine world of the play. Bradshaw's Ophelia broke in on Laertes' (Guy Lankester) rebellion brandishing Polonius' (Dennis Quilley) staff. "Beware Of entrance to a quarrel," she cried from up-left, then launching a stunning attack of her own. She wore the formal, fur-trimmed gown in which Polonius had been killed. As in Pearce's depiction, the father's clothes signaled at once a wish for protection and the futility of that wish.

Bradshaw simulated Polonius' death and lay down, her hands folded in front of her. She was her father's alter ego, acting out something she only understood physically, and attempting to compensate for the lack of ceremony after his death, as Laertes does verbally. Since Polonius was not played with a beard (the line about his beard had been cut), Ophelia's reference to a "beard... white as snow" was the projection of old age and natural death into her mimicry. She rose, leaving Polonius' robe and shoes on the imaginary grave and scattered fragments of Hamlet's letters on the imagined corpse. Hamlet had previously torn them up and put them in her purse. This substitution of letters for the flowers Ophelia distributes had been used by Diane Venora in the Kline production (1990). Here it was poignant because the line "that's for remembrance" was directly linked to one of Hamlet's love letters. Truth became a liar. To complete this sequence, Gertrude (Sara Kestelman) dropped her own wedding veil and bouquet on Ophelia's grave, neatly objectifying Gertrude's heartbroken conflation of wedding bed and grave. Caird added "maimed rites" to the visualization of the script, stressing their significance to the world that *Hamlet* explores.

Hamlet contains its audition pieces for the title role. Michael Redgrave, Michael Pennington and Kenneth Branagh, for example, graduated from Laertes to the role of Hamlet. Pennington has gone on to double Ghost and Claudius. Sarah Bernhardt played Ophelia and later Hamlet. Probably the only actor to audition for Ophelia by playing Hamlet was Diane Venora, who played the title role for Joseph Papp and Ophelia later in the Kevin Kline production. She graduated to Gertrude in the Almereyda film.

Hamlet cannot always tell us what his play is about. I don't think he knows. If we watch Ophelia carefully, though, we will get a sense of what the production is doing. She knows, but she can only communicate her meanings and those of the play in ways that force the audience, like Elsinore, "to move the hearers to collection."

Counterclockwise from uppper left: Mrs. Lessingham, 1772; Ophelia with lute; William Poel production, 1900; Gertrude Elliott, 1913.

*Asta Nielsen and
Lilly Jacobsson,
1920.*

*A. Bromley Davenport
and Muriel Hewitt,
1925.*

*John Barrymore with
Rosalinde Fuller,
1922.*

*Lillian Gish,
1936.*

Top: Bootless, Jean Simmons prepares to cruise down the river, 1948. Bottom: Simmons and Laurence Olivier, 1948.

Top: *Anastasia Vertinskaya, Kozintsev, 1964;*
Bottom: *Vertinskaya, 1964.*

Counterclockwise from top: Vertinskaya and Innokenti Smoktunovsky, 1964;
Nicol Williamson and Marianne Faithfull, Richardson, 1969; and Bruce Cromet
and Michele Farr, Alabama Shakespeare Festival, 1982.

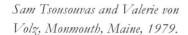

Sam Tsousouvas and Valerie von Volz, Monmouth, Maine, 1979.

Richard Monette and Marti Marsden, Stratford, Canada, 1976.

Laser Lindtner and Tina Hartvig, Olso, 1983.

Top: Roger Rees and Frances Barber,
RSC, 1984. Bottom: Lycyna
Stankiewicz, Tomaszewski Mime,
Poland, 1979.

Top: Helena Bonham-Carter, Zeffirelli, 1990. Bottom: Ethan Hawke and Julia Stiles, Almereyda, 2000.

Kenneth Branagh and Joanne Pearce, RSC, 1992.

VI

ಿತ್ನ

Reading *The Tempest* toward Production

i

A play by Shakespeare should be read only as a prelude to performance. The words on the page are a "script," designed to be activated by the imagination of a director and by the voices and bodies of actors. Reading, then, is a preliminary activity that opens into the imagination and realization of a performance, not a final action.

It follows that "readers" must place themselves in the role of director. How would I translate these words into a production of this play? The "reader" must become the actor. How do I read this line? And, of course, one hears the meaning when one hears an actor read the line. Antony, in his funeral oration after the assassination of Caesar says, "He hath brought many captives home to Rome, Whose ransoms did the general coffers fill" (III.2.90-91). If the actor emphasizes the first syllable of "coffers" he presents a fact. If he emphasizes "general," he is saying that Caesar did not add the ransoms to *his* treasury, but to that shared by all Roman citizens. "Did this in Caesar seem ambitious?" (III.2.93). The plays are replete with such moments where Shakespeare gives actors choices and options about how a line can create meaning. Try, for example, putting a different emphasis on each syllable of Antony's "If you have tears…" (III.2.168) and notice the different meanings Antony assigns to the crowd with each different stress.

Shakespeare wrote for a stage that included a broad platform, open to the audience on three sides, a "discovery space" upstage (where a king could try to pray and statues could come alive), an "above," or balcony, where representatives of besieged towns would parley with their enemies, or where Juliet would sigh for Romeo, a trap door for the appearance of supernatural beings, and entrances/exits stage left and stage right. His platform had its areas of definition: Up center was a position of power that controlled the rest of the stage. Down right (to the spectator's left) was a position of vulnerability, where Hamlet stands in the second scene of that play and where Rosalind stands when banished by Duke Ferdinand, who is up center. Down front is a place from which an actor communicates with the audience, in soliloquy or aside. Some soliloquies might be delivered as a "stream-of-consciousness," like Hamlet's berating of himself ("O, what a rogue and peasant slave am I!": II.2.549:), and some might be to the audience, as in the same soliloquy when Hamlet, more calmly, talks about people "sitting at a play" (II.2.589) who have confessed to murder. It is possible that a mixed convention inhabits the stage simultaneously: Claudius's effort at prayer might be "to himself." Hamlet's decision not to kill the King at that moment might be to the audience. I have seen Claudius' soliloquy powerfully delivered to the audience, however.

Shakespeare's stage did not incorporate an elaborate set—as do plays by Chekhov, Ibsen, O'Neill, Shaw and other playwrights. The proscenium sets of post-Shakespearean playwrights, with their "realism" and limited field-of-depth, resemble the space available on a television screen. Shakespeare's plays occurred "in space," and the scripts—with a few exceptions like *The Tempest*—do not include elaborate stage directions. The language created place, time and mood. "The deep of night is crept upon our talk" (IV.3.225), says Brutus to Cassius, even though it is a long afternoon on London's Bankside as Richard Burbage, as Brutus, says these words in an outdoor theater illuminated by natural lighting.

Shakespeare's stage represented the medieval and late 16th Century view of the cosmos and suggested the reaches of eternity. It had its "heaven"—the zodiac on the ceiling above the stage—its earth—the stage itself—and its "hell"—the area below the trap door. Those areas could be used conventionally, as in a play like *Hamlet*, where purgatory is described, or *Macbeth*, where damnation is often mentioned, or for a play that questions the very assumptions that the stage depicts, like *King Lear*. Some awareness of the original space—its actual and conceptual attributes—will help a director in adapting a Shakespeare script to the space the director has available. (Nagler 1958, Gurr 1970, rev. 1980)

Shakespeare's plays cannot be read like novels in which a Dickens or Conrad or Hemingway creates a setting and describes the characters who inhabit it. Nor are the plays merely poetry, except when characters in *Love's Labour's Lost*, or *As*

You Like It, or *Much Ado about Nothing* or *Hamlet* actually write poems, and often bad poems at that. Shakespeare writes a lot of prose, but most of his plays are written in *dramatic* poetry: unrhymed iambic pentameter, which is a line of five units, each unit composed of an unstressed and stressed syllable. Shakespeare varies this rhythm, of course, so that it does not become a monotonous metronome.

The opening of Laurence Olivier's great 1944 film of *Henry V* creates a London of Shakespeare's time that may not be historically accurate in every detail but that gives us a wonderful, bustling sense of what it may have been like for people coming across the Thames from the city to a new play called *Henry V*. The film includes a wonderful shot—borrowed from a hundred "backstage" films—of Olivier as Richard Burbage clearing his throat and stepping into the view of the Globe audience. They applaud the great actor Burbage, who bows, pauses, and then assumes his role as Henry V. It is a film, of course, but the moment captures the transition from person to actor to character in which we the audience must also participate. When we go to a play we suspend our disbelief. We don't believe that what we are experiencing is "reality," but we lend ourselves to the fiction that the actors are creating.

And we must do something like that when we "read" a play. We read it toward our own imagined direction of the script and performance within it.

ii

Shakespeare's plays are full of characters who claim contact with supernatural power: the exorcist, Pinch in *The Comedy of Errors*; the witch, Margery Jourdain, and the conjurer, Roger Bolingbroke in *II Henry VI,* the magician, Owen Glendower, in *I Henry IV*, the Weird Sisters in *Macbeth*; and Soothsayers in *Julius Caesar*, *Antony and Cleopatra* and *Cymbeline*. But no such character dominates a play as Prospero does *The Tempest*. It is as if Shakespeare has been saving the magic for one grand finale.

This "most difficult of plays," as Robert Smallwood calls it (1999, 240) usually receives two modes of treatment, with little in between: either a "spangled" version, with all kinds of visual effects designed to simulate the magic world of the enchanted island, or a spare production (Trewin 1978, 268) perhaps similar to Shakespeare's original. That might have been indoors, of course, and the Blackfriars facility might have permitted a more spectacular approach than did the outdoor Globe. Still, Prospero "on the top" and the banquet disappearing "with a quient [quaint] device" (as the 1623 Folio stage directions say) are possible on Shakespeare's stage, with its upper level and its trap door.

I prefer the plain style *Tempest*, with touches of thunder and music as the original directions call for, but with an emphasis on the language. The words should not be drowned out. Nor should they be upstaged by vivid visual effects. Shakespeare writes so beautifully no where else, except possibly in *Antony and Cleopatra*. I am not claiming that language is fundamental to the script, however. Action, as Aristotle says and as silent film versions of the plays prove, is always primary. But language and plot are interconnected in *The Tempest* more intimately than in other scripts.

When the Boatswain asks "What cares these roarers for the name of king?" (I.1.16-17) he is suggesting that Nature is superior to the politics of man. Each generation must re-learn that lesson. The opening scene also suggests that the ways of the sea are not the ways of the court: "You are a counselor; if you can command these elements to silence, and work the piece of the present, we will not hand a rope more. Use your authority" the Boatswain says sarcastically to Gonzalo. (I.1.21-24) It is a truth that anyone who has read the sea-stories of Joseph Conrad will recognize. These insights should not be drowned out by a director's tape-recorded storm. Nor should we be blinded as we listen to the lines.

Here is Susan L. Fischer's description of the opening of the 2006 RSC production, directed by Rupert Goold: "As the theatre darkened, the BBC shipping news broadcast a severe storm warning of 'Cyclonic 7 with gales of possible hurricane strength for Northern Iceland' across an oversized radio projected on a huge scrim. Gray waves then crashed on the projection scrim… and a radar dial transformed into a porthole through which the audience peered below-decks at a video of the King's capsizing ship with its panicking crew and passengers aboard. A red warning light and fading beeps accompanied the final cry of 'We split!' … The sequence ended with so-called 'white noise' whirling on a scrim that was alternately seen to be 'charting a tornado or brainwave interference'." (Fisher 2007) I did not see this production, but it strikes me that special effects were substituted for language at the outset. We also seem to get remarkable "distance" from the event depicted—a video viewed through a porthole. Do we see Ferdinand abandon ship? Do we hear anything besides the final cry? Nunn's *Twelfth Night* (1996) gives us a shipboard scene before the wreck, and thereby explains the potential interchangeability of Viola and Sebastian. What does the opening of this *Tempest* provide other than a display of directorial ingenuity irrelevant to the issues the play will explore?

One aspect of Prospero's magic is that he can summon music: "A solemn air, and the best comforter To an unsettled fancy, cure thy brains, Now useless, boiled within thy skull!" (V.1.58-60) Music in the play should not be an accompaniment, as in an old Hollywood love scene, but an element of control, a magic designed to flow into the inner being of those who hear it. It settles the minds even of beasts, as Lorenzo says in *The Merchant of Venice*. If "any air of music touch their ears, You shall perceive them make a mutual stand, Their savage eyes turn'd to a modest gaze by the sweet power of music." (V.1.76-78) But *human* nature must be capable of hearing the music, and not all men are. As Caesar says of Cassius, "he hears no music" (I.2.204). In *The Tempest*, Antonio seems incapable of the transition from inner storm to tranquility that the play's meteorology charts and that Prospero hopes to induce within his enemies. Antonio validates what the others have won. He remains outside the circle of harmony, as do so many other characters in comedy, possibly Egeus, certainly Jacques, who is "for other than for dancing measures" (V.4.192), Shylock, Malvolio, Don John and Parolles.

In "reading" this play, one must ask whether Prospero ever contemplates revenge against his enemies. He is certainly angry as he recounts past history for Miranda—"that a brother Should be so perfidious!"(I.2.67-68)—but I find no evidence in the play that he has to fight off the impulse to punish those who deposed him with anything other than the pain of their own guilt. Most observers argue that Ariel persuades Prospero toward mercy:

> if you now beheld them, your affections
> Would become tender.
>
> Dost thou think so, spirit?
>
> Mine would, sir, were I human.
>
> And mine shall.
> Hath thou, which art but air, a touch, a feeling
> Of their afflictions, and shall not myself,
> One of their kind, that relish all as sharply,

Passion as they, be kindlier mov'd than thou art?
Though with their high wrongs I am struck to th' quick,
Yet with my nobler reason 'gainst my fury
Do I take part.

(V.1.18-27).

My own sense of Prospero's progress is that he has *never* during the course of the play considered a physical revenge like that Hamlet contemplates as the latter puts his sword up and leaves the kneeling Claudius. (III.3.87 ff.) *The Tempest* cancels Hamlet's revenge. "The rarer action is," says Prospero, "In virtue than in vengeance." (V.1.27-28) Prospero descends from his god-like status, as does Cupid in the Masque, who resolves to "be a boy right out" (IV.1.101), but I see no evidence that Prospero's rage is likely to overcome his control. Something else happens.

Prospero has already—intellectually—decided against revenge at some point during his twelve-year exile. He would hardly encourage love between his daughter and Ferdinand were he thinking of harming Ferdinand's father, King Alonso. He tells Miranda that he will not harm so much as a hair on the heads of those she thinks she saw sink on that ship. (I.2.29-31) What occurs is more subtle. When he sees Gonzalo weeping at the plight of his party, Prospero's humanity catches up with him:

Holy Gonzalo, honorable man,
Mine eyes, ev'n sociable to the show of thine,
Fall fellowly drops.

(V.1.62-64)

There, he is no longer the god-like character who can raise storms and who can decide whether or not to revenge himself against other people ("Vengeance is mine, saith the Lord": Romans: XII.19), but a human being. As occurs so often, his own emotions are pulled forth by the display of grief shown by someone else. Just as the actor playing Lady Macbeth must chart her course to the hallucinations of Act Five, so the actor playing Prospero must show how he gets to the tears he sheds in response to Gonzalo's. As some characters emerge from the sea—a symbol of the unconscious—Prospero's emotions arise from within him. Human tears have the same amount of salinity as does the salt water of the sea. Robert Smallwood. however, isolates an earlier moment for Prospero's decision, or recognition, in discussing Adrian Noble's 1998 production: "Suddenly, provoked by his puzzled observation of Ferdinand and Miranda together, Ariel asked 'Do *you* love *me*, master,' and touched him on the breast." (Smallwood, 238) Thus Ariel's glimpse of what human love is rekindled Prospero's dormant memory of it and predicted his later "And mine shall."

Caliban raises a special problem for the "reader" of the play. He is a "salvage [savage] and deformed slave" in the First Folio's list of characters. But how do we depict him? Trinculo, coming upon the recumbent Caliban, apparently assumes that Caliban is a fish ("he smells like a fish": II.2.26), but what Trinculo *says* is "his fins like arms!" (II.2.34), *not* "arms like fins." In other words, Caliban's "very ancient and fish-like smell" (II.2.25) causes Trinculo to anticipate further fish-like characteristics that are not there. Caliban is a "monster" (II.2.30, and several times after that) and a "strange beast" (II.2.31), but that strangeness is in the eye or nose of the beholder. The possibilities for Caliban embrace a wide range. Miles Potter in John Hirsh's Stratford, Canada, production (1982), as depicted on a "Page to Stage" cassette is a refugee from a tidal pool. Teagle Bougere was a handsome African-American in the 1995 George Wolfe production in New York. Bougere's Caliban had eyes on Carrie Preston's Miranda. She was not averse, so Ferdinand was a timely addition to the island's population. At the end of that production, Caliban went happily off with Aunjaune Ellis's beautiful Ariel—an unusual addition to the play's happy ending. Here, Caliban was not one of the characters left out of the comic circle at the end of the play. The middle ground is represented by Warren Clarke in the BBC version (1980). He is a pot-bellied bum, lacking only a sixpack to complete his characterization.

Does Caliban stay on the island at the end, staring off after the departing sails, or does he go off to Milan with the rest? He has learned too much to return to his symbiotic relationship with his island. But can he ever be part of the sophisticated society of the Italian Renaissance? Shakespeare raises the question of the value of education ("You taught me language...") and the shortcomings of colonization through Caliban ("and my profit on 't Is, I know how to curse": I.2.365-66). Caliban would seem to be, as Matthew Arnold has it, "between two worlds, one dead, the other powerless to be born."

The Tempest raises the issue of genre. That means, simply—What kind of play is this? In the broadest sense, it is a comedy. It ends happily and with the promise of a marriage. Some call it a "tragi-comedy," in the mode of plays that were popular at the end of Shakespeare's career. In the tragi-comedy, everything seems to move toward tragedy, wherein the protagonist would, though his own volition, bring negative forces down upon his head. The best example would be Macbeth, who knows that his murder of Duncan will elicit a cosmic response. Yet he goes ahead anyway, and pays both a temporal and an eternal price for his crown. Prospero almost repeats his initial error. Twelve years before the play begins, neglect of the world and fascination with his art brought about a conspiracy "one midnight" (I.2.128) that deposed him. Again, as he is rapt in the masque that he has created for Miranda and Ferdinand, Caliban and his confederates approach. "All's hushed as midnight yet." (IV.1.207) *This* time, however, Prospero wakes up as "The minute of their plot Is almost come." (IV.1.141-42) In other words, Shakespeare creates the possibility for another fall, also caused by Prospero's too-narrow focus on his art, but cancels it just in time by having Prospero become aware of his potential error before it can harm him—and Ferdinand and Miranda, who embody the future. The play also fits the configurations of "romance," that moonlit world that Nathaniel Hawthorne discusses in "The Custom House," in which "reality" picks up shadows and shadings that change it into something between the tangible and the illusionary. Here, as in Shakespeare's other final plays, including *Antony and Cleopatra*, apparent death is a prelude to reconciliation with self and others and new life for the individual and for society. Cleopatra imagines herself returning to her original meeting with Antony, where they can begin again without the troublesome interference of Octavius. At the end of *Cymbeline*, Posthumus, seemingly beheaded, emerges from battle to rejoin Imogen. Thaisa, "supposed dead" (V.3.36) returns to Pericles. Death seldom occurs in these plays: Cloten in *Cymbeline* and Mamillius in *The Winter's Tale* are exceptions. Apparent death does occur, so that a sense of rebirth can suffuse the final scenes. The last plays usually occur in a pagan world, the better to incorporate soothsayers, oracles and magicians. In *The Tempest*, the pagan vision, as manifested in Prospero's Masque, can be said to be overtaken by the Christian imperative of forgiveness. That is an ultimate "comic" result, as in Dante's *Divine Comedy*. It is a good idea, then, in considering *the Tempest*, not to argue too strenuously for one genre or another, but to permit various definitions to suggest how the different but reinforcing ways in which the play works. Genre merely tells us what can and cannot occur within the work of art. *The Tempest* is wide enough and deep enough to incorporate several different labels.

iii

Most readers of *The Tempest* will have no difficulty in identifying the "Christian" content of the play. Prospero puts his enemies through a penitential experience ("heart's sorrow":III.3.81) and promises a "clear life ensuing." (III.3.82) Antonio seems to be impervious to the pressure to repent, but Prospero is perhaps the chief beneficiary of his own plan. He yields to Ariel's suggestion that a "human" would "become tender" at the plight of the King and his party, and Prospero agrees, finally shedding tears in response to those of Gonzalo. As his eyes "Fall fellowly drops," the humanization of Prospero is complete.

Less available to a modern audience is the play's neo-Platonic context. The effort to transcend human nature or to discern Nature's secrets, to release its essence involves magic, of course, and takes us as the play does to the intersection of magic and science and to the borderland between what is legitimate and what is an offense against God. We discern the issue in the splitting of the atom, which created an ethical problem that is still very much with us, as is the solving of the genetic code and the attendant issue of cloning. Nowadays, "magic" is "science," which threatens so-called Christians who find it easier to argue with Charles Darwin, whom they think they understand, than with Albert Einstein, whom they know they don't. For Shakespeare's time, a fine line existed between the work of Frances Dee, who defended himself against charges that he was a practitioner of the black arts, and the bargain that Marlowe's Faustus makes. Faustus achieves the ability to amaze the lesser nobility with his skills, but he cannot participate in the sacraments and he is ultimately dragged off by devils to a fiery underworld. Prospero claims to have opened graves and let their sleepers forth (V.1.48-49)—which would be black magic—but his control of wind and wave, while like that of Macbeth's Weird Sisters—is used ultimately for benevolent purposes. It should be added that his own human nature survives, even triumphs over, his godlike proclivities.

It can be said, then, that the "Christian" context proves superior to the magical, but only after the magical has been permitted to do what it can with the "fraughting souls" (I.2.13) with whom the play opens. And, of course, some magical qualities are attributed to basic Christian rituals, even if Richard Hooker, the great Anglican apologist, does not claim that any wine has been transformed to the blood of Christ.

No play has ever combined traditions as this one does, unless it be the also syncretic *King Lear*, where death cancels Christian insight, where a coming to life from "the grave" (IV, 7, 46) precedes a crucifixion. Like *King Lear*, the *Tempest*'s blending of traditions makes interpretative choices difficult. Alonso is both right and wrong when he says, "These are not natural events." (V.1.229) A magic storm has coerced human nature out from under the issues of rank and politics and into recognition of less superficial priorities—positively for most of them, even if only the evil core of Antonio remains impenetrable. Auden has Antonio say, "I am myself alone," and he becomes that terrifying entity best exemplified in Shakespeare by Iago—the personification of evil. Antonio's evil, though, is motivated, or has been in the past. At the end, it seems to be the product of mere habit.

Since *The Tempest*, of course, the great lesson of repression has been codified. Lady Macbeth learns a sterner lesson than her husband because her repression has been stronger. She experiences damnation even as her body lives: "Hell is murky" (V.1.34). *The Tempest* is a critique of rationality—but a milder one than *Hamlet* or *Macbeth* delivers. Prospero—in weeping at the sight of Gonzalo's tears—discovers a saving humanity within himself. Or, it discovers him. As the King's party emerges from the sea to be saved—if they will be—so saving salt springs from Prospero. "[F]ellowly drops" signal his reentry into the circle of humanity that for a while he has patrolled from above.

iv

The play observes "unity of time" (that is, the action supposedly occurs during "real time"), and some directors show the sun slanting across the stage as the play's day passes. *The Tempest* also casts a final light over much of what Shakespeare has done before and sends him into the twilight of his retirement at Stratford. A controlling magician who can make himself invisible and who has a spirit to serve him?—Oberon in *A Midsummer-Night's Dream*. The reunion of relatives who thought the other drowned?—Sebastian and Viola in *Twelfth Night*. An island that threatens to descend to anarchy, as does Cyprus in *Othello*? A father who, like Alonso, kneels and asks his child forgiveness?—King Lear with Cordelia. An attempt to kill a sleeping king?—the murder of King Hamlet and of King Duncan. But the murder of King Alonso is prevented, and *The Tempest* cancels Hamlet's revenge. "The rarer action is," says Prospero, "In virtue than in vengeance" (V.1.27-28). The play shows us *Hamlet* with the ending that might have occurred had Claudius confessed during "The Murder of Gonzago." The *Tempest*, then, is not only a superb emanation of Shakespeare's imagination, it is a recapitulation of his career, a gift to the audience that had buoyed him for some twenty remarkable years. If people wish to hear Shakespeare's voice as Prospero "drown[s] his book" (V.1.57) and, in the Epilogue, steps toward his humanity by becoming a mere actor hoping that the play has pleased its audience. That is their privilege.[1]

v

We get an enticing glimpse of an early production of *The Tempest* from an account book in 1611. It calls for "a curtain of silk for the Musick House at Whitehall." We know that the play was performed on Hallowmas Eve, 1 November, 1611, for King James at his residence at Whitehall. (Barnet 1987, rev. 1988, Kermode 1964, Law 1920) The curtain of silk may well have been for the musicians who played the "sweet airs" (III.2.138) and "Marvelous sweet music!" (III.3.19) that pervade the play. The silk would have made the players and their "twangling instruments" (III.2.139) invisible, as the script suggests they are, but it would have offered no obstruction to the "Solemn and strange music" (III.3.17, s.d.) trembling across the stage. In fact, that is how the play should come to us today: not a riot of color and visual effects, but a combination of eerie sounds and superb language emerging from a space that does not try to substitute for our own imaginations. When we come to a play, we agree to suspend our disbelief, and that suspension is unusually demanded by this script. The "soft music" (IV.1.59, s.d.) and the "solemn air" (V.1.58) contrast, of course, with the "tempestuous noise of thunder and lightning" (I.1, s.d.) of the opening storm and the "strange, hollow, and confused noise" with which the wedding masque vanishes (IV.1.138, s.d.). Shakespeare talks of "hearing" a play. *The Tempest* insists that we listen.

The play, like so many of Shakespeare's scripts, suffered from attempts to "improve" it. The John Dryden-William Davenant version—to which William

Pepys refers in his diary of 1667-69—began with this stage direction: "a thick, cloudy sky, a very Rocky Coast, and a Tempestuous Sea in perpetual Agitation. This Tempest (supposed to be raised by Magic) has many dreadful objects in it... several spirits in horrid shapes flying down amongst the sailors, then rising and crossing in the Air. And when the Ship is sinking, the whole House is darkened, and a shower of fire falls upon 'em... accompanied with Lightning and several Claps of Thunder, to the end of the Storm." (Furness 1892, 392) Thus are we robbed of the possibility that this is a natural as opposed to an elfin storm. In Shakespeare's script, we don't know that it is Prospero's storm until he so informs Miranda. The rest of the late 17th century script, available in the Furness Variorum Edition, represents a "marked coarsening and vulgarization of the original," as John Palmer says. (1968, 18) It tends to subordinate the themes of enchantment and slavery to misogyny. Thomas Shadwell's operatic version (1674) featured a chorus of devils and a ballet of winds. David Garrick revived Shakespeare's play in 1756, cutting only 442 lines and adding only 14. That showed remarkable restraint, given Garrick's proclivity for "improving" the inherited scripts. Charles Macready restored Shakespeare's script for good with himself as Prospero in 1838.

The 19th century demonstrated two tendencies of *Tempest* production that continue to this day. Charles Kean's 1857 production was so elaborate that it lasted for five hours—and this play is short. In the Shakespeare canon, only *The Comedy of Errors* is shorter. William Poel, by way of contrast, staged a bare, "Elizabethan" production, causing George Bernard Shaw to recognize that "The best scenery you can get will only destroy the illusion created by the poetry." (Barnet 1987, 222-23) Bernard Beckerman agrees: The play "glows in austerity. The less spectacle it has, the more wondrous it seems. It is easy to be seduced into giving form to the mysteries of the island, but that is a temptation to be resisted." (1976, 57) Keith Sturgess argues that "the magic island should not be scenically realized. ...It is a symbolic landscape... Utopia... Garden of Eden... desert place... possession [and] prison." (Vaughan and Vaughan 1999, 107 ff) Production, then, awaits the imagination of a spectator for its completion. That is something that directors should remember when dealing with this or any play of Shakespeare's.

Prospero, of course, defines the quality of the isle. Lois Potter notes that modern directors tend to "distrust [an] unproblematically presented authority figure." (Potter 1992, 450) The range that Prosperos inhabit is suggested by Anthony Dawson: "The disillusioned, weary, or even bitter Prosperos will necessarily adopt a different accent from the more traditional benevolent ones"— one sometimes "exaggerated," the other "sentimental." (1988, 231) The great 20th century Prospero was John Gielgud, who played the role for Peter Brook (1957) and Peter Hall (1974). He "looks into the future and sees... the destruction of the great globe itself with a shuddering fear," said Harold Hobson. (Hirst 1984, 55) He was "a haunted figure out of El Greco, a man filled with anguish... armed with a sword, set off for Milan, not as one who would live in easy retirement, but as one who would continue to struggle against evil." (Barnet 1987, 225) Lois Potter recalls "not Prospero's forgiveness but his aged bitterness." (1992, 450) Some felt, however, that Gielgud's magnificent "vocal skills were somewhat of a hindrance in the role [making] it difficult to believe in any spontaneous reaction to events." (Hirst, 58) Charles Laughton's Prospero (1934) was a "serene, majestic octogenarian." (Pringle 1998) Derek Jacobi (1982) "found it hard to exchange the role of an omnipotent magus for that of a mortal duke." He was "still smoldering with resentment." (Halio 1988, 42) John Wood (1988) played a "retiring, almost reluctant Prospero." (Pringle 1998) Michael Bryant for Peter Hall (1988) was aware of the "deeply sinful nature of dabbling in magic." (Potter, 450) He "yearned for God's forgiveness." (Beyenburg 1995, 203) "Max von Sydow (1970) was tempted to smash Antonio's face with his staff before he decided to forgive him." (Beyenburg, 203) Von Sydow manifested, for Potter, "tyrannical colonialism." (Potter 1992, 250) Timothy Wright in Cheek by Jowl was a "director forcing actors to improvise according to his changing moods." (Beyenburg, 203) Ian McKellen was "life-battered, weather-beaten... wryly disillusioned." (Nightingale 1999, 36) According to director Peter Hall, Prospero is "in a struggle with himself... He play[s] God... performs black magic... Caliban represents his own fear of lust and sensuality." (Southbank, 1988) Stephano, Trinculo and their plot are a surprise to Prospero, Hall says (Southbank 1988). That means that Hall's Prospero must improvise, making tactical plans that further his grand scheme for the King and his party. And, as the play shows, Prospero almost forgets to confront the unexpected conspiracy. Through Ariel, he easily thwarts the threat to Alonso from Antonio and Sebastian. Yet he almost succumbs to Caliban.

At the end, as an occasional production demonstrates, Prospero can stand with Ariel and beg the audience to "set *us* free." That means that the audience must respond so that Prospero's project can be completed just beyond the end of the action. Ariel must be empowered by the "Gentle breath" (Epilogue: 11) to "fill" the "sails" of King's ship (Epilogue: 11-12) and provide "auspicious gales" (V.1.314) that will permit Prospero and company to catch the "royal fleet far off." (V.1.316) If Ariel is included, the audience carries the imagery of Prospero's return with them as they leave the theater. It is we who have permitted that return to civilization. Thus the experience of the dramatic continuum, in which the audience participates, is reinforced.

Dennis Kennedy makes a distinction between metaphoric and metonymic modes of production. (1993, 266-67) The metaphoric approach sets the play in a world meant to reinforce meanings in the script. The metonymic technique is neutral or eclectic about where or when, but supplies specific suggestions of concept or theme within the production, often through a "single or detachable image." (Kennedy, 226) Kennedy's example is Peter Zadek's 1987 *Richard III*, where "the semicircular arena look[ed] like a cutaway barrel, with wooden slats curving upwards from the sawdust floor to the flies, making a graphic metaphor of claustrophobic space." (Kennedy 275) This "suggestive" approach usually works best for television, which lacks a field of depth that can accommodate either a location or a detailed set and which relies on editing of close-ups, two-shots and reaction shots that virtually defies analysis. In Richard Eyre's *King Lear*, for example, Ian Holm's Lear wore the Fool's cap even after the Fool had uttered his final line (III.6.85), thus reiterating the equation between the two characters. In Robert Strane's production of *The Tempest* for Asolo Theater (Sarasota, Florida) in 1980, Prospero's equipment included an astrolabe. It was not until the late 18th century that Captain James Cook perfected the sextant and made longitude available to the sailor. Strane's attention to detail rewarded the auditor who had seen many productions by placing the play in a precise historical context. In spite of Prospero's magic, the play's vision is limited to a moment when certain ways of seeing—emotional and intellectual azimuths—were still unavailable. Suffice it that the metonymic mode almost invariably works best for stage and television, each of which can be overwhelmed by too much detail within limited fields of width and depth.

J.C. Trewin suggests that productions of the play tend to be "spangled or plain." (1978,.268) I would suggest a third category—a "concept," or "metaphoric" production. The latter might be a "science fiction" version, a la the film, *Forbidden Planet* (1956), or a production that put Shakespeare's play in a futuristic setting, like that that Bernard Knox describes in the mid-1950s: "the shipwreck scene took place in a spaceship, and the action which occurs away from Prospero's cell was seen [by him] on a giant television scene." This interpretation, said Knox, matched Shakespeare's script, which replaces "the normal laws of the operation of matter [with] a new set of laws invented for the occasion." (Barnet 1987, 164) Prospero's magic could be appreciated at a moment when saucers were flying, when television was suddenly epidemic, and when the concept of being "lost in space" could be grasped by an audience staring at the black-and-white zone of television-land. The play will always pick up the interests and anxieties of an audience, whether blatantly, like the one that Knox describes, or more subtly, simply by dint of the suggestiveness of performance. Performance invariably occurs in time and within a specific historical moment, and production cannot be isolated from those contexts.

One of the best productions of the play that I have seen was Richard Sewell's at the Theater at Monmouth in 1970. It was spare visually and accompanied in its transitions from scene to scene by snippets of James Mason Neale's 1854 translation of St. Theodulph's hymn, "All glory, laud, and honour," a Palm Sunday anthem. That made a "redeemer king" of Prospero for those who knew the words. We knew that the action was occurring within a benevolent context, even if the positive impulse was being challenged by disbelief and evil. It was an "Anglican" *Tempest*, appropriate to a play that was written as the King James Bible was being completed. And that was Sewell's concept. Caliban was pagan. At one point John Fields' Prospero angrily knocked a large fish from a post. It was Caliban's sacrifice to Setebos. This Prospero was that old testament "type of Christ"—Elija, Samson—who was going about the defeating of the pagan gods. The music reinforced a moving, "old-fashioned," thematic interpretation of the play. The production would seem reactionary these many years later and it was certainly not exploring radical possibilities in 1971. It did, however, express brilliantly one of the depth-structures of the inherited script.

vi

I want to move on to three productions that incorporated the three approaches to the play—plain-style, spangled, and conceptual.

Sam Mendes's production for the RSC (1993-94) was not accompanied by spectacular effects. It began with Ariel swinging a lantern. The motion summoned wind, storm and the pitching decks of a ship. We were "invited to think about actors making *The Tempest*," says Robert Smallwood. (1996, 176) We moved from the actor, to the fantasy he created, to the "reality" that the fantasy was for the men on the ship. Alec McCowen, Prospero, stood above and behind, in command. Ariel stood stage-center. The Boatswain was down front. A hierarchy descended toward us, the audience. We were the sea—the unconscious awaiting activation—and the ultimate authority to whom Prospero prays at the end. The theater, including the auditorium, became a community.

And the production was unabashedly theatrical. Stephano and Trinculo were Prospero "offshoots," the former "a mad parody of Prospero," (Billington 1994, 38) the latter a failed ventriloquist from Yorkshire with a look-alike puppet. The payoff, of course, was that when Ariel shouted "Thou liest!" (III.2.70) Trinculo thought that the wooden head had come alive. David Troughton's Caliban was afraid of the puppet, as if it were another of Prospero's spirits. The masque became a puppet show within a life-size proscenium. The "sunburn'd sicklemen of August" (IV.1.134) turned out to be Caliban and company, having hidden within the illusion in order to perpetrate their ambush. This was a "stagey" moment, somewhat alien to the production's unobtrusive mounting, but it integrated the Masque with the "making a play" approach that dominated the production. And it made its point: as Prospero almost lost himself in his art, his enemies were permitted to invade it. The fictive layers were stripped away suddenly, as Prospero remembered "the foul conspiracy" (IV.1.139). Here, art was shattered by a reality latent in the art form and the moment suggested how Prospero had invited a threat by ignoring it until it was almost too late. As he had been "rapt in secret studies" twelve years earlier (I.2.77), here he lost himself again.

According to Thomas Larque, Michael Boyd's RSC production at the Roundhouse in 2002 showed a Prospero who "apparently lost control of his own masque, which has apparently revealed the human appetites that Prospero himself suppresses… [He] agitatedly breaks off the entertainment, having been reminded of Caliban and the conspirators." (2003, 17) Prospero becomes then, like Hamlet, the artist who is most affected by the work of art he has designed for others. Patrick O'Gara's production for the Illinois Shakespeare Festival (1996) achieved a Jungian integration, according to Justin Shaltz: During the Masque, "Prospero begins to emerge from the potential vengeful brutishness of Caliban, represented by masculinity, and ascent to the spirituality and forgiveness of Ariel, represented by femininity. [The Masque] symbolize[s] a visual crossroads for Prospero." (1996, 29) This approach seems too allegorical and very premature, but it does signal the movement from storm to calm that the play and its chief character chart.

Mendes' Ariel, Simon Beale, was a heavy, pajama-clad Maoist, who yearned for a status beyond the freedom/service equation the play asserts. The play created a wonderful metonymy when Ariel, restless for his release, was given a pinecone by Prospero. This reminded Ariel of the pine tree in which he had been encased for twelve years. This Ariel really yearned for love, not freedom. He spoke of "*your* affections" (V.1.18), as if Prospero had none. And, at the end, he lingered, aware that while he may have been leaving one vacuum, he was about to enter another. He looked back as if upon a dream or a memory from childhood—an uncompleted space that must remain incomplete. The a-human freedom "where the bee sucks" (V.1.88) was suddenly not as enticing to a spirit who had begun to absorb "a touch" (V.1.21) of human feeling. Ariel was linked to Caliban, who also yearns for freedom but comes to despise the agents of his enlargement, Stephano and Trinculo.

Most of the critics, however, found McCowen "dispiritingly low-key" (Hanks 1994, sec. 6/1) and "dangerously under-driven." (Taylor 1994, 38) But the energy often displayed by Prospero had been provided by Mark Lockyear's Stephano. McCowen's understated Prospero asked us to fill in the emotions. He did not display the anger resident in so many Prosperos, indeed resembled Ronald Colman explaining Shangri-la to Jane Wyatt. In other words, his performance matched the plain-style of the production.

George Wolfe's version (1995) was, as Pia Lindstrom said, "a mishmash of styles." (1995) John Lahr claimed that "we leave the theater remembering the sound of drums and the spectacle of gargantuan Brazilian saint-goddesses, but not one vivid line of poetry." (1995, 121) It was, said Clive Barnes, "spectacle rather than poetry, glitz rather than passion." (1995, 27) I kept looking for Carmen Miranda. And add to that tumult that Carrie Preston played Miranda as if auditioning for "The *Gilmore* Girls" and you have a design for disaster.

Patrick Stewart, however, worked against the deafening frenzy, and delivered a beautifully developed Prospero. His quirky magician could convince us that he had to decide against revenge *again* after deciding that he would not harm "an hair" (I.2.30) of his enemies' heads. If the production around him had a rationale, it was that it reflected Prospero's turmoil. His opening narrative was not the cadenced account of a McCowen, narrating an historical event, but the jumpy outburst of a man who had long-repressed his story. Prospero forgot Gonzalo's name in his opening, but remembered it much later.

"Gonzalo," he said to Miranda as Gonzalo wept at the plight of the King and his party. Prospero had to discover the Gonzalo in himself during the course of the play. When Prospero's passion met Gonzalo's compassion, the name came forward. He had resisted the earlier analogues of pity—Miranda's for those on the wreck, Ferdinand's for Alonso, Ariel's for the King and his party, but Gonzalo finally reached him, and Prospero's eyes expressed the continuum in "fellowly drops" (V.l.64). As his enemies had come out of the sea, tears came unbidden to Prospero's eyes for Gonzalo. This moment, celebrating Prospero's embrace of "fellowship," was the emotional climax of the play.

At the end, Prospero discarded his finery, adding it to the pile of trash that Stephano and Trinculo had filched. Stewart said "Now I want…" (Epilogue, 13) paused and watched the set rise to the flies. The lights came up on the tiny man standing there on the empty stage. This was an old device, of course, but it paid off in Stewart's discovering his character's deepest nature only moments before he became a mere actor hoping that we would set him free. I found this ending powerful, even as I wished that that the set and the circus attendant to it had been discarded long before.

Caliban escaped Ralph Berry's edict that "Caliban must [either] fit into the history of the white man [or be an] outcast." (1993, 129) The command that Caliban trim Prospero's cell and Caliban's promise to "seek for grace" (V.1.295) were cut to facilitate his linking up with Ariel. The two slaves leaped off to some Never Never Land, out of time and history, to create a world parallel to but very different than that of the future king and queen, Ferdinand and Miranda.

Ron Daniels production for the American Repertory Company (1995) featured a huge compass—about 40 degrees worth—curving into a great dune. This was all that remained, it seemed, of some giant craft that had crashed into the island at some moment of its prehistory. The "concept" was that all of the characters were survivors, not just the Prospero and Miranda who have escaped their "sea-sorrow." (I.2.170). Survival lay ahead for King Alonso and his party. They had entered a moment when the past suddenly meant nothing—"What cares these roarers for the name of king?" (I.1.17-18)—and where the future was an improbability. The problem, however, was that the compass blocked the center of the stage, making the area down left the primary playing area. The "concept," however, paid off, in that the bottom of the compass became the site of power here. Since at least eight of the play's characters, are, talk of, or would be rulers, their moment in the sun or their basking in dreams of sway occurred in this spot. Thus was a "theme" reinforced by simple placement on stage. And that is how directors tell an audience what their version of this play is "about." They use the stage—the visualization of space and of relationships within it.

Prospero stood on the compass for much of his disquisition to Miranda. Caliban's cave was behind the compass. Dark forces lay behind the white man's inventions. Caliban spoke of being his "own king" (I.2.342) from that central spot and assumed his leadership of the anti-Prospero conspiracy from there. Gonzalo gave his "Had I plantation of this isle" (II.1.143) disquisition on Utopia from there. Antonio and Sebastian plotted their regicide from there. Prospero drew his magic circle there, and summoned Ariel from there. Ariel had freed himself, however, and Prospero's promise of "calm seas and auspicious gales" (V.1.314) seemed frail without Ariel to summon them. Ariel's absence, however, led to Prospero's hope that "Gentle breath of *yours* my sails Must fill."(Epilogue, 11-12) We were where the storm and the sea had been and now became the many-handed god to whom the former magus prayed. He had no other source of magic.

In spite of the obstacle that the compass represented, the concept would have worked had it not been for Paul Freeman's Prospero. He was of the "old school" that went out with the solos of Donald Wolfit and the quavering recitations of Maurice Evans. He sounded like a 78 rpm record playing amid the very different dramaturgy and acting styles of the mid-1990s. He ranted and raved and glinted opaquely out at the audience, a berserk colonizer out of Conrad stumping around the sand like Robinson Crusoe, leaving no "r" untrilled. Jessalyn Gilzig's Miranda was infected by this one-man frenzy and could hardly have been accused of not attending to Prospero's story. If anything, she over-reacted, already a nervous wreck on the basis of a mere narration. Only Benjamin Evett's calm and cleanly-spoken Ariel helped the early moments of the script to make sense.

The production finally modulated toward coherence. Freeman delivered the "revels" speech calmly and "in context." It was not just another rip-roaring rant or recitation of a well-known anthology piece. And Freeman paused before he asked Ariel "Dost thou think so, spirit?" after Ariel spoke of being "human." (V.1.20) This was not the spiritual wrestling to which Stewart subjected his Prospero. Yes, Freeman's Prospero said: that's what I meant when I first raised the storm. I had to wonder why Freeman displayed so much sound and fury earlier.

While, clearly, I argue for minimalist productions that permit changes in character to be displayed and discerned, a post-modernist approach to this script can incorporate the latest technology. Frances Teague says "Because Prospero's magic is his only source of power, the way that his magic is presented becomes an index to his character." Teague suggests that Prospero as "artist" deploys magic "as an aesthetic event like a masque or ballet." For the "tyrant," magic is "darkly alarming" And for the "incompetent sorcerer," "the magic is comic and inadequate." She goes on to describe a production directed by David Saltz, wherein "Prospero's magic is the perfect metaphor for contemporary digital media." While I am not certain that any metaphor can be "perfect," the mode of production sounds interesting: "Every movement [Ariel] made was picked up by the sensors she wore and was transmitted to a large scale computer animation that followed the performer's lead," so that Ariel became a "virtual puppet." As Saltz says "In one scene... Ariel transforms into a monstrous harpy; in another, she becomes the waves and thunder of a sea storm, and in yet another she creates a spectacular wedding celebration that vanishes with the snap of a finger—'such stuff as dreams are made on.'...The use of the remote control wand heightened the sense of a largely passive Prospero, who could summon up visions but could not take part in them." (2001, 21-22) While Prospero can be played as an unmoved mover, I am more convinced that he is most the beneficiary of his own project to touch the hearts of others. Prospero, like Duke Vincentio, should not inhabit some zone outside of the dramatic action. The Saltz experiment is one I wish I had witnessed. It sounds, though, like the substitution of one performance for another, with the emphasis largely on the substitute.

vii

The Tempest raises many questions, some of them unique to this script. I will briefly deal with the issues of the Masque and gender.

Anthony Dawson asks "How does one find a style [for the Masque] that fits credibly with the overall conception [of the production], whether the emphasis is on colonialism, magic, symbolic representation and renewal, or weary and resigned futility?" (1988, 237) The Masque offers a contrast to the play around it, of course, as the short, rhyming lines of "Pyramus and Thisbe" collide with the blank verse of *A Midsummer Night's Dream*, and as the stilted couplets of "The Murder of Gonzago" contrast with *Hamlet*. The plays within-a-play in *Hamlet* and *A Midsummer Night's Dream* are interrupted, and each furthers the themes of the play that surrounds it. This is not obvious in the also interrupted Masque. When Cupid breaks "his arrows, Swears he will shoot no more, but play with sparrows, And be a boy right out" (IV.1.99-101), as Iris reports, "he swears he will no longer be a god," as Kittredge's note says. (1939, 135-36) Cupid refuses to infect Ferdinand with venereal desires and could be said to represent the sublimation of that lust prior to its authorization by ritual. Cupid's decision *within* the Masque predicts Prospero's decision in the play to descend from godhead and meet his enemies on the plane of humanity. The Masque should, I believe, have an effect on us similar to that it has on Prospero. We have overheard Caliban's plans with Stephano and Trinculo, and we, as well, forget about it until Prospero remembers. In other words, no matter how a director treats The Masque, it has to be at once part of and apart from the play surrounding it. Its apartness is signaled by Prospero's command "No tongue! All eyes! Be silent." (IV.1.59) Other inner plays permit and sometimes invite audience commentary, as do 'The Play of the Nine Worthies," "Pyramus and Thisbe," and "Gonzago." But not the Masque. Later, after Ferdinand has questioned Prospero about The Masque, Prospero says, "Hush and be mute, Or else our spell is marr'd" (IV.1.126-27). The point, of course, is that we, as audience are meant to pay attention to the inner play and not to watch its audience, as in *Hamlet*.

While productions of the play are notorious for raising the issue of colonialism—which David Kastan argues is product of our own back-projection on the script (1998, 93-101)—it seldom explores the question of gender as does a comedy like *As You Like It*, with Rosalind, already a boy actor, playing a boy who insists on being a stand-in for the "absent" Rosalind. In 2000, Vanessa Redgrave played Prospero at the Globe in London as a conventional male. (Collins 2001, 12-13) Redgrave did not, then, disturb the "father-daughter" dynamics of the script. Shakespeare has plenty of father-daughter combinations—Minola/his daughters, Capulet/Juliet, Shylock/Jessica, Egeus/Hermia, Polonius/Ophelia, Brabantio/Desdemona, Lear/his daughters, and so on—and some father-son combinations—Henry IV/Hal, Hamlet/Hamlet, Polonius/Laertes—and a lot of mother-son combinations—Tamora/her sons, Constance/Arthur, Duchess of York/Richard III, Duchess of York/Aumerle, Volumnia/Coriolanus, Queen/Cloten—but few mother-daughter combinations. Thiasa and Marina, Hermione and Perdita meet after long estrangement, and Cymbeline's Queen is an "Evil-eye'd" stepmother to Imogen. (I.1.72)

Demetra Pittman in the Ashland production of 2001 played Prospero as woman. Antonio became Antonia (Linda Alper). Prospero was *not* happy at the developing love between Ferdinand and Miranda, although she had encouraged it. She was "a mother who struggles against the impulse to step in… and supervise her daughter's life. [T]he incipient loss of her daughter overwhelms any pleasure in her project's unfolding." This Prospero "finds refuge in magical power from the pain of human relations." This Prospero did not give up "her beloved magic," but left the objects of its manifestation—staff, book, and robe—"for the island's new monarch, Caliban." This strange variation on the ending cannot have been merely the result of a change in Prospero's gender, but a placement of perversity in "the feminine," which was reluctant to put any trust in the male world, even though it was a sister who has been the betrayer, but then sanctions Caliban's accession to island kingship. Somehow—I know not how—this production "reflects an old-fashioned reading of the play, crediting Prospero with a moral journey… and the harmonious reconciliation of all the play's contestants for power." But somehow the issue of Prospero's harmony seems to have remained unresolved. Interestingly, this production's Gonzalo (Richard Farrell) went native. "As he describes his utopia, Gonzalo transforms himself by degrees from a grave counselor to an exuberantly barefoot beachcomber." It would seem, on the basis of report, that this script does not lend itself to the alteration that Alan Armstrong reports: "Good wombs have borne bad *daughters*." (2002, 25-26) *King Lear* will support that thesis, but will *The Tempest?* That question may still await a production that can answer it. Perhaps Julie Taymor's forthcoming version with Helen Mirren as Prospero will give that convincing answer.

viii

Monmouth's first production was of *The Tempest* thirty-six years ago. It occurred while a thunderstorm crashed and burned outside. I still recall my surprise that such a superb offering should find its way to this needle point of a town in central Maine.

The latest version was a "plain" as oppose to "spangled" version of the play. The costumes carried the imagery, particularly for the Queen (Alonsa) and her party, who were dressed for their destination, but not for a shipwreck. Off stage rattles and thumps, discretely employed, articulated the magic of the island. No effort was made to put the text to any allegorical uses, Christian or colonial.

A sure sign of amateur direction in Shakespeare, though, is a pause between scenes. To create such a break after the hunting down of Caliban and his confederates is legitimate. It permits hilarity to drain off prior to the solemn ending. But earlier pauses seemed to be just a matter of not getting actors on stage in time. An audience has to be educated to the continuity of Shakespeare's dramaturgy. The first line of a new scene hits the last syllable of the final line of the previous scene. We are constantly engaged by the seamless flow of action. Otherwise, people applaud tentatively at scene's end and destroy the continuum between spectator and stage. On the night I attended, the curtain was ten minutes late. Such tardiness also encourages an inattentive audience by violating the contract into which a Shakespearean spectator enters, however half-consciously.

Bill Van Horn's Prospero functioned at top decibel from the outset. His opening narrative was painful to him, and his admonitions to Miranda were really his own admission that he was having trouble telling the story. That interesting approach created a problem: he overpowered the small auditorium, in contrast to the relatively soft-spoken rest of the cast. Van Horn modulated his delivery for his "revels" speech and for his colloquy with Ariel about humanity and revenge at the beginning of Act V. But when he spoke to Gonzalo about "fellowly drops," he shed no tears, merely mentioned them. Salt would have surprised this Prospero and the moment would have been very moving. And when Van Horn needed power, in his "elves of groves" speech, for example, he had already used it up, and much of what he said merely blasted on by. Tracie Merrill was a very good Miranda, facially responsive without "acting," and challenging her father from the stance of a maturity that Prospero was slow to acknowledge. Her "My affections Are then must humble" was a rebuke to Prospero, not a tentative admission of love. Victoria Caciopoli's Ariel was splendid, precise in movement and diction, signaling a subtext of skill and invention that could accomplish all of Prospero's complicated commands. The play crackled when she was on stage. Janis Stevens' Alonza combined amazement with enjoyment during the final set of revelations, the latter a quality I have never seen in the character. Stevens dominated the stage during her few moments. Dustin Tucker's Trinculo sometimes spoke directly to us, a permissible technique, given Shakespeare's stage and Trinculo's role as jester. The sequence with Caliban's gabardine was very funny—Tucker on top, his legs over Caliban's shoulders as the latter crawled around wondering whether he had become the monster Stephano describes. During the "Thou liest!" interplay, drunken Stephano (Michael Anthony) missed Trinculo, but the latter was hit anyway by Ariel's slaps, transmitted across thin air. It was a neat parody of how blows are often faked on stage, Ariel clapping her hands as Trinculo reeled. Caliban (Adam Pena) was merely a good looking young man somewhat skimpily attired, so that remarks about monstrosity were in the eye of the beholder. I hoped that perhaps Caliban and Ariel might get together at the end as did Aunjanue Ellis and Teagle F. Bougere in George Wolfe's New York City production (1995), but no such luck. Mark S. Cartier's Antonio and Charles Waters' often inaudible Sebastian projected no menace at all, so that the "Macbeth rhythm," as G. Wilson Knight calls it, did not resonate here. It was interesting, though, to hear Waters, an African-American, deliver the lines about Claribel's abhorrence of the King of Tunis.

The opening scene occurred in one of Monmouth's ornate boxes (down right) and was free of line-annihilating sound effects. That the Queen's party actually handled sheets and lines, though, blurred the Conradian distinction that the scene makes between the way things work on a ship and the way they work on land. I admired the effort to put on a complete Wedding Masque, though here it was a trifle ponderous, and I don't think anyone could recognize that a malign Cupid represented a threat to Miranda and Ferdinand before resolving to be "a boy right out." The Masque tells of a godlike persona becoming human and thus predicts Prospero's own progress toward those tears he sheds on seeing Gonzalo.

This was a good production whose primary virtue was a modesty of design that showcased some excellent acting.

ix

The Tempest has not fared well on film or television. Television is a "realistic" medium and does not ask us to suspend our disbelief. Furthermore, its limited field of depth permits only the most simple of special effects. The spectacular needs space. Film could work for this script, of course. The opening storm at sea threatens the ship as passengers and crew believe it does. The camera tracks across the waves, leaving the ship boiling in the distance, and discovers Prospero and Miranda observing the isolated zone of wind and rain that surrounds the ship. And so on. The language would have to be squeezed and the camera privileged, but that is what film must do. *The Tempest* would make a great contemporary film, but no director has dared undertake it. Sir John Gielgud had this to say about the play as potential film: "I think *The Tempest* would make a wonderful film and have my own ideas about how it would be done. The play has to be set in several, unidentifiable locations: marshes one minute, cornfields the next, then cliffs and sea, and finally sands." (Cook 1985, 164) We learn from this how flexible Shakespeare's platform stage could be, and also that Gielgud's vision was betrayed by Greenaway's *Prospero's Books*. Gielgud begins with the space in which the action occurs, knowing that space defines what can occur within it. We notice when we read the play that different characters respond to the same environment in very different ways. Film, which by its very nature, *has* space as other media do not, and the fluidity of camera that can isolate individual reactions to the same stimuli should be a superb vehicle for this most imaginative of Shakespeare's scripts. And what good composer would not leap with the alacrity of an Ariel for the chance to compose the score for this film?

The earliest of the silent films on the British Film Institute release of 2000 is the weakest, a 1908 *Tempest,* directed by Percy Stow in Great Britain with an unknown cast. It begins with Prospero in a small boat at the side of a larger boat receiving (we assume) Miranda and a large book. He "seeks refuge on an island" and appears in front of some patently phony rocks with Miranda in one arm and the book in another. Immediately, we notice film's reliance on the iconic tradition that preceded the printing press. We assume, perhaps, that Prospero's book is an illuminated manuscript full of occult material that somehow survived medieval suppression. Blessedly, the film goes on location. Prospero finds Caliban eating roots and subdues him. Ariel calls to Prospero from an unconvincing imprisonment inside a tree, and Prospero frees her. Ten years pass by in the time it takes to read the title card. Caliban woos Miranda, but Ariel, in the guise of a muskrat, chases Caliban away. The scene suggests the techniques of visual transformation that film would achieve later, as Jekyll becomes Hyde, a man changes to a werewolf, or James Cagney feels his face grow marv'lous hairy as Bottom becomes an ass. Prospero creates a spell in a poof of smoke from which three doves fly forth. A ship, viewed through an opening in a cave, founders and sinks, much to Miranda's distress. Ferdinand, however, swims to shore, sheds his cape, and looks about, shading his eyes. Miranda sees Ariel as the script suggests she does not as Prospero sends his spirit off to fetch Ferdinand. In a series of dissolves that imitate Georges Meiles—the inventor of trick photography—Ariel plays a game of hide and seek with Ferdinand, who fears that Miranda will become the same diaphanous creature. She is real, though, and the two embrace at first sight. Prospero celebrates, then separates the two. Ferdinand carries several small logs, then gives up. Miranda arrives and helps him lug a larger log a few feet. They pause to smooch. Prospero comes down the path, shakes hands with Ferdinand, and blesses the couple. Antonio's party, resting on the grass, is treated to a disappearing picnic. Prospero and this group become "Friends once more." Ariel is released and dances happily into the woods. Prospero shakes hands with someone we assume to be Ferdinand's father. A long boat slides in past the obvious flat and all climb aboard (including some from the "water" on the other side of the boat), except for Caliban, who wants to go with the departing people but is shoved back to the island.

What this film leaves out is, basically, the *evil* to which Prospero responds. "A genial Prospero forgives all," says Kenneth Rothwell, (1990, 283) but for what? For all we know, he and the baby handed to him could be the first ones off a sinking ship. The film, however, is an interesting experiment in the simplification and visualization of the inherited story. Its use of location and special effects—like the disappearing and reappearing Ariel—demonstrate Stow's awareness that his new medium is free of stage conventions. And the title cards outline the scenario that the actors will mime—a more effective approach than the one some directors of silent Shakespeare employ: quoting lines from the play in advance of the scene's visualization. The silent films support Aristotle's contention that *action* is the basic component of drama.

The BBC-TV series was unjustly panned. It does include an excellent *Measure for Measure*, which is in many ways a soap-opera and therefore eminently "televisual," Derek Jacobi's splendid Richard II, Robert Lindsay's superb Iachimo in *Cymbeline*, and Jane Howell's wonderful *Henry VI* sequence, where a playground set becomes at once a place for politics and a sardonic commentary on that old profession. But *The Tempest* (1980) is dull and dark. A metonym for the production is that a dead apple orchard was imported for the set. Michael Hordern's Prospero is an annoying Mr. Badger. He "puts everyone asleep as effectively as he does Miranda," Maurice Charney suggests. (1980, 287-96)

The opening scene is filmed, as opposed to taped, yet presents no sense of emergency. Masts, sails and sheets appear under the opening credits, but the rain falls straight down, as if the ship were safely moored in a windless harbor. Film, if carefully scaled, can work on TV, of course, but BBC wastes four minutes and forty seconds of it here. Most of the words are inaudible, so that the point about "authority" (I.1.25) and "the name of king" (I.1.18) are useless amid the "roarers" (I.1.17) of the sound-effects.

The production tends to fall between stage, which can incorporate long speeches, and film, which demands visual equivalents of the language. Even in an oral medium like TV, Prospero's exposition is tedious, although Pippa Guard does the best she can as listener. She delivers the "Abhorred slave" speech (I.2.351 ff.) as Folio suggests she should and frightens even Prospero. Having seen Hordern in Clifford Williams' tame 1978 RSC *Tempest*, I thought that a muted Prospero might work on TV. But the irascible-schoolmaster model fails here as well.

But even weak productions sometimes reward careful observation. Television's limited field of depth prevents movement within its space, but the framing of shots in this production is sometimes effective. As Miranda and Ferdinand (Christopher Guard) exchange the sight of first love, Prospero, camera right, tells us that he must prevent "too light winning." (I.2.451) The camera creates a simultaneity of response and counter-response that lends a sudden and unexpected texture to the moment. Antonio and Sebastian plot in a two-shot that frames Alonso and party, the target of the conspiracy. Trinculo's lines about Caliban (II.2.144-173) are delivered as sour asides, a technique that lends surprising "interiority" to the jester. Nigel Hawthorne as Stephano is very funny as he tries to "think" while dead drunk. Warren Clarke's "Be not afeard" (III.2.144) is splendid. His Caliban expresses a sense of selfhood that is symbiotically interfused with his island. One senses the source of his grievance against Prospero. He tells us that this was a magic place even *before* Prospero arrived to subjugate him. The banquet disappears beneath the harpy's wings of David Dixon's Ariel, so that Prospero's "A grace it had, devouring…" (III.3.84) has a visual antecedent. Miranda's "How beauteous mankind is!" (V.1.183) is to Antonio (Derek Godfrey). She recognizes the resemblance to her father. This camera work neatly sets up Prospero's bitter "'Tis new to thee." (V.1.184).

A spritelier version is the 1960 production, directed by George Schaeffer, with Richard Burton as a sonorous Caliban, Tom Poston as an amusingly befuddled Trinculo, and Lee Remick as a luminous Miranda. Roddy McDowell's Ariel is sometimes an annoying insect that Prospero must brush away, a victim of early TV's effort at special effects. At one point, McDowell is dropped too soon by the boom on which he's been "flying" and makes a miraculous crash landing. Evans' Prospero is a tremolo recitationist of the old school. Jack Gould noticed one issue of translating the play to the small screen: "closeups [are not helpful with a play] that requires reporting that is fanciful not factual." (1960, 63) Of course, TV tends to be "factual," and blurs the line between fact and fancy as *The Tempest* does so often. We suspend our disbelief on TV only for kiddie cartoon shows, presidential news conferences and Fox News. The production ends with Evans speaking the "revels now are ended" speech, an understandable directorial decision given television's tendency toward simplification and prime-time wrapping-up.

The Bard production (1985) begins with Prospero's thinking up a linear storm represented by two blue streamers, pulled up and down by spirits. This could work on stage, but on a naturalistic medium, Prospero's calming of Miranda is irrelevantly ex post facto. And, again, the sound drowns the lines of the opening. The production is placed on a stage resembling Tudor England—balcony and discovery space included—but it never works out an effective relationship between its stage-like premises and the ever-present television camera. A difference always exists between being in the space where the performance is occurring and having a camera, which is never neutral, mediate between our eyes and what the director chooses to show us. Admittedly, a stage director will show us, via lighting and sight-lines, what he wants us to see, but we are always aware, when watching a TV show, that it was made in the past. A live performance is being created as we observe it and, given the openness of Shakespeare's stage, we participate in it with our emotions and imaginations.

Efrem Zimbalist Jr., Prospero, is a television actor notable for his portrayal of an FBI officer in a long-running TV show of the '70s. Perhaps as a carryover from this role, he is mildly ingratiating—the public servant pretending to be concerned for the public welfare. He does not modulate his Prospero at the beginning of Act V, a relaxation of god-like capacity toward the human insight that is at last ready to meet a compassionate equivalent. He is blandly consistent.

But, again, the production is worth watching. William Hootkins plays Caliban with understated precision—an excellent style for a medium that punishes hyperbolic acting. The scene between Caliban, Stephano and Trinculo—and Ariel—(III.2) is excellent. Ariel is in full view but the stage-like premises permit us to accept his invisibility. A lithe dancer, Duane Black, as Ariel would have been excellent in live production. The banquet is replaced by skulls, but we are looking at Prospero when the substitution occurs, so that the off-camera transition comes as an effective surprise. The characters in the Masque become the dog-faced furies that chase Caliban and his confederates. This "doubling" provides a brief glimpse of the plasticity of the "bare island" on which the action occurs.

The Tudor façade keeps forcing us to unsuspend the disbelief that the stage-like setting and the front-on camera work encourage. Director William Woodman never varies his lighting, so we experience no contrast in visual tonality. The entire production would have picked up energy had it been played in front of a live audience. Such an event, even televised, can simulate the experience of theater, as in Joseph Papp's versions of *King Lear* and *A Midsummer*

Night's Dream, several TV productions of plays done on the Stratford, Canada, main stage, and RSC's televised *The Comedy of Errors*. The sense of living people responding to what is happening on stage can add to a television viewer's enjoyment and overcome the "in the can" feeling of most TV drama.

The animated version (1992) is disappointing—the cartoon format has already conditioned us to "things invisible to see," so the magic is merely more of the same, not like the special effects that can startle us in *The Wizard of Oz*, *Vertigo*, or *Raiders of the Lost Ark*. This animated production uses puppets—each frame reflecting a slight adjustment in the figures. The value of these animated versions may be, as Laurie Osborne argues, that they teach a young audience how to respond to film and to Shakespeare on film. (Osborne 1997, 1998, 73-89) The best of the animated versions—*Hamlet*, *Richard III* and *The Taming of the Shrew*—are masterpieces of condensation and narrative drive. An alert viewer of the animated *Tempest* will notice a unicorn munching on the foliage.

Fred Wilcox's *Forbidden Planet* (1956) shows that the man who gets hold of magical powers is likely to be destroyed by them. It is a science-fiction version of *Dr. Faustus* and still worth watching in spite of the evolution of the genre at the hand of many intelligent designers since 1956. The special effects, by the MGM master A. Arnold Gillespie, feature a horizon different than any viewed on Earth, and are particularly vivid. Pauline Kael, who saw them all, calls *Forbidden Planet* "the best of the science fiction interstellar productions of the 50s." (Jacket cover)

Derek Jarman's *The Tempest* (1980) is set in a ruined wing of Stoneleigh Abbey. The film was trashed by Vincent Canby as "very nearly unbearable" (1980, c20), but praised by Walter Coppedge in 1998 as an effort "to detemporize the classics… to get away from the limitations of time." (1998, 12) Assuming the film becomes commercially available, students will have a chance to mediate between Canby and Coppedge.

Paul Mazursky's *Tempest* (1982) features John Cassavetes's mild mid-life crisis, a vibrant debut by Molly Ringwald and Raul Julia's wonderful Kalibanos. Its resemblance to Shakespeare's play is tentative and at times forced. At one point, Ringwald tells a friend, "We're studying *Macbeth* at school. It's unbelievably boring!"

Among the most ludicrous of versions of the script is Peter Greenaway's

Prospero's Books (1992). It does have the merit of a reprise of Gielgud as Prospero. Otherwise, Greenaway substitutes the crawling, squirming insides of books—as if their covers were rocks that had been lifted up—for whatever the script may be saying. He imposes television upon film, a blatant reduction of scale and artistic premises as he gives us a seemingly interminable Home Shopping Network sequence, in which actors so out of work that they have pawned their very clothes present fishes and bananas to Ferdinand and Miranda. Within this misconception, Greenaway can do nothing with Caliban. We get a standard new critical version of the play. Suppose Greenaway had pursued Caliban's suggestion that Prospero's books must be seized, that they are a source of power, and had depicted a contest for control of the media. Seize his books—and then his television station! That's what rebels do these days. As it is, even Miranda's potential to bring forth a brave brood for Stephano is hardly an issue here. The isle is full of naked people presumably prepared to give delight and not get hurt. That this film has become the favorite of the theorists argues that it was not made to bring a new interpretation of a complicated script before audiences, but to attract the avant-garde to its gimmicks. Not much time will go by before the film is seen for the travesty that it is.

Worth considering in detail, because it illustrates the problems with "adaptations" of Shakespeare recast into a familiar or contemporary setting, is *The Tempest*, which aired on NBC in December 1998. Recent "straight" films of the plays—Branagh's *Love's Labour's Lost* and Taymor's *Titus Andronicus*, for example, have failed at the box office. We are likely, then, to get more *O*s, more *(Ten) Things I Hate About You*, and more *Romeo Must Die*s. I enjoyed the latter as satire, though most critics seem to have taken the film at face value. And *(Ten) Things* has such a slender connection to its source, that Shakespeare and the film do not collide in the traffic pattern. The NBC *Tempest*, however, demonstrates vividly the fallacy of linking the play to a specific time period. That is true, even though the NBC script eschewed the language of the play. It did pursue the *praxis*—that is the action, or plot.

It is set in the Confederacy of 1865. The thematic links with the American Civil War would seem to emerge from the "freedom-bondage" concept that runs through the play and illustrates in different ways the conflicts of Ariel, Caliban, Ferdinand and Prospero. Here, we have an irrelevant Gator Man, played by J. Pyper-Furgeson, who wants his bog back, and an Ariel, played by

Harold Perineau, who combines Caliban *and* Ariel. The "spirit" can become a crow at any moment he chooses, but he also does a lot of the domestic chores. An unfreed slave, who learns about the Emancipation Proclamation two years after it has been issued, he wants to join Grant's army on the way to Vicksburg.

The production resembles a narrative of Haitian voodoo thrust upon a Civil War reenactment, or perhaps a nightmare of Mr. Hightower, Faulkner's preacher in *Light in August,* whose sermons keep rumbling off into the dust of one of Jeb Stuart's cavalry columns. The voodoo is promising (a la Gloria Naylor's *Mama Day*), but the production places the narrative in a specific 1865 and makes Ulysses Grant an unseen sub-hero, thereby introducing a host of issues the script does not raise and blurring beyond distinction what the script does invite a production to explore. A specific historical moment is seldom a good environment for the translation of a Shakespeare script to any medium, and that is particularly true for television, where a limited field of depth cannot accommodate background. A specific historical moment may suggest a superficial metaphor but soon collides with the hard facts of the play itself that torpedo the linkage below the waterline. Here, it doesn't matter.

The special effects "from the same masters who dazzled in last spring's miniseries, *Merlin*" (Williams 1998, 2), are tame and tiny, as they must be on a medium that lacks the scale for the spectacular and that usually translates the supernatural in to the psychological. (Dessen 1986, 1, 8) We learn all that we need to know when we are told that "the teleplay is by veteran TV writer James Henerson, whose work [includes] '*I Dream of Jeannie*' and '*Bewitched*'" (Bobbin 1998, 2)—two shows that emerged from the very different personae of their resident witches.

The major problem with the production is its remarkable lack of believability. Television is a medium of soap operas that treat in tedious detail the reasons for meaningless actions, or that show persons whose stories reveal the poverty of the human experiment. Peter Fonda's Gideon Prosper is a victim of both strains of these twin displays of futility. The sudden effort to lynch him—he is, after all, chief landowner of the area—is as improbable as his deliverance from the rope. We infer that the abortive lynching has been instigated by Prosper's evil brother—but inference is a difficult process for television. I believed for an instant that the narrative would be a version of Bierce's "An Occurrence at Owl Creek Bridge," and that *The Tempest,* would be a long dream within a short drop, but, no, Prosper actually does escape to a nearby swamp, there to live in exile. In the theater, we suspend our disbelief for the moment. Film can ask us to do that. Television can, as well, though it is a stretch. Still, the words "once upon a time" can weave a spell to which adults will willingly lend themselves.

But Prosper's motivation to stay in the swamp grows more and more implausible as he is pressured to develop a conscience. The effort here is to parallel the development of Shakespeare's Prospero, as various characters present their own compassion to him, but NBC's Prosper is more a puppet of the plot—a Pinocchio—than a recognizable character struggling with a moral or ethical dilemma. Why does he object to his daughter's elopement with her handsome Union officer? Prospero has reasons for slowing the romantic pace of Ferdinand and Miranda, but to change the motive into a sudden hatred of Yankees is to introduce yet another irrelevancy to the story. Since the swamp is right around the bend from the old plantation, Gideon can go after his usurping brother at any time. His excitement at hearing that his brother is near is incomprehensible. Has Prosper been laboring in some fog of amnesia until then? After Prosper's storm, Katherine Heigl's Miranda, little homemaker that she is, gets herself off-camera by saying that she is going to check on the house. We remain breathless until she returns to report that nothing of the vine-woven, bark-covered Tarzan treehouse has perished. At another moment, after Gideon is plugged through the breastbone by his brother, Anthony (John Glover is a terrible shot until asked to shoot offhand from a rocking boat), I thought that we were going to be asked to clap our hands and say that we believe in "Dat Ole Black Magic." Prosper recovers, however, without audience intervention.

At the end, rewards are handed out. The production answers the still-vexed question of Caliban by showing that Gator Man gets his swamp back because he had courage. I thought that Gideon would hand the cowardly blusterer a purple heart. As Prosper, Miranda, and Fred leave the island, Gator Man stands on his deck. No one waves goodbye. What does work is Anthony's sneering refusal to accept his brother Gideon's hand at the end, even though a firing squad awaits him. But we wonder, given this blank Prosper and this perfidious Anthony (who has committed far worse than *The Tempest*'s Antonio), why the hand has been offered in the first place. Since the action had seemed to be influenced by a voodoo priestess appearing as a face out of flames, the sudden advent of a "Christian" set of values has not been prepared for. *The Tempest* may be more pagan or cabalistic, more Giordano Bruno or Cornelius Agrippa, than a reflection of Richard Hooker and the reformed church, but it does have a strong Christian rhythm. How could it not? "After all," as Barnaby Dobree, writing of the final plays, says, Shakespeare "belonged to a Christian country; he had been brought up on the Bible; so its ideas, its familiar phrases, would naturally occur to him." (1961, 148) Even an explicitly pagan play like *King Lear* has deep Christian undertones. Here, we cannot believe in either pole of the play's syncretic value system.

I sought some equation between Gideon Prosper and the Bible's Gideon. The first name cannot have been chosen at random, after all. In the Book of Judges, Gideon is one of the citizens oppressed by the Midianites. After a lot of negotiation with God, which involves tearing down the altar of Baal, tests in which a fleece left out over night is alternately wet with dew when the ground is dry or dry when the ground is wet, and the reduction of his army from 22, 000 to 300 (so the Israelites can't brag about what *they* have done), Gideon drives the enemy out, killing most of them, including the princes, Oreb, Zeeb, Sebah and Zalmunna. It is a great story, but I could not find any parallel between it and this version of *The Tempest*. The first name apparently sounded "southern," "old-fashioned" and biblical.

The production reminds us of our own dispensation by constantly interjecting, at what the directors must have deemed moments of unbearable suspense, commercial breaks. Many of them were for what must be the worst television shows imaginable. If the spots selected to promote these shows are so crashingly unfunny, for all of the artificial laughter that floats around them like dead leaves, why would anyone be tempted to watch them? At other moments, since the production appeared only a dozen shopping days until Christmas, the mosquito-buzzing swampland of the Mississippi Delta was juxtaposed against the snowflakes, balsam trees, colored lightbulbs, and other clichés of a white, middle-class Christmas.

Freeing the slaves was necessary and overdue, but it was only a secondary reason for the American Civil War. Did the production meant us to infer the knowledge that the brave new world of Reconstruction became a version of the old world very quickly. What on earth is executive producer Raskin talking about when she says, "We loved the banishment and the isolation, in this case, in terms of North versus South"? (Williams 1998, 2) That statement signals incoherence at the heart of the project.

I asked myself a) whether the production would have been successful without any knowledge of *The Tempest* to get in the way, and b) whether the production enhanced our sense of the source. In each case, I answered no. The production itself is tedious, elongated beyond its intrinsic content and centered on a mere Scrooge. Its connections with the original script are so tenuous or simplified that it distorts rather than illuminates. Unlike other works of art—painting and sculpture, for example—the plays of Shakespeare permit us to inhabit them in our time and, inevitably, *with* our time. This production simply abandons its originating source—Shakespeare's play—and gives us a far lesser thing in its place. This production was like one of the sources of Shakespeare's plays, awaiting the alchemy of his genius.

It will be objected, rightly, that my critique would not even occur were it not for the production's linkage with Shakespeare's play. True—without that connection this *Tempest* would have passed unnoticed, its radical inconsistencies merely those of television melodrama. Our expectation of the medium is a fragment of Aristotle's "final cause"—the effect of the work of art on the observer. This *Tempest* can be said to have met our expectations for television, which are low. Television is in its infancy—and likely to stay there. We learn about it, however, as it encounters the Shakespearean script and struggles to find the right balance between a heavy concept and a bare stage.

Perhaps it goes without saying that so far no film or television production has recreated the effect of music emerging from players invisible behind silk. *The Tempest* awaits a film-maker with the vision and courage to show us "how" the script means on film. Perhaps Julie Taymor, who has already directed a brilliant *Titus*, will show us how it is done.

x

Roger Warren says that "theatrical interpretation of Shakespeare is a continuing process. Each new production makes its own discoveries." (1990, 243) Dennis Kennedy agrees: "One way to imagine the scenographic history of Shakespeare is to see it as a series of attempts to make a home for the otherness of the texts." (1993, 310) Every production of a play makes an effort to give the script "a local habitation and a name." The names and habitations vary, of course, through time and with cultures. *The Tempest* is a play of surpassing "otherness," and that is a quality that changes as history and culture decide what is "other" and what is not. Ralph Berry suggests that "Our experience of [The Tempest] will suggest fragments of a great allegory." (1993, 138) The play touches the "boundaries of both Prospero's magic and the ephemeral magic of the theatre," says Anthony Dawson. (1988, 241) Usually, the fabulous quality of the magic is enhanced by the spareness of the setting that surrounds it. What the play's allegory may be will be variously described by different auditors of even the same production and by those who will hear the play on stages not yet built, in ages yet unborn.

VII

Shakespeare on Film: The Web of Allusion

i

The great modern medium, film, has brought some magnificent versions of the plays to us, as only film can, with the language greatly reduced, the spectacle greatly increased. Less remarked are the ways Shakespeare pervades films not ostensibly based on any of the plays. In previous sections of this book, I have argued for "archetypes"—central ideas in the scripts that must be recognized and that must flow into the values that inform a particular production. They do not have to be the same archetypes, of course, but *Hamlet* must explore the question of identity. *Richard II* must examine the probably insoluble dilemma of a bad king. *Henry V* should look at the qualifications that gather around "successful" kingship. *The Tempest* suffers, I believe, if Prospero remains an "unmoved mover."

I would suggest that Shakespeare provides a basic cultural background for film itself and that the frequent allusions to and uses of Shakespeare in film demonstrate the ways in which a medium for which Shakespeare did not write reaches back to touch a source of artistic energy that comes forward in time to inform the moment at which the reference is made. The allusion is an acknowledgement, unintended or consciously made. Some allusions ask simply that we recognize ourselves within a cultural continuum, that is, to sense the link between the line from an old play and its meaning in the immediacy of a moment in a film. Other allusions are more substantial, asking us to experience a "source" even as we respond to a work of art on screen. This response approximates the experience of spectator in the late 1500s of one of Shakespeare's history plays—an awareness of "source" combined with a simultaneous perception of the drama at hand.

Shakespeare is not our contemporary, but he becomes a co-inhabitant of our culture through film. That our American culture has been "teened" in the past sixty years or so argues that *Romeo and Juliet* would be the most frequently adduced of Shakespeare's plays in recent films. And, as I will suggest, it is.

To make the argument for Shakespeare's pervasiveness in film, I must provide examples, of course. Since I wrote *Shakespeare Translated*, a look at recent and older, unnoticed adaptations of and allusions to Shakespeare in films, I have found several more. Some, I grant, are little more than transitory allusions. Others, though, are useful ways of interrogating the film in which they appear. I will include some of the former instances by way of illustrating how the latter work in their films. It is entirely possible that I do not grasp the full significances of any particular allusion.

The most interesting, of course, are those where the Shakespeare play deeply informs the film, serving as a model for the plot or as an organizing metaphor for the film's narrative. *Shakespeare in Love*, of course, uses Shakespeare for both purposes, providing a version of *Romeo and Juliet* and employing the script of the play to capture the film's exploration of gender roles and to provide its final sequence, in which fictional farewells reinforce what is happening in the lives of the actors.

Seldom is a reference to Shakespeare merely random, although its application may sometime be a product of a critic's ingenuity rather than a screenwriter's intention.

Zola's version of *King Lear*, *La Terre*, was filmed in 1919 and released in 1921. Directed by Andre Antoine, the film reduces the Lear story to the world of the small farmer. The old farmer, Pere Fouen (Armand Bour) divides his land in return for a promise of a pension, along with an allotment of wine. Things go immediately wrong, of course, when the pension is refused, the wine turns out to be undrinkable and the beneficiaries' hospitality turns hostile. This is a disjointed film, hard to follow, and imprecise in the points of view that the camera is simulating. The film falls far below the standard that the silent screen was beginning to set just after World War I. It does give a good sense of farming before machines became available, though it all seems like a throwback to the world of Millet. Ironically, about the only element of coherence in the film is the pursuit of the Lear story. Those who know the main plot of the play can follow some of the action in the film. Otherwise, the *King Lear* narrative adds nothing to the film. Watching it is a grim and unrewarding experience.

One would expect Shakespeare to appear in films that feature actors who also played Shakespeare, particularly films that originate in Great Britain or that include British actors.

In Zolton Korda's magnificent *Four Feathers* (1939), Ralph Richardson's blind Captain Durrance, ostensibly reading Braille, recites Caliban's speech to Frederick Culley's Dr. Salton. Caliban says "I cried to dream again." Richardson says "I cried to sleep again." And then, having showed off his prowess with Braille, he says that he learned the speech at school. Is this a subtle undercutting of the film's depiction of courage, cowardice and chauvinism, signaled by Durrance's having not memorized the speech quite accurately? At the end, after all, C. Aubrey Smith's General Burroughs is caught out for his fibbing about Balaclava. The substitution of the word "sleep" for "dream" may suggest a wish for oblivion.

In *Kind Hearts and Coronets* (1949), Alec Guinness recites Rosalind's "who time gallops withal" as he is about to go to the gallows for a murder he did not commit. Reprieved at the last minute, he stands outside the jail's gate, wondering whether to join the woman who has delivered his alibi or the wealthy woman to whom he is married. He is then reminded that he has left his diary in his cell. It describes the many murders of which he *is* guilty. The sound of hoofbeats recurs as poetic justice gallops in.

In *The Lavender Hill Mob* (1951), Stanley Holloway, who had been Olivier's Gravedigger, recites, "O polish'd perturbation, golden care, that bring'st the ports of slumber open wide to many a watchful night." Holloway's Alfred Pendlebury is the accomplice of Alec Guinness's Henry Holland. They are melting gold and casting it into imitations of cheap Eiffel Towers for export. Both, of course, will go to gaol, but Holland will enjoy a carefree year in Rio before he is led in handcuffs back to England. The lines from *II Henry IV* allude, of course, not to the crown but to the souvenirs cast to make and ultimately mar their fortunes.

The reference to Shakespeare may be so brief that only the most alert of ears will pick it up. In *Theodora Goes Wild* (1936), for example, a tipsy Theodora (Irene Dunne) enters Michael Grant's apartment and asks Michael (Melvyn Douglas), "Are these your etchings?" Grant says, "They are," and paraphrases Touchstone, "Poor things, but my own." The line argues the cultural sophistication of the character using it. Charles Van Doren (Ralph Fiennes) uses the same line ("A poor thing, but my own") in explaining his complicity in playing a fixed game to his father, Mark (Paul Scofield) in *Quiz Show* (1994).

A similar allusion may occur in *The Maltese Falcon* (1941), when Humphrey Bogart holds the supposedly golden falcon up and says "Such stuff as dreams are made of."

Another conventional use of Shakespeare occurs in Ernst Lubitsch's *Cluny Brown* (1946). As the Butler (Ernest Cossart) argues that Cluny (Jennifer Jones) be fired for her clumsiness—she has even dusted the eye out of one of Sir Henry Carmel's hunting trophies—Belinski (Charles Boyer) rises and quotes *The Merchant of Venice*: "The quality of mercy is not strained. It droppeth as the gentle rain from heaven." He raises his glass. "To Shakespeare," he says. Cluny is spared, but Syrette the Butler is appalled. The man had actually risen from the table and addressed him as a *person*! But Belinski, the Czech emigre, and Cluny, the apprentice plumber, end up married and living in the egalitarian U.S.A. The film is a subtle study of England's stultifying class system as it existed just before World War II.

Another conventional rendering occurs at the end of *Sherlock Holmes and the Secret Weapon* (1943). The RAF lumbers off to Berlin, equipped with the Tobel Bombsight that Professor Moriarity had hoped to give to Germany. Basil Rathbone (Tybalt in George Cukor's 1936 *Romeo and Juliet*) recites, "This fortress built by nature for herself, this earth, this realm, this England." John of Gaunt's speech becomes, as so often, a paean to patriotism. It had been spoken by Leslie Howard's Pimpernel in the 1934 Korda film, as the Scarlet Pimpernel awaits execution at the hands of Citizen Chauverlin's (Raymond Massey) firing squad. The Pimpernel, of course, has so arranged things that the squad is made up of his own men.

A more complex intrusion of Shakespeare into the Holmes mythology occurs in *The Seven-Percent Solution* (1976). Having deciphered Holmes' (Nichol Williamson) dream and having experienced Holmes' deductive powers, Freud (Alan Arkin) tells Dr. Watson (Robert Duval) that "We are such stuff as dreams are made on." Holmes had earlier told Freud, "You enjoy Shakespeare." Here, Freud uses the line from *The Tempest* to define the field he will study. The methodology will be that of Sherlock Holmes. Holmes' repressed memory had been of Moriarity making love to Holmes' mother. Moriarity, here Holmes' math tutor, permits Freud to show Holmes what his tutor actually taught him, via a long-delayed insight. The quotation from Shakespeare suggests that Freud's career, for all of the fame he has already achieved, is really just beginning. The time is just before 1900, the date of the publication of *The Interpretation of Dreams*.

In *The Doctor's Dilemma* (1958), as the artist Louis Dubedat (Dirk Bogarde) is dying, Sir Ralph Bloomfield-Bonington (Robert Morley) remarks "I think it is Shakespeare who says that the good that most men do lives after them, the evil lies interred with their bones. Yes, interred with their bones." His inversion is meant to be recognized by the auditor, of course. Sir Ralph is a fool. In Shaw's play, Sir Ralph goes on to deliver a version of Macbeth's soliloquy worthy of "the most celebrated thing in Shakespeare," as Twain's Duke calls Hamlet's soliloquy. Sir Ralph's further excursion is cut from the film, which is, after all, a film and is winding up:

> Tomorrow, and tomorrow, and tomorrow,
> After life's fitful fever they sleep well
> And like the insubstantial borne from which
> No traveler returns
> Leave not a rack behind.
> Out, out brief candle,
> For nothing canst thou to damnation add.
> The readiness is all.

One of Shaw's coercive stage-directions claims that Sir Ralph's speech is "too sincere and humane to be ridiculed." That impossible cueing is not what the film suggests.

Shakespeare also appears in unlikely black-and-white contexts and centrally in more than one.

Trouble for Two (1936) features a prince in disguise, Florizel of Bohemia (Robert Montgomery), who joins a "suicide club." The film is based on Robert Louis Stevenson's short story, "The Suicide Club." What MGM adds to the story is a love plot in which the princess to whom Florizel had been engaged in an arranged marriage arrives in London incognito. The story merely mentions a failed love affair suffered by the young man who introduces Florizel to the Suicide Club. MGM borrows the princess from *The Winter's Tale*. In the film, Rosalind Russell's character, unlike Perdita, knows who she is, of course. Russell administers a love test to Montgomery, a la *As You Like It*. At the end of the film, Montgomery must fight, mano a mano, for his kingdom, as Prince Hal must do at the end of *I Henry IV*. Earlier, Montgomery had been admonished by his father, the king (E. E. Clive) for his carefree ways. While the other hints of Shakespeare may be coincidental, the centrality of *The Winter's Tale* to the film's narrative is obvious. This is an intriguing film which begins with expectations of Nelson and Jeanette but quickly becomes a fog-bound London thriller.

In *Ball of Fire* (1941), the naive professor, Bertram Potts (Gary Cooper) gives Sugarpuss O'Shea (Barbara Stanwick) a ring, with an inscription inside. "See how my ring encompasseth thy finger. Even so thy breast encloseth my poor heart. Wear both of them, for both of them are thine," a lengthy sentiment for the inside of a ring, as Potts explains. Later, given a choice, Sugarpuss discards the huge diamond given her by her hoodlum fiancé, Joe Lilac (Dana Andrews) and retains the ring Potts has given her. Professor Gurkakoff (Oscar Holmolka) explains to Potts that this means that Sugarpuss really loves Potts! Potts does not realize that his lines of love emerge from the stunted Richard III, so Sugerpuss's preference for the professor signals her rejection of Lilac and any sinister connotations surrounding her new relationship. Suffice it that things do end happily.

In *In a Lonely Place* (1950), Charlie Waterman (Robert Warwick) arrives at Dixon Steel's (Humphrey Bogart) apartment, thirsty for a brandy. He recites Sonnet 29:

> When in disgrace with fortune and men's yes,
> I all alone beweep my outcast state,
> And trouble deaf heaven with my bootless cries,
> And look upon myself and curse my fate…

He puts Steel to bed and concludes with "For thy sweet love remembered such wealth brings, That then I scorn to change my place with kings." Steel's lover, Laurel Gray (Gloria Grahame) tiptoes in and whispers, "then I scorn to change my place with kings." It is a sweet moment in a film in which Gray must finally discard her Jekyll and Hyde lover. It is also a brilliant performance by Grahame in a moving and unsentimental film. Robert Warwick had played Montague in MGM's 1936 *Romeo and Juliet*.

In *Blackboard Jungle* (1955), based on the novel by Evan Hunter (Ed McBain), Glenn Ford recites part of Henry V's speech before Harfleur and gets the job teaching at an inner city school. His knowledge of Shakespeare contrasts with the illiteracy of the students he inherits as he steps into the jungle of this school. Ford's character must finally "imitate the action of the tiger" in confronting a knife-wielding student (Vic Morrow). Was the contrast between the Harfleur that yields without a fight and the vicious students who manifest only violence intended? Certainly the contrast between "education" and brute resistance to it is clear. Another intentional contrast is that between the idealistic Ford and the school's cynical faculty, represented by Louis Calhern, clearly waiting things out until retirement.

As You Like It appears briefly in *Never Been Kissed* (directed by Raja Gosnell, 1999). Josie (Drew Barrymore) and Jason (James Franco) go to the senior prom as Rosalind and Orlando. "Shakespeare?" one of the teenagers asks. Since Josie is back in high school as a 25-year-old reporter for the *Chicago Sun-Times*, some element of disguise and deception is involved in her characterization. She is not disguised as a male, though, in her undercover role or—as is quite obvious—in her prom costume as Rosalind. The film is relatively successful in arguing the necessity for a transition from the vicious teen hierarchy of high school into responsible adulthood. Josie represents that transitional figure, as do Rosalind and, through her tutorial, Orlando, in the play.

American Pie (directed by Paul Weitz, 1999) deals with four high school seniors determined to lose their virginity before the graduation that looms ahead. Their English teacher (Clyde Kusatsu) summarizes the *Henry IV-Henry V* transition this way: "So, once Hal becomes king he has to take on the responsibilities of leadership and turn his back on his old drunken friend, Falstaff. You see, Hal is going through a rite of passage, much as you all are. So make the most of your time together. You'll miss it later." This is perhaps to reduce Hal's transition to Henry V to the ultimate banality, but the students are—however obliviously—embracing their teacher's advice. But their version of rite of passage might be more accurately captured in the final line of *The Merchant of Venice*. No Nerissa, however, appears among the characters of the film. Each of the lads does, in anticipated or unexpected ways, fulfill his version of rite of passage.

Hamlet, of course, appears often in films.

Kenneth Rothwell, having seen the Hal Roach *Bromo and Juliet* (1926) at the Folger, says that this is one that Shakespeareans "should probably avoid." (1990, 248) I did enjoy, though, the Cop (E. J. O'Connor) suddenly materializing on the balcony and chasing Charley Chase's Romeo back down the ladder. The film also includes a *Hamlet* scene—Hamlet and the Ghost, a staple in 19th and early 20th century theaters. Here, Hamlet and (presumably) Horatio enter, cueing the moon. "Every night when yon full moon rises," says Horatio. A quarter moon is hauled up, with a drunken Charley, a fugitive from "Pyramus and Thisbe," sacked out in its curve. He climbs off and walks away along a wall, pausing to bow to Hamlet and Horatio, who bow back. Hamlet, staying in character, says, "This is the hour when my father's ghost doth walk." Charley grabs the sheet from the actor playing the Ghost and staggers out on to the wall, pursued by the Cop, who by this time is enjoying his dramatic debut and also wears a sheet. We identify him by the outstretched arm with the billy-club in it. The film has recently been restored with a new musical score by Turner Classic Movies and premiered on 2 April, 2007.

In *The Arizonian* (1935), a placard for a show in the territories circa 1880 promises "Hamlet and the Ghost." The Ghost is a terrified Negro who says, "I ain't gonna play no ghost!" just before the stage manager puts a sheet over his head. So the film plays on that stereotype, as well as giving us a stagy Hamlet (D'Arcy Corrigan), wearing a dark outfit and black yarmulke. Hamlet cries, "Angels and ministers of grace defend us," as the sheeted apparition appears, to the understandable hilarity of the cowboys attending. "I'll call thee Hamlet, being a thing immortal as itself," he proclaims before the scene is obliterated by the raucous spectators shooting six-guns into the air. Singer Margot Grahame comes out and shouts, "You cowards! If I had a gun I'd shoot back at you!" She is persuaded, though, to sing the immortal "Roll along, covered wagons, roll along," and the good-natured crowd soon joins in. The *Hamlet* sequence is a cut above the work of the King and Duke in *Huckleberry Finn*, but not by much.

The play is a handy device for labeling a fool a fool. In *My Son, My Son* (1940), the British Colonel (Stanley Logan) says, "Wasn't it Kipling who said 'To be or not to be—that is the question.'" The war correspondent (Brian Aherne) says, "No. I believe it was Shakespeare." Since the film deals with a failed relationship between father and son, the allusion to *Hamlet* may be intentional. Since the film deals with World War I, the allusion to Kipling in the mouth of a stupid senior officer is probably intentional.

In *My Favorite Spy* (1951), a conventional Bob Hope flicker and the last of his "My Favorite" series, Hope doubles as a smalltime comic and an international criminal. At one point, he picks up a skull and says, "Alas, Poor Yorick! To sleep, perchance to dream." A hole in the back of the skull prompts "Popped your cork, huh?" Hope then says, "Looks like a fellow I know who sings," a dig at Bing Crosby, of course. Perhaps the disquisition to the skull mirrors Hope's dual roles in the film. The skull becomes, as Hope says, his "straight man." The moment predicts Robin Williams' similar parody some 35 years later on *Saturday Night Live* ("Doctor, I think we have a malpractice suit here!").

Another allusion to *Hamlet* occurs in *Our Man in Havana* (1959), when Dr. Hasselbacker (Burl Ives) says, "One may smile and be a villain." He refers to Captain Segura (Ernie Kovacs) a thuggish member of Batista's constabulary in pre-Castro Cuba. It is an apt comment, since Segura is not just another sadistic functionary. At the end, he hands Jim Wormold (Alec Guinness) an incriminating slug—the one Wormold has used to kill his enemy. But it was Segura's gun that Wormold had stolen and used, so the policeman delivers a complicated message about his power and his humanity. He is also in love with Guiness's daughter (Jo Morrow). Like Claudius, Segura is more than a mere stereotype.

Stay (2005) is a "psychological thriller" directed by Marc Forster. A psychiatrist, Dr. Sam Foster (Ewan McGregor) is searching for Athena (Elizabeth Reaser), an aspiring actress. He finds her rehearsing as Hamlet with Rosencrantz (Sterling Brown). They are doing the scene in which Hamlet complains that "Denmark's a prison." The important lines for this film are "There is nothing, either good or bad, but thinking makes it so," and "I could be bounded in a nutshell and count myself a king of infinite space where it not that I have bad dreams." Athena complains to Foster that she is playing Ophelia. "Things get tough, she jumps in the drink. Hamlet hogs all the good lines." The allusion to Ophelia underscores the film's preoccupation with suicide. The rehearsal points not just at the indistinct line between good and bad and is not just metaphor for "bad dreams." Since Rosencrantz forgets where he is in the script and repeats "A prison, my lord?" the rehearsal points at the film's repetition of moments within it. In fact, after Foster has chased Athena out of the theater, he returns to find her rehearsing the same scene with Rosencrantz. That she would prefer to play Hamlet suggests the transfer of roles that occurs in the film. Foster is trying to keep a suicidal college student, Henry Letham (Ryan Gosling) from committing suicide. But as he tries, Foster suffers a massive attack of transference, as his psyche is invaded by Letham's. They become alter egos, speaking each other's lines and exchanging physical positions. It is indeed a bad dream in which levels of reality and illusion alternate within the minds of the two characters.

At the end, Letham is apparently successful in killing himself, although the film seems to tell us that he has been dead all along as a result of the car crash with which the film begins. Has the first death been "real?" The three days after the initial auto accident become, perhaps, a numinous projection of a person for whom suicide is superfluous.

The film borrows heavily for its ideas and effects from directors like Cukor (*A Double Life*), Fellini (*Juliet of the Spirits*), Hitchcock (*Vertigo*), Kurosawa (*The Bad Sleep Well*) and Ramis (*Ground Hog Day*). Director Forster employs doubling in the minor roles to create an eerie sense of deja vu in the auditor. The *Hamlet* sequence provides a grounding, or, to be more accurate, a point of view with which to observe the film's kaleidoscopic surrealism. And perhaps *Hamlet* and its shifting meanings are constantly relooping like a siren down the canyons of a city through our culture seeking a future that it captures and redefines.

I was surprised when Turner Classic Movies included *The Man from Laramie* (1955) in its program of Shakespeare translations on 15 December 2005, along with *West Side Story*, *Forbidden Planet* and *Kiss Me, Kate!* I recalled the film as a great western—one of the many that Jimmy Stewart made in the 1950s—but not as having derived from Shakespeare. TCM host Robert Osborne suggested that the film's subplot was borrowed from *King Lear*. The film is not included in Robert Willson Jr.'s excellent book, *Shakespeare in Hollywood: 1929-1956*, which, except for a brief epilogue, ends its discussion with films of 1955 and 1956; nor is it listed in Kenneth Rothwell's exhaustive list of films in his superb *History of Shakespeare on Film* (2004), or in his earlier *Shakespeare on Screen*, with Annabelle Melzer (1990).

The film does, though, owe a debt to *King Lear*.

The Internet Movie Database contains this comment, from T.M. West: "[Director Anthony] Mann wanted to make a western about *King Lear* (which he never did), but it was not this one, although you can feel he was toying with the idea." It may not have been Anthony Mann who was toying with the idea, but rather screenwriter Philip Yordan. Yordan had already written two scripts based on *King Lear*: *House of Strangers* (1949, with Edward G. Robinson as a patriarch banker in the '20s and '30s, who watches his sons deny their responsibility for the indictable mess he has made), and *Broken Lance* (1954, with Spencer Tracy as a rancher, who observes a similar situation in a 19th century western setting). One must be cautious with Yordan, of course, because his name appeared in place of many of the blacklisted screenwriters who worked, literally, in his basement during the McCarthy era.

Yordan would seem to be the source of the link between *The Man from Laramie* and *King Lear*. Dave, the sadistic scion of a vast empire (Alex Nichol) destroys the wagons and shoots the mules of Will Lockhart (Stewart). Dave's father, the ranch owner, Alec (Donald Crisp), promises to pay for the damage. That is not, however, Lockhart's goal. He wants to discover who is selling repeating rifles to the Apaches. His brother and his cavalry unit have been wiped out by Indians using this advanced weapon. Crisp blames his foreman Vic (Arthur Kennedy) for not watching Dave more carefully and threatens to fire Vic. Vic replies that Alec has promised him half the ranch. It was never put in writing, says Alec. Vic, however, has always yearned to be Alec's son. Vic kills Dave, and Will, of course, is accused of the murder. Dave and Vic are the ones who have been selling the rifles to the Indians, as Will discovers.

A respondent to the Internet Movie Database, Mackjay, notices the resemblance to "the subplot of Gloucester and his two sons." "Whether the Shakespearean connection is intentional or not, it works extremely well," Mackjay says. The link with the Edgar-Edmund-Gloucester subplot of *King Lear* might indeed seem almost a coincidence were it not that Alec, the doting father, goes blind. In the film, the blindness is necessary so that Kate Canady (Aline MacMahon) can take care of Alec. She's never stopped loving him, of course. The blindness in the film means more, then, than its obligatory introduction in Jane Smiley's dreary *A Thousand Acres*.

King Lear's subplot gives Yordan a context within which to rework the theme of filial shortsightedness and to reformulate the tug-of-war between two "sons" for the father's affection—and estate.

The parallels are imprecise, but they are there, and the borrowed plot greatly enhances the film.

ii

The question of gender in the Shakespeare film begins to be asked at the beginning, in 1900, when Sarah Bernhardt, as Hamlet, duels with Laertes (Pierre Magnier). Bernhardt is, obviously, a woman. Asta Nielsen in the 1920 *Hamlet* (director, Svend Gade) is a woman disguised as a man for dynastic purposes. The deception is not revealed until Horatio (Heinz Stieda) discovers an anatomical detail at the end of the film, which he keeps to himself, even as he recognizes that he loved Hamlet as a woman and that she loved him as a man.

Film itself has adopted gender disguise so as to make it a convention, even if we do not suspend our disbelief as we observe the working out of the motif. One notable gender switch is Greta Garbo's sultry male disguise in *Queen Christina* (1934) finally grasped by John Gilbert. The early 1980s saw *Tootsie* (1982) in which Les Nichols (Charles Durning) falls for Dustin Hoffman's Dorothy Michaels, *The Year of Living Dangerously* (1983), an incoherent film partially redeemed by Linda Hunt's moving portrayal of Billy Kwan, and *Yentle* (1983), in which Barbra Streisand plays a girl disguising herself as a boy to get into the male-only school that teaches the Torah.

The only male character in a Shakespeare play who plays a woman is *Merry Wives'* Falstaff. Bartholomew, Flute and the Boy in *Hamlet* are boy actors. A recent male impersonator on film was Robin Williams in *Mrs. Doubtfire* (1993), who impersonates a middle-aged nanny to maintain contact with his children. Whoopi Goldberg, in *The Associate* (1996), is a woman financial wizard whom no one will credit because she is a woman. She assumes a persona—looking very much like Marlon Brando—and is initiated into the exclusive all-male Peabody Club. She unmasks gradually during her acceptance speech. She takes her gloves off before she doffs her mask. Her hands are *black*, My God! the men exclaim. Then, the further enormity hits them. We've initiated a woman! A *black* woman! Only the black waiters applaud in a neat reversal of class distinctions. In *She's the Man* (2006), Amanda Bynes disguises herself as a boy so that she can play soccer. The film exchanges one set of stereotypic assumptions for another. An amusing moment occurs, though, when the Sebastian figure (James Kirk) shows up and is amorously accosted by the Olivia character (Laura Ramsey). "I think I'm going to like this school," he muses.

In a version of *Victor/Victoria* (1982), Julie Andrews performs the triple play of being a woman disguised as a man performing as a female impersonator. A 1935 *Victor/Victoria, First a Girl*, has a distinct Shakespearean inflection. Victor (Sonnie Hale) is a frustrated Shakespearean actor who shows Elizabeth (Jessie Matthews) photos of himself as Hamlet (holding a skull), Shylock (looking like Henry Irving) and Richard II in full armor. "That's during the battle," he says. The script writer must have meant Richard III. Victor auditions unsuccessfully for a play by reciting Antony's funeral oration, changing his voice as the theater director responds to the sketch of a set. "Higher." "Lower." Hale does show off his versatility. When Elizabeth balks at playing a woman, Victor says "There is a tide in the affairs of men—and women—which, taken at the flood, leads on to fortune." "Tides go out, don't they?" Elizabeth replies. While dancing with the Princess (Anna Lee), Victor slightly mis-quotes *The Rape of Lucrece:* "O, Opportunity, like guilt, is great," he says. He goes on to say, "Is love a tender thing? It is too rough, Too rude, too boist'rous, and it pricks like thorn." He shakes the Princess. "If love be rough with you, be rough with love." "*As You Like It*," he says. "I don't," she replies. The lines, of course are a conflation of Romeo and Mercutio. At the end, after Victor has triumphed by taking Elizabeth's place and proving that "she" is a man, the Princess promises to back him in *Hamlet*, he dons a wig and says, "*Hamlet?* I'll be the greatest Cleopatra the world has ever known!"

The film is a remake of a 1933 German film, *Viktor und Viktoria*, which starred Renate Muller. The 1935 film does have one good song, "It's Written All Over Your Face," performed by the winsome Matthews, and composed by Maurice Sigler, Al Goodhart and Al Hoffman. Matthews also dances well but needs an Astaire opposite her to complement her grace. That bruited pairing never came off, of course. The score is good, but cannot compare with those that Porter, the Gershwins, Berlin, Kern and Fields, et al were composing during the '30s for Fred.

Last Summer in the Hamptons (1996, directed by Henry Jaglom) is collection of subplots with a documentary effect. The members of a theatrical family squabble as they prepare a mournful Chekov play for performance on the last summer that they will own their East Hampton estate. It will go the way of many cherry orchards. A visiting actress (Victoria Foyt) meets a midwestern director (Kristoffer Tabori), who is planning a blackbox production of *As You Like It*. "Is there a part in it for me?" she asks. He mentions Rosalind, "a difficult part," Celia and Phoebe. "Do you do comedy?" The actress does not know.

But she reads a play by one of the family members, Jake (Jon Robin Baitz), and insists that she play the lead, Angelo, a gay male, as Angela, a woman. She cannot then play Rosalind, of course, but she does change the gender of a character in another play, forcing Jake to "perform a sex-change operation on my play," as he says. *As You Like It* thus serves as metaphor for a new play about to appear. The concept of gender fluidity that Shakespeare's play embodies is an archetype for energies feeding into drama yet unborn.

Shakespeare is central to *Stage Beauty* (2004), directed by Richard Eyre and adapted by Jeffrey Hatcher from his play. The film depicts the late 18th century transition from male actors in women's roles to women on stage. It is a fascinating study of gender and gender confusion. Mr. Kynaston (Billy Crudup) is homosexual, and possibly bi-sexual. The character himself is not certain. What is certain is that he has trained for years to play women's roles, notably Desdemona. He easily depicts "the five stages of female subjugation." Maria (Claire Danes), his dresser, says that Desdemona "would fight" (as few Desdemonas ever do, but as Imogen Stubbs did in her version of the role). Maria is emerging from a sense of who a woman is intrinsically, as opposed to the gestural depiction that the stage presents. The latter has become stylized and stereotypical. Kynaston is challenged by Maria, who plays the woman's roles vicariously from backstage. She can play Desdemona only at a tavern, in a travesty of the great stage on which Kynaston and Betterton (Tom Wilkinson) perform. But, to the delight of a spate of spaniels, Nell Gynne (Zoe Tapper), who has acting ambitions of her own, convinces Charles II (Rupert Everett) to outlaw male actors in women's roles. Later, at the court, we see her playing a male to King Charles in drag. The convention whereby women could play in court masques but not on public stages is reversed.

"A woman playing a woman?" Kynaston complains. "Where's the trick in that?" Impersonation has become its own art form. And it is not just that Kynaston believes in his art. Emotionally, he believes that "women do everything beautifully." That belief makes the death scene difficult for him. But Maria is ascendant, Kynaston reduced to playing bawdy woman's roles in a dingy music hall. The two have reversed positions. "She did what she did first. You did what you did last." Maria, though, is in love with him. When challenged, poor Kynaston cannot play male roles. He reverts to the gestures that are by now conditioned reflexes. "It is the cause…" is accompanied by an elaborate wave at the "chaste stars." His training has not merely dictated confusion about his own gender, but has denied him the ability to play the man. In other words, without his ability to act the female role, he has no role, on stage or off. He loses his male lover, Buckingham (Ben Chaplin) who has insisted that Kynaston wear a blonde wig and tells him, "I always thought of you as a woman. I don't know who you are now. I don't think you do." Buckingham is getting married, he tells Kynaston. "The King is coming. Dryden is writing a sonnet." Dryden may be writing an ode for the celebration, or a song, but not a sonnet. Maria rescues Kynaston after he is beaten by order of an angry Sir Charles Sedley (Hugh Griffiths), who had taken him for a whore and tried to pick him up. Maria and Kynaston alternate sexual roles, as she tries to ascertain who is the male and who the woman. Maria enlists Kynaston to help her with her Desdemona. She can parody Kynaston's performance, but it doesn't work. A man playing a woman uses a complicated code accepted by an audience. A woman who attempts to use that code comes off as parody. But Maria cannot craft her style from "Nature." She has no subtext. She must figure out who she is as woman and as woman playing woman's roles. The two issues are interfused, of course, but the question of the actress demands a transition from acquired skills that destroy the performance. Kynaston insists on replacing Betterton in the title role and, in a brutal bedroom scene, almost kills Maria. It is almost a reprise of Ronald Colman and Signe Hasso in *A Double Life* (1947). The theater audience is fearful and we, the film auditors, cannot be sure what is happening. Maria's "Nobody. I myself" emerges from its play but also suggests that her own ambition to act has resulted in her apparently real death on stage. The sudden transition from 18th century decorum to Stanley Kowalski is anachronistic and implausible, but it reinforces the substitution of women for male actors, that is, a movement toward greater naturalism on stage. It is the court and its more liberal conventions that become suddenly anachronistic.

The film repeats a gesture of the right hand, palm up. At first it is Kynaston's Desdemona, signaling that the play is not over yet. Then it is the battered Kynaston, whose hand quivers with the vestiges of life. Finally, it is Maria's Desdemona, who may be dead. The hand captures the fusion of illusion and reality, on stage and off, with which the film plays.

Kynaston's plight exemplifies Jennifer Drougin's insight that "the tensions negotiated by Shakespeare's gender-bending characters and the slippages that produce the comedic moments of his plays… are important to understand because they can so easily turn to tragedy in real life." (2008, 51)

"Slippages" occur in comedy, when the breeches role is close to being exposed as "in drag" for the characters on stage. Slippage cannot occur in tragedy, since the only female character to assume a male guise is Cleopatra when she dons Antony's "sword Philippan." The tragedy to which Drougin alludes is that of Brandon Teena who passed as a man and, when found out, was beaten to death in Nebraska. His story was made into *Boys Don't Cry* (1999), directed by Kimberly Pierce and starring Hillary Swank as Brandon. Drougin says that the "principles of Shakespearean comedy are not transferable to real life." (2008, 51) The female impersonator who has been conditioned to that role, professionally and imaginatively, whether in tragedy or comedy, can translate to "real life" only in that guise, unless, as Mr. Kynaston does, he uses his biological maleness to confound the disbelievers. But he may have trouble believing in himself—that is the self as a he. Mr. Kynaston, for all of Maria's coaching and encouragement, is still not sure. Eric Vilain conjectures that "sexual orientation is probably much more hard-wired than gender identity." (Rosin 2008, 66) The film does not give us an easy either/or response to the distinction.

Obviously, the issue of gender has biological premises. Mr. Kynaston insists on that for all of his mimetic skills. He is also homosexual, perhaps bisexual, and that equivocal orientation could be said to have contributed to his decision to be a female impersonator. But to what extent is gender a construction? And to what extent does perception contribute to that construction, as in the case of Buckingham in this film? Kynaston's performance convinces us at the end that he does not know who he is, as opposed to the "regular guy" A. O. Scott makes of him. (8 Oct. 2004) The film, then, complicates the ending of a Shakespeare comedy. Gender relationships are restored when Rosalind appears in a wedding dress or when Viola is told to don her "woman's weeds." We continue to suspend our disbelief about the gender of the actor. But at the end of *Stage Beauty*, our belief in gender confusion is confirmed.

Finally, Shakespeare's approach to gender anticipates modern adaptations of the Narcissus myth. Christopher Lasch (1979) argues that contemporary narcissism involves copying the behavior of persons perceived to be successful. When Whoopi Goldberg, for example, decides to created a male persona— Robert Cuddy—in *The Associate*, she purchases an elegant silver golf trophy and the head of a rhinoceros, fabricates an autographed photo of Barbra Streisand, and loads them all into a new Mercedes convertible.

Rosalind, in assuming male disguise, accounts for who she may prove to be beneath her disguise:

> Lie there what hidden woman's fear there will,
> We'll have a swashing and a martial outside
> As many other mannish cowards have
> That do outface it with their semblances.
>
> (I.iii.117-120)

That "other" places her in the company of "mannish cowards." But Rosalind accounts for "interiority"—something deeper than stereotype—and thus predicts the process whereby Orlando can become more than just the narcissistic lover.

Portia is more confident, and more contemptuous:

> I have within my mind
> A thousand raw tricks of these bragging Jacks,
> Which I shall practice.

The characters at once assume a male persona and deconstruct the role they are assuming. Rosalind's seems to be the healthier, more androgynous attitude, but we have to account in Portia's case for a) the imposition of her father's will upon her, and b) the quality of suitors thus far exhibited, perhaps excluding Bassanio, perhaps not. In each instance, the characters employ the imitation of behavior they have witnessed and see through that narcissistic stance.

iii

Recent interpretations of *Romeo and Juliet* reflect two cultural tendencies. The first is an emphasis on the teenage world as a separate society, independent of the adult world. When I was growing up, the teenage years were transitional, a movement toward getting a driver's license, getting drafted, being old enough to drink. The second way the play is used nowadays is to suggest cross-cultural relationships, those that ignore racial, economic or religious differences: *West Side Story* (film, 1961) and *China Girl* (1987), for example. The play tends to reflect multiculturalism and egalitarianism. The play yields to our archetypes, but, in doing so, often disguises itself as something it is not. In other words, as often happens with plays like *Henry V* and *Julius Caesar*, *Romeo and Juliet* becomes a victim of the imposition upon it of meanings that muffle those that *are* there in the script—"households alike in dignity," for example. Any translation of a Shakespeare play into teen norms or political correctness is likely to suffer a reduction. That *Romeo and Juliet* seems to contain our societal impulse toward equality and the breaking down of walls that separate us is probably a good thing, but that it has become our paradigmatic Shakespeare play is troubling. That fact argues a certain immaturity in the culture that selects the play. I won't attempt an analysis that links that preference to the cardboard approximations of humanity that Hollywood gives us these days or to gun violence or to our proclivity for war even as Bush claims "I am a man of peace." Links do exist, though, between how a society behaves and the art that it prefers at any given moment in its history.

In *Shakespeare Translated*, I suggest that the Tchaikovsky *Romeo and Juliet* overture that suddenly sounds behind Johnny Weissmuller's Tarzan and Maureen O'Sullivan's Jane in *Tarzan the Apeman* (1932) signals "probably the first time… that film emphasizes the radical differences between the two lovers, as opposed to the 'both alike in dignity' context of the Shakespeare play" (2005, 34) Wrong!

In *The Red Mill* (1927), Marion Davies' Tina, a scullery maid becomes "Juliet" (several times in the title cards) to Owen Moore's Irish aristocrat. The film includes some amusing balcony scenes, including one borrowed from *Much Ado*, from which wrong conclusions are drawn. The film's subplot also borrows from *Romeo and Juliet*, and includes a marriage to a bemedaled aristocrat forced upon a young woman (Louise Fazenda) by her Burgomaster father. This one is interrupted at the last minute, a la *Girl Shy* (1924), *The Garden of Eden* (1928, where the interruption is only temporary), *It Happened One Night* (1934), *The Man in the Iron Mask* (1939), *The Philadelphia Story* (1940), *Arizona* (1940), *Christmas in Connecticut (1945)*, *Angel on My Shoulder* (1946), (just too late) *What About Bob?* (1991), and *Dr. T. & the Women* (2000). In *Arizona*, William Holden says "Go ahead" to the Judge (Edgar Buchanan), who is about to marry him to Jean Arthur. Holden's order comes after the nasty Warren William, who is waiting for a showdown with Holden, shoots a shot glass to bits. In *The Graduate* (1967), the interruption comes as the would-be groom is about to kiss the bride to complete the ceremony. In a variation on the convention, *Carefree* (1938), Fred Astaire substitutes at the last minute for Ralph Bellamy and leads Ginger Rogers down the aisle. She has a black eye from a Bellamy right hand that Astaire had ducked. In *Top Hat* (1935), Bates (Eric Blore) confesses that he posed as a clergy man in marrying Dale (Ginger) to Beddini (Erik Rhodes). That means that Jerry (Fred) and Dale can dance off happily together. In *The Red Mill*, The Burgomaster's daughter escapes with her working class lover (Karl Dane).

Even as early as 1927, then, *Romeo and Juliet* was reconfigured to fit the aspirations of an egalitarian society. In this case, Juliet is Cinderella, without the royal background that the older versions of the Cinderella story provide her.

Only recently, I would have argued that the linkage between teenage America and *Romeo and Juliet* began with Franco Zeffirelli's magnificent 1970 film version, in which he cast inexperienced actors in the leads. The teenager as independent entity as opposed to transitional figure had been confirmed in the late 1950s by retailers and advertisers suddenly aware of a vast, new market separate from and often at variance with that of adults. The generational gap that Zeffirelli's film emphasizes had been deepened in American society and abroad by divisions about the war in Vietnam.

But I would have been wrong.

Reefer Madness (AKA *Tell Your Children*) is a profoundly awful 1936 film warning of the deadly effects of marijuana. In it, Mary (Dorothy Short) and Bill (Kenneth Craig) are using *Romeo and Juliet* as to provide language for their own courtship.

"What o'clock tomorrow shall I send to thee?"
"By the hour of nine."

Mrs. Lane (Mary MacLauren), Mary's mother, interrupts this tender moment. Bill subsequently gets hooked and Mary dies as a result. Bill's mourning of Mary as she lies on a couch could be a miming of Romeo in the tomb. At Bill's trial, the Principal (Joseph Forte) is asked whether he can give an example of Bill's instability. "Yes. During a discussion of *Romeo and Juliet*, he broke into hysterical laughter." Perhaps it was not just reefer madness that overcame Bill at this moment, but an awareness that his and Mary's story paralleled that of the doomed lovers of Shakespeare's play. The film does not tell us that, of course, but it firmly links the play with its modern moment.

It is coincidental, of course, that the film was made during the same year as the Cukor-Thalberg version of the play, infamous for its casting of superannuated Norma Shearer and Leslie Howard in the leads.

In *Dramatic School* (1938, director Robert B. Sinclair), the students are inevitably rehearsing the balcony scene. The teacher, Gail Sondergaard, interrupts them to show how it is done. She had played the role at sixteen; rather; she says "I spoke the lines." She lacked the maturity to really depict Juliet. Unfortunately, Louise (Luise Rainier) falls asleep during Sondergaard's demonstration. Louise has been working nights in a factory to support her acting studies. Sondergaard threatens to expel her from the school. Meanwhile, the notorious playboy Marquis Andre D'Abbencourt (Alan Marshall) woos Louise, so that the modern Romeo and Juliet story of a linkage between disparate social and economic strata seems about to play itself out. But he jilts her for a dancer. She returns to her apartment to find Annette (Marie Blake) weeping over *Hamlet*. "I did love you once," Annette reads. "Indeed my lord," Louise replies, "you made me believe so." She should not have believed him. Sondergaard is passed over for the part of Joan of Arc—"Too mature," is the euphemism. She has "Lady Macbeth and Andromache" to look forward to, the impresario (Henry Stevenson) tells her. But magnanimously, she gives the role to Louise, who triumphs. The Marquis comes back hoping for a reconciliation, but Louise turns him down, content to have escaped from her daydreams and look at her name in lights on the marquee outside the National Theatre. The film is notable for the early film appearances of Paulette Goddard, Lana Turner, Anne Rutherford and, in an uncredited non-speaking role, Dick Haymes.

In *Shakespeare Translated*, I argue that Romeo and Juliet has become the vehicle of our adolescent culture. As I also suggest, the play does pop up earlier than the 1950s, however. I have recently discovered more instances.

In *This Man is Mine* (1934), Irene Dunne looks at the black eye that her husband (Ralph Bellamy, who had a habit of socking actresses on screen) has delivered to Constance Cummings and says, "I'm sure that Romeo took a poke at Juliet now and then too." Romeo and Juliet simply stand in for stock lovers and their quarrels here. As William Holden says to Bing Crosby in *The Country Girl* (1954), "They start out as Juliet and grow up to be Lady Macbeth."

In *Marry the Girl*, a deeply forgettable Warner B-flick of 1937, David (Frank McHugh) quotes Romeo to Virginia (Carol Hughes):

> O speak again bright angel! for thou art
> As glorious as this night, being o'er my head
> As is a winged messenger of heaven
> Unto the white-upturned wond'ring eyes
> Of mortals that fall back to gaze on him
> When he bestrides the lazy-pacing clouds
> And sails upon the bosom of the air.

She is innocent of the source of the lines and merely compliments David on his verbal facility. They end up together once the film itself mercifully ends.

Romeo and Juliet appears more substantially in *The Goldwyn Follies* (1938). Producer Adolphe Menjou hires small-town girl Andrea Leeds over an ice cream soda to give him an honest response to his films. Her first assignment is to watch a dance sequence in which the Capulets (who love ballet and lascivious lute music) dance against the Montagues (who love jazz, here represented by a tenor sax and tap dancers). The sequence ends with the twosome of Romeo and Juliet (Vera Zorina) in a very balletic sequence miming death in each other's arms. "Do they die that way?" Leeds asks. "It's always ended that way," Menjou replies. "How would you change it?" he asks. "I'd want them to get up and then have their parents forgive them, and be married and be happy." "No one ever thought of that ending for *Romeo and Juliet*" Menjou exclaims. Friar Lawrence thought of that ending, of course, as did the late Susan Snyder, admittedly much later than 1938. Snyder argues that the play replicates Shakespeare's comic pattern. (1970) Menjou gives the order. "I want the hearts of the world beating with love and triumph!" It is a Hollywood ending. The music for the sequence, by Vernon Duke, is mundane, nothing akin to the dynamic Prokokief ballet of only two years earlier. Duke tries to sound like George Gershwin, who could not finish the film and died shortly after it was made. The film itself is utterly forgettable. It even manages to squander the final songs that George Gershwin wrote, "Love Walked In," and "Love is Here to Stay." Since small town girl Leeds falls for short order cook Kenny Baker, the film does not feature a "modern" Romeo and Juliet romance between different classes or races within its main plot.

Romeo and Juliet makes a surprise appearance in *Huckleberry Finn* (1939). It is used in place of "the most celebrated thing in Shakespeare." Huck (Mickey

Rooney) plays Juliet in a balcony while Romeo (Walter Connolly) tears a passion to tatters below. Romeo inadvertently pulls the balcony down and Juliet, advertised as Mrs. Sarah Siddons of London, is shown to be a boy. Both Romeo and Juliet must flee the angry audience. The sequence is another illustration of how poor Huck is deceived by the rapscallions. The scene is, interestingly, played for pathos rather than for laughs. It shows the King's frustrated wish for things grander than he has attained and, at the same time, his con-man's need to dupe both his boy-actor and his audience. The 1960 version of *Huckleberry Finn* eliminated the Shakespearean element, except for two lines by Tony Randall's King: "he was untimely ripped from the cradle" and "thus we knit the raveled sleeve of friendship."

In *The Corsican Brothers* (1941), Mario (Douglas Fairbanks, Jr.) climbs through the window of Isabelle's (Ruth Warrick) room. "How did you get here?" she asks. "With love's light wings did I o'erperch these walls," he explains, "For stony limits cannot hold love out." The linkage goes a bit further than just his clambering up to second story windows. He is an outlaw and she is sought in marriage by an odious aristocrat (Akim Tamiroff—no "man of wax"). Later, to save Mario's life, a doctor (H.B. Warner) administers "a drug, a desperate chance" to make him appear dead. Fairbanks plays both brothers—one an extraverted young man who has been raised in Paris, and his twin, an introverted figure who experiences his brother's life vicariously and describes himself as his brother's "shadow." Fairbanks skillfully distinguishes between them. The film is based on Dumas' 1845 novel, a "double story" like so many in the nineteenth and early twentieth century that were beginning to explore the unconscious as a living presence within the psyche, particularly the archetype that Jung would call "the Shadow"—Poe's "William Wilson," Dostoyevsky's "The Double," Wilde's "Dorian Grey," Robert Louis Stevenson's *Dr. Jekyll and Mr. Hyde*, Hardy's "The Trumpet-Major," James' "The Jolly Corner," Conrad's "The Duel," and Lawrence's "The Prussian Officer," for example.

In *Girl Crazy* (1943), Danny Churchill (Mickey Rooney) clowns around for Ginger Gray (Judy Garland) by quoting from *Romeo and Juliet*: "He jests at scars that never felt a wound. But soft, what light from yonder window breaks? It is the east, and Juliet is the sun." The lines have no ostensible purpose except perhaps to remind us that the film delineates the "modern" version of the two lovers, in which they come from different backgrounds. Danny is a wealthy playboy from New York. Ginger is a girl of the golden west, of the desert college to which Danny has been exiled. She is the daughter of the dean of the impoverished institution. The film has some good moments—Judy singing the Gershwins' poignant "But Not for Me," during the 'boy loses girl' phase of the film, and the great trombone of Tommy Dorsey.

In *My Foolish Heart* (1949), a melodramatic tearjerker that does incorporate a great song sung by Martha Meers, Eloise (Susan Hayward) and Mary Jane (Lois Wheeler) are reading *Romeo and Juliet* in their college dorm. "Romeo, banished!" The line has a foreboding quality, since Eloise's boyfriend, Walt (Dana Andrews) is separated from her by the inexorable rhythms of world war and ultimately killed in a training accident. A greater power than anyone can contradict comes between them.

In *The Court Jester* (1955), Danny Kaye, in a moment of confidence induced by a spell, backs Ravenhurst (Basil Rathbone) up with a dazzling rapier, and shouts, "Ravenhurst, you rat-catcher!" The allusion would be incomprehensible unless we remembered that Rathbone had played Tybalt, to whom Mercutio delivers the taunt in the Cukor *Romeo and Juliet* (1936). Rathbone, Hollywood's premier swordsman was very impressed with Kaye's quick mastery of sword play.

The recreation of the myth, in which the two lovers bridge racial, religious or economic divides is represented by *Inventing the Abbotts* (1997), in which, after myriad meanderings, the boy from the wrong side of the tracks, Doug (Joaquin Phoenix), marries the girl who lives in the big white house, Pamela (Liv Tyler). The link between their story and Shakespeare's lovers would be coincidental, were it not that Doug proudly shows Pamela the stage set he has designed as his project at Penn. I thought it was a set for *Death of a Salesman*. Wrong! It's for *Romeo and Juliet*. Pamela immediately mentions the loft of the barn to which the two had climbed to consummate their relationship. It becomes in the film the equivalent of Juliet's bedroom. At this point in the film, we may recall that there's been a lot of climbing in and out of bedroom windows so far.

In *All I Wanna Do* (aka *Strike*, 1998), about a teenage rebellion at a girl's boarding school, Tinka's mother (Barbara Radecki) tells Tinka (Monica Kenna) of the aristocratic young man who is coming home from school for Christmas and suggests that it is time for Tinka to get together with him. Tinka, meanwhile, sneaks out of the window of her dormitory room to the balcony, where she joins her townie boyfriend, Snake (Vincent Kartheiser), who wafts her away in a cherry picker. This configuration again represents the "modern" *Romeo and Juliet*, wherein the girl again, in this case, opts for the boy of her choice rather than someone from a "household alike in dignity" to hers.

I should point out that "cross-cultural" pairing is standard in recent teen flicks, whether they refer to Shakespeare's play or not, as in *Save the Last Dance* (2001), where a white girl, Sara Johnson (Julia Stiles) moves to Chicago and has a relationship with an African-American from the South Side, Derek Reynolds (Sean Patrick Thomas), a reprise for Stiles of her Desi Brable opposite Mekhi Phifer's Odin James in *O* (1999, released 2001). Other similar pairings of teens with dissimilar backgrounds include that of a wealthy daughter of a congressman, Nicole Oakley (Kirsten Dunst) with Latino jock, Carlos Nunez (Jay Hernandez) in *Crazy/Beautiful* (2001) and of a blonde sorority girl, Carolyn McDuffy (Christina Ricci) with the mentally retarded Pumpkin Romanoff (Hank Harris) in *Pumpkin* (2002). In these films, Hollywood reflects its own wish for an America that will accept such pairings as a matter of course. A variation of this pattern occurs when the prom king and major jock of the school ditches the prom queen and begins to date a less conventional choice, a previously undated freshman (Molly Ringwald), as in *Sixteen Candles* (1984), or an introverted artist (Rachel Leigh Cook), as in *She's All That* (1999).

In *Teaching Mrs. Tingle* (1999), a twisted morality play in which some good ideas are perverted to accommodate a "happy ending," Mrs. Tingle (a wonderfully mordant Helen Mirren) watches Jo Lynn (Marissa Coughlin) say "Romeo, Romeo, wherefore art thou Romeo" to Mrs. Tingle's Pekinese. "What's your name? It isn't Romeo," Jo Lynn says. "You could never play Juliet," Mrs. Tingle says. "You haven't the commitment, the soul." "That's the Tingle we all know and love!" Jo Lynn sneers. "You haven't got the heart," Mrs. Tingle continues. "At least I have a heart," Jo Lynn responds. Later, as she begins to manipulate Jo Lynn, Mrs. Tingle says, "You aren't very quick, Jo Lynn. You might just make a good actor after all." The allusion here would seem to be to the one play to which teenagers "relate" and to the one role to which a teenage actor might aspire. Had the students' attack on Mrs. Tingle trapped them in Grandsborough, as she is trapped, the film might have made a valid point. All should be punished. And Grandsborough looked to me like a very pleasant middle-American town. It was hardly an Appalachia being blasted away by the coal companies.

Suffice it that *Romeo and Juliet* is alive if not always well in the filmic canon.

Suffice it that "Shakespeare on film" is an expanding field, even if few new Shakespeare films are making their way to the theaters these days.

VIII

❦

Three Recent Productions

i

William Shakespeare's Merchant of Venice, directed by Michael Radford, designed by Bruno Rubeo, photography by Benoit DelHomme, with Al Pacino, Jeremy Irons, Joseph Fiennes, Lynn Collins, Zuleikha Robinson, Kris Marshall, Charlie Cox, Heather Goldenhersh and Mackenzie Crook.

As You Like It, directed by Kenneth Branagh, designed by Tim Harvey, photography by Roger Lanser, with Richard Briers, Kevin Kline, Brian Blessed, Bryce Dallas Howard, Romola Garai, Adrian Lester, David Oyelowo, Alex Wyndham, Jimmy Yuill and Alfred Molina.

King Lear, directed by Trevor Nunn. PBS, 25 March 2009. With Ian McKellen, Romola Garai, Frances Barber, Monica Dolan, Jonathan Hyde, Sylvester McCoy, William Gaunt, Philip Winchester, Ben Meyjes, Julian Harries and Guy Williams.

Any hope that new films of Shakespeare would encourage something like the remarkable explosion of the 1990s that produced Luhrmann's *Romeo and Juliet*, Stoppard's *Shakespeare in Love*, and Taymor's *Titus* has been dashed by the films themselves—Michael Radford's murky *Merchant* and Kenneth Branagh's radically mis-placed *As You Like It*. Neither film helped us to cross the bridge that metaphor creates, between where the script is—ascertained, for all the debate about the script of a play like *Hamlet* or *King Lear*, and edited, as invariably it is, for a specific production—and where we, the individual spectator, may be. Television, however, continues to be a good medium for Shakespeare when stage productions are remounted for TV. That holds true even for as vast and complicated a script as *King Lear*, a "film made for the small screen," according to the PBS website for Nunn's 2009 version.

Radford's *The Merchant of Venice* evoked a division of opinion on the

Internet. David Kaplan claimed that it "moves briskly." *Jam!* also found it "brisk." *Movie House* praised its "clarity." Peter Bradshaw also found it "lucid." (*Guardian*) James Christopher, however, compared the lovers, Portia and Bassanio, to "actors trying to sprint under water." (*The Times*) *Slant* found the film "a morass of paralyzing drudgery." *Slate* called it "deeply boring." Neil Smith described it as a "gloomy, long and slightly draining haul." (BBC) Steve Rhodes found it "dry and disappointing." (*Internet Review*)

I come down in the latter camp. This is an often incoherent film, undermined by shadowy production values, shaky characterizations and dubious editing of the inherited text.

Venice is a night-shrouded swamp, except during the day, when, for some reason, the only business being conducted is at the brothels. And where is Belmont? At one point it seems to be within an easy swim of the city, but at other moments it lives across a wide expanse of water. If Portia is a version of faraway treasure, she exists in the imagination of that sea-faring adventurer who was an Elizabethan hero. Bassanio describes her as having "sunny locks" that "Hang on her temples like a golden fleece." "And," he says, "many Jasons come in quest of her." These references—which I did not hear in this film—take us back to that fabulous epoch when the Greeks were discovering the rich world around them. We see Portia's palace on a hillside—hardly a beautiful mountain—under the moon and a few stars, a version of Gatsby's estate. The fabulous is reduced to the merely grand. Soon the locations become generic not dynamic, and the montage becomes merely a convention of this dull production. Contrast Zeffirelli's brilliant camera in his sun-drenched *Romeo and Juliet*, and the superbly timed cross-cuts in *Shakespeare in Love* that conflate rehearsals of *Romeo and Juliet* and the love affair of Will and Viola.

The film opens with an account of the treatment of Jews in Venice in the 16th century. The ghetto gate locks with a decisive clang, as the Torah burns below the title cards. Thus is the spectator permitted to distance him/herself from what is to follow. Thank heavens we are not like that! But why not let the narrative find its contemporary resonance—or not—as it may? The play itself makes clear enough the status of Jews in Venice. In his novel, *Will in the World*, Stephen Greenblatt supposes that Shakespeare might have attended the execution of the Jew, Lopez, in 1594 and derived his concept for the play from that grisly event. (2004) Perhaps so, but like Radford's opening exposition, that possibility is irrelevant to the way the play steps forward to speak to the living. We must respect Elizabethan "meanings," insofar as we can recover them, but we cannot permit them to substitute for our own response to the plays as performed in media undreamed of in Shakespeare's dramaturgy anymore than we should press Shakespeare's scripts into our own contemporary meanings. We can count ourselves fortunate that Radford choose not to frame his film with Lopez's execution.

The chief victim of the editing is Portia. Much of her excited greeting of Bassanio is given as soliloquy, and it is inaudible. She is robbed, though, of her most significant early line. Nerissa reminds her of a Venetian who had visited once upon a time. Portia replies, "Yes, yes, it was Bassanio—as I think he was called." It is a very funny line because it captures her excitement at the memory and her immediate recognition that she has betrayed that excitement. Watch Joan Plowright deliver it in the Miller production. For Lyn Collins to lose the line is for the production to lose the beautiful princess waiting on her mountain for her prince to come. While we know that Bassanio is on his way, we do not know that she is hoping he will come. We do fear that she is likely to be given away before he gets there.

Portia is denied her racist "Let all of his completion chose me so" after Morocco exits. The edge that the line can give to a Geraldine James (in the Hall production of 1989) or to a Deborah Findley (in Bill Alexander's 1987 RSC production with Anthony Sher) can combine with her resentment of her father's control even after death to send a convincing Portia off to the trial at Venice. Collins is very good in the trial scene, but we have not been prepared for her sudden emergence. When Portia is a mature woman, as is Joan Plowright in the Miller production, a lot of her motivation can be taken for granted. She has been waiting a long time for someone to release her from the magic spell of the caskets.

Gabriel Shanks complained of the film's "incomprehensible moments of feigned levity." Had all of Gobbo material been excised, the film would have been strengthened. Radford does cut the discussion between Lorenzo and Jessica of all those ill-fated lovers (Troilus and Cressida, Pyramus and Thisbe, Dido, Medea, Endymion, et al) probably because he realizes too late that lights, camera and action command in film, not language. To his credit, Radford does cut Shylock's long and incomprehensible disquisition on Laban's sheep.

Radford misses another opportunity as the trial begins. "Which is the merchant here, and which the Jew?" Portia asks. She has never seen either man. Antonio and Shylock step forward. "Is your name Shylock?" Portia asks. Suppose that is directed to Antonio? "*My* name is Shylock," Shylock says, insisting on the identity that has so often been undercut, and will be again. As rendered in Radford's film, Shylock merely says, in effect, "Yes, I am Shylock." And so a potentially exciting moment becomes merely dull.

Portia is robbed of her "Your wife would give you little thanks for that, If she were by to hear you make the offer," an aside she delivers in response to Bassanio's protestations of love for Antonio. That aside helps to establish her subsequent nastiness about the ring. As the *Movie House* reviewer said, "Had I been Bassanio, I would have asked Portia whether her imaginary lawyer also handled divorces."

The attempts of the two early suitors, then, acquire only local tension. Morocco is a caricature, a Mohammed Ali with entourage. Aragon is disgusting and should have hit the cutting-room floor. In the Peter Hall production, the suitors arrived flamboyantly, as if versions of the ultimate Mulberry Street Parade. After their wrong choices, they huddled under dim blue lighting, as if they and their entourages had been stricken by some fatal thunderbolt and were being driven to a negative afterlife. Here, the scenes are merely obligatory preludes to Bassanio's correct choice. In a production I saw in Valencia in 1999, the Bassanio doubled in disguise as Morocco and Aragon—a tour de force that made his deliberation as the "real" Bassanio very amusing. In the Jonathan Miller production, Charles Kay's Aragon is a senile old man—no doubt politically incorrect enough to elicit the ire of the AARP. As he opens the silver casket, however, he pulls out a mirror and looks at himself. "What's here? The portrait of a blinking idiot!" In the Radford film, the caskets sit impressively under a portrait of Portia's father, but the production does not respond to that controlling presence, particularly after Bassanio's correct choice. It is time for a changing of the guard, time to put that portrait in the attic, but that opportunity is ignored here. Suffice it that I kept redesigning this stultifying film as it dragged its slow length along.

Pacino pulls his Shylock down from a Roy Cohn or a Herod, and his rasping complaint contrasts effectively with Jeremy Irons' aristocratic rumble of a voice. Pacino delivers the "Hath not a Jew eyes" powerfully. He is angry all the way, and revenge is the culmination of a diatribe. Warren Mitchell in the BBC-TV version reads the speech as a running joke and then turns savagely on his listeners as he says, "And if you wrong us—will we not revenge?" The speech does not reflect shared humanity. It argues shared *in*humanity. Pacino, however, does nothing with "I would not have given it for a wilderness of monkeys," after he learns that Jessica has traded away the ring Leah had given him when he was a bachelor. Radford adds "her mother" here. Olivier has a photo of Leah on his desk and the implication is that she had died in delivering Jessica to the world. Shylock's greatest speech, before the Venetian Senate as he explains why he pursues a losing suit against Antonio, is, as Pacino handles it, merely a monotonous explanation. It is actually at once very amusing and macabre, a justification of actions emerging from irrationality that demands some awareness on Shylock's part of the darkness he is articulating.

At the end, three characters are excluded from the comedy. Antonio—who has *not* been told that all his ships have come in—is left alone in the moments just before dawn gilds the tip of Belmont's palace. Antonio can be incorporated, of course. At the conclusion of a 1970s production at The Other Place in Stratford (with Patrick Stewart as Shylock), Antonio took Bassanio's hand and placed it in Portia's. He was "giving her away," fulfilling the role of her absent father and also surrendering any claim to Bassanio's love. In the Radford film, Shylock, now a reluctant Christian, is left on the street as his fellow Jews close the door of their temple upon him. Then we see Jessica run to the waterside to look across at Venice. She fingers the turquoise ring that she had supposedly traded for that monkey. We had seen the exchange in a flashback as Tubal described it. Apparently that had that been Shylock's hallucination. Let Antonio and Shylock be excluded from the final harmonies. And make an exile of Jessica too, since she may be between two worlds—one dead, the other powerless to be born. But why confuse us by apparently refuting something we have already seen? How did she get that ring back? The play suggests that, while Bassanio and Gratiano too easily surrender their rings, Shylock would never have parted with the turquoise. But what point is Radford making with Jessica here? At the end of the Olivier version, Jessica is alone, listening to her father sing the Kaddish, the Yiddish prayer for the dead. That ending is as powerful for the production as a whole as Shylock's off-stage howl of anguish had been for the trial scene.

A good recent *Merchant* is Trevor Nunn's Royal National Theatre version, remounted for television, with Henry Goodman and Derbhle Crotty, a production emerging from the ennui of Venice and the boredom of Belmont in the 1920s. Probably the best available *Merchant*, however, remains Miller's 1974 television production with Laurence Olivier. The latter has not sufficiently toned down his stage performance for the cool medium, and the editing makes Shylock's motive too clear: it is Jessica's desertion. But Shylock's effort at assimilation is powerfully suggested. Miller kept reducing the hook in Olivier's nose in rehearsal. Shylock looks almost like the other Venetians and mimics their aristocratic accents. But he will never be one of them.

Merchant is a difficult script—a "problem play" because it raises issues that cannot be resolved within the assumptions of comedy. Orson Welles started a version of *Merchant*, and fascinating snippets of that unfinished film appeared on a Bravo documentary in 2000. Radford's entry is unlikely to encourage more Shakespeare to the screen. To make a great Shakespeare film, the director's imagination must collide explosively with the inherited script, as Kozintsev's did, as Kurosawa's did, as Welles's did with the *Henry IV* plays, as Olivier's and Branagh's did with *Henry V*, as Zeffirelli's and Luhrmann's did with *Romeo and Juliet*, and as Taymor's did with *Titus*. Radford does not come close.[2]

ii

Although Branagh's *As You Like It* was conceived as a film, it ended up on HBO. Yet it seems "televisual" in its shots and in its limited use of shots. And *As You Like It* should be an easy play for television. Its scenes tend to be one on one confrontations, usually featuring Rosalind discussing things with Celia, being banished by Celia's father, or encountering Jacques and Orlando in the Forest of Arden. Its shots, therefore, are televisual—closeups, two shots, reaction shots, an occasional rack shot—a point-of-view technique where one part of the frame is out of focus—and the wrestling match that was a staple of early television in the U.S. Since it has few "big" scenes, *As You Like It* does not require the field of depth that television does not provide.

The play was, of course, designed for a stage. Language tells us where we were. "Well, this is the Forest of Arden!" Rosalind exclaims, and so it is for our imaginations. In 1978, BBC made the mistake of going on location to sunny Scotland, so that we watched people tripping over real roots and heard birds chirping whether in court or woodland. Comments about how cold it was seemed wildly incomprehensible in the sun-infused highland springtime. (Bulman 1988) Television is not a "location" medium. In 1992, Christine Edzard placed her film in the London dockyards, brutally mocking the pastoral mode. That production was redeemed by the performance of winsome Emma Croft as Rosalind/Ganymede.

Branagh chooses nineteenth century Japan for his version. He seems aware that a film made for television, as this one turned out to be, must retain TV's tight focus so that even location—in West Sussex—does not doom the production. What dooms it is Branagh's bizarre decision to place the script in Japan. This location robs Rosalind of her great speech about donning male attire. She knows that "hidden woman's fear" may lie beneath her "swashing and martial outside." Her faint much later confirms her knowledge of herself. The feminine subtext becomes the energy that drives her to insist that Orlando surrender his fatuous idealization of her for something that permits relationship to work. Her line "Alas the day! What shall I do with my doublet and hose?" must be surrendered to directorial concept. The play shows her doing much with her male disguise as she insists "You must call me Rosalind!" before she finally doffs it for her appropriate and longed-for wedding dress. Orlando must move from adolescent to man before she can rejoin her feminine self. Shakespeare's exploration of gender—stereotypes and intrinsic qualities—gets lost here. For how to make the issue central to our experience of a given script, see Trevor Nunn's 1996 *Twelfth Night*, in which Imogen Stubbs "plays the man" and shows how difficult it is for *men* to attain the attributes that make up the stereotypic male. If Lasch is correct in his study of narcissism (1979), the narcissist studies the habits, manners, and dress of people perceived to be successful. Nunn shows Viola doing just that. The goal, of course—the result of comedy—is the annihilation of such superficiality and role-playing. (Coursen 1998, 198-215)

Rosalind's use of disguise is far more creative than that of Imogen (in *Cymbeline*), who is told that she must assume "a waggish courage, Ready in gibes, quick answer'd, saucy, and As quarrelous as the weasel," but finds that "a man's life is a tedious one." In *The Two Gentlemen of Verona*, Julia's disguise as a "well-reputed page" puts her in the painful position of "unhappy messenger" between her beloved Proteus and Sylvia. She must prove a "false traitor to" herself until things get straightened out at the end. *Twelfth Night*'s Viola discovers that her disguise as Cesario is "a wickedness." She is trapped in it until Sebastian comes upon the scene. Portia (in *The Merchant of Venice*) sneers at the male role she assumes: "I have within my mind A thousand raw tricks of these bragging Jacks Which I will practice." Portia puts her male role to good use in the trial scene and also uses it to gain the upper hand in her relationship with Bassanio and revenge herself for the victimization imposed upon her by her father's will. But Branagh's placement of the script in Japan robs Rosalind of her very specific outfit and accoutrements and of her awareness of who she continues to be underneath all that, even as she reassumes the name of Rosalind. And so the central dynamic of the script is simply not there in this production. The editing of Rosalind's part represents something far more damaging than just the "abbreviation" that New York *Times* critic, Virginia Heffernan, called it. (21 Aug. 07)

Branagh begins with a submarine coup against the Duke Senior, Roz's father, scenes that the play itself does not provide. It is brutal and confusing. We are told that the Duke Senior has already fled to the Forest of Arden before he makes his narrow escape. The opening is incomprehensible, as is the sudden introduction of Audrey (Janet McTeer) and William (Paul Chan) in the Forest. Who are they? This footage should have been cut. Branagh also deletes Touchstone's bawdy parody of Orlando's bad verses, thereby robbing teachers of the opportunity to point out that Touchstone's is the only way to demean poetry that is already self-mocking. Having produced a film which incorporated the entire conflated text of *Hamlet*, Branagh seems unwilling to trust Shakespeare's language here. While film is not a linguistic medium, this one could have included some of the deletions. Television, as this one was destined to become, can incorporate more language than film simply because words are needed to supplement the paucity of the imagery and because TV emerges from radio, not the photograph. Rosalind is also robbed of her effort to suggest to Silvius (Alex Wyndham) appropriate male behavior by misconstruing the love letter that Phoebe (Jade Jeffries) has insisted that Silvius deliver to Ganymede. That calls for some skill in the acting of it and in our inferential ability as spectators, but I would have liked to see the actors given the chance to deal with the lines.

What does work wordlessly is Kevin Kline's seedy Jacques as he wanders away from the others gathered around Adam (Richard Briers), whom Orlando

(David Oyelowo) has just carried into the encampment. Adam represents a sharp refutation of Jacques' clichés about the oblivion of old age. Jacques seems to realize that his speech about the meaningless of life is itself meaningless, refuted by the vitality exploding in the Forest. Adam is old and hungry, even toothless as he admits, but hardly an example of drooling second childhood.

At the end, Jacques is not given his cogent summary of the four marriages, perhaps because Branagh realized how much film he had squandered in the murky opening. And Touchstone's tour de force disquisition on "if" is cut. It is late Elizabethan, not a commentary on mid-century Japan. The emptiness of its formula, however, nicely recapitulates the hollowness of Jacques' treatise on the Seven Ages of Man. And so a segment of the script's commentary on itself is just not there in this production.

Given its talented cast, this one might have worked had Branagh not given himself such bad advice about his concept. Except for the occasional incongruous oriental face or abandoned pagoda, the concept does not intrude once the action gets to Arden. Bryce Howard is a lovely and amusing Rosalind, even if we don't for a minute believe that she's a male. We'll accept the fiction on stage because we "suspend our disbelief," but when Ms. Howard doffs her cap, her disguise goes with it. She becomes a pre-Raphaelite beauty. Romola Garai is a smashing Celia, looking like a 19th century version of Ophelia. Jimmy Yuill as Corin holds his own with calm authority against Alfred Molina's over-the-top Touchstone. Brian Blessed doubles as the legitimate and usurping Dukes, though his bad brother seems far too thuggish to be redeemed by the Forest's magic atmosphere as we are told he is.

Branagh betrays his lack of understanding when—in his HBO interview—he calls the play's central romance "beautiful and silly." It may be beautiful, but his editing of Rosalind's part at the service of his a priori concept is what makes it silly.

iii

King Lear is not an easy play for television. Its range, its complexity of plots, and its lack of any defined worldview permit it to work in the indeterminate space of an undefined stage, like that of Shakespeare, and in the ample conceptual area that film provides. A literal and limited frame like that of television imposes limits, however. The play did produce two great black-and-white films, almost simultaneously in the early 1970s. Peter Brook's brutal interpretation looks and feels like a documentary about the Nazi invasion of Poland. Grigori Kozintsev's magnificent version was filmed in 70 mm SovScope. The two films allow us to see each in contrast to the other and thus to sense the borderlands of this vast script—from a close-up and negative exploration of human evil set loose by bad decisions to a more expansive vision in which higher values compete with iniquity. In Kozintsev, virtue loses, but that does not mean that it does not exist. In Brook, though, it does not exist.

One of the better television versions remains the Papp-Sherin version of 1973, a televised stage production that incorporates the audience within its frame and thus captures some of the energy that live performance creates. James Earl Jones is a powerful Lear and Raul Julia a wonderfully menacing Edmund. Lee Chamberlin's Cordelia had marched at Selma and really wants to confront "these daughters and these sisters." The production suffers from a belatedly imposed "Christian" interpretation, as souls flutter up from Central Park and off to heaven. The 1982 BBC production features a fussy CEO Lear in Michael Hordern and crowded frames that resemble a football huddle waiting for the wrong play to be called. The 1983 Thames version is an homage to Olivier and suffers from obtrusive cello chords which undercut rather than reinforce the language. We see a great actor in his last role, but we do not see much more than that.

One can expand the size of a television screen, but the medium remains conceptually limited. It cannot incorporate special effects—a squiggly beamup hardly qualifies—and it relies on a basic grammar of shots: close-up, two-shot, reaction shot, and the occasional rack shot and establishing shot. A recent version of *King Lear, King of Texas*, was bound to fail. It features a pint-sized Lear (Patrick Stewart) who decides—against any modicum of common sense—to divide his vast cattle ranch. Vast cattle ranches worked well in the great cowboy flicks of days gone by, but they get reduced to Archie Bunker's living room on television. And, historically, by their very nature, cattle ranches resisted division.

The way to go with any televised Shakespeare script is to take a production from a small theater and reproduce it for the minimalist medium of television. Richard Eyre's Royal Shakespeare production of *King Lear* at the tiny Cottesloe in London was remounted for television in 1998. Economy of scale works beautifully here. Ian Holm dons the Fool's white cap once the Fool departs. Thus the production, via a simple metonymy, suggests the complex progress of Lear's soul. Holm's understated but sensitive readings need more resistance from Victoria Hamilton's Cordelia. It is Lear who dooms her, after all, by insisting that they go obliviously off to a prison controlled by Edmund. That fulfills Lear's dream of resting in Cordelia's "kind nursery," but Cordelia, for all of her forgiving qualities, is not characterized as either a purveyor of or a sucker for elevated rhetoric. But this is a production worth revisiting.

Trevor Nunn's production, with Ian McKellen, was apparently difficult to understand. One poster complained of "marbles in the mouth," as if the actors were Eliza Doolittle under the tutelage of Professor Higgins. I know the script fairly well, having taught the play for fifty years, so hearing the words was not a problem for me. I did question the editing. Cordelia's asides in the beginning, as she hears Goneril and Regan prostitute themselves with words of love, are cut. Her "Nothing, my lord," comes out as a surprise to us as well as to the on-stage audience. Also cut is Edmund's attribution of the Lear thesis to Edgar ("I have heard him oft maintain it to be fit that, sons of a perfect age, and fathers declining, the fathers should be as ward to the son, and the son manage his revenue"). A Gloucester, still stunned by the opening scene, is convinced, as his shouting "O villain, villain!" tells us. But not here. If you are going to include the Gloucester subplot, why rob Edgar of his magnificent description of the view from the cliffs of Dover? It's that that convinces the blind Gloucester that he is on the edge of eternity. And just because Lear says, at the end, "My poor fool is hanged," it is not necessary to stage the hanging. Why report Edmund's death if Albany's contrast of that "trifle" with the death of Lear and Cordelia is cut? The payoff for the editing, though, is the retention of most of Kent's role. That permits Kent (William Gaunt) to develop as a laconic ally of Lear, a "reflector" of the main character, as Henry James would put it. The final voice-over, as Edgar ends the play, is a potent epilogue, a pessimistic closing of the play and a projection of the play's questions into the final silence, which is ours.

McKellen charts his movement toward madness well, using a finger to point toward a disintegrating cortex. Frances Barber and Monica Dolan are wonderful as Goneril and Regan, dark-haired adventuresses who obviously have neither reverence nor time for old men. "Age," as Lear says, "is unnecessary." Their competition for Edmund is powerfully depicted. The forthright

Romola Garai as Cordelia does seem to be, as McKellen claims in his interview on PBS, the child of a second marriage. And it is at his former wife that he gazes so hopefully at the outset, at least as McKellen explains his subtext. The marriage auction between Cordelia, Burgundy and France is brilliantly mimed.

My favorite scene here is the chaotic rumble at the hovel, as Edgar, playing Mad Tom, the Fool, orchestrating an imaginary trial, and Lear going bonkers, run amuck. It feels like an episode at some indeterminate hour between midnight and dawn at the Deke House bar. Lear's forced awakening in the hovel ("This rest might yet have balm'd thy broken senses") into the "hard cure" of nightmare is nicely contrasted to his later rebirth ("You do me wrong to take me out of the grave") and dawning recognition ("I think this lady to be my child, Cordelia"). The reconciliation between Lear and Cordelia is moving, as Lear admits his vulnerability and reveals a sweetness that had been latent in his character until now. The play, after all, is the story of the brief adulthood of this old man. The process cannot begin until he is no longer king. McKellen develops his understanding of that truth across a considerable spectrum of emotion. The saber battle between Edgar and Edmund is exciting and does seem dangerous, as stage combat seldom does. The time, it seems, is Russia, just before the Revolution, a fitting moment, suggesting the breaking of nations.

This production represents the third major collaboration between Nunn and McClellen. The *Macbeth* of thirty years ago, originally produced at the tiny stage—The Other Place in Stratford and remounted for television, is probably the best version of that play available. And, of course, while its crimes strike heaven in the face, its viewpoint is close-up, as Lady Macbeth (a superb Judi Dench) plots to entice her husband to murder, as Macbeth is tempted, and, at the end, as he roams alone in his castle like a trapped bear, even as she seeks for light in the gloom of damnation-while-still-alive ("Hell is murky"). A decade later, again in a studio production, McKellen played an Iago chillingly detached from the evil he was fomenting. And, again, *Othello*, for all of the Moor's grandiloquence, calls for tight camera angles. It ends, as the great A.C. Bradley says "in a close-shut, murderous room." (1904, p. 145)

The current *King Lear* is a very good production of a play whose dimensions are simply larger than those that television can accommodate. But, for generations, the play was thought to be too large for the stage as well. It was not until the end of World War II, with the Holocaust and the Bomb, that the play became available to us as a vehicle for performance. It is still too large for our imaginations and for the formats in which we recreate them, but history has proved to be just as incapable of being phrased or framed. And so, *King Lear* will continue to challenge us, defeat us, and permit us to take it on again. It is, like Lear's, a learning process.

Conclusion

Branagh's *As You Like It* does not account for the way in which the issue of identity—specifically the awareness of, the construction of, and the performance of gender—is central to *As You Like It*. Instead, his "bright idea" of placing the script in medieval Japan smothers its possible communication to us via the "doublet and hose" of the script and the disguised Rosalind's skillful interrogation of the infatuated Orlando. Radford simply dumps the concept of anti-Semitism on us as a given, a burning Torah. The Shakespeare script is a given in one sense, but the words are there to be peopled by actors. The script is there as something to be explored by a director, not as a set of assumptions to be presented to us as an announcement. Announcements in Shakespeare can be "givens"—like the Chorus in *Romeo and Juliet* which warns us that the zodiac is not inscribing a comedy here, or they can be examples of naive narration—like the Chorus to Act IV in *Henry V*. *The Merchant of Venice* does not play well if un-interrogated by a director.

Nunn's *King Lear* suffers from the inevitable diminution imposed upon this titanic script by the domesticating effect of TV. More domestic and scaled-down contexts like *Macbeth* and *Othello*, each play focused on a debate between two characters, prosper under Nunn on the small screen. But, then, so does his magnificent *Antony and Cleopatra* of 1972, which uses billowy curtains, cushions and reclining people for Egypt and armor, marching feet, and focused faces for Rome in metonymies that serve as effective backgrounds for the language and superb acting. It fails in its depiction of Actium, but then few would claim that battle sequences are Shakespeare's greatest strength. The opening Chorus to *Henry V* suggests that he knew as much.

I would suggest that if you hear remarks about "how clever" the director was to set the play in this or that place, you will have experienced a production that called attention to itself. Twenty years ago, for example, a *Romeo and Juliet* set in Belfast and featuring a love affair between a

Protestant and a Catholic would have been a case in point. Juliet would have had to have been the Catholic, simply because of her frequent use of the offices of the Church, though Romeo would have had to know the Friar. But the play itself is given a Catholic setting, primarily because it is set in Italy, but also to emphasize the potential resolution that the Church can offer. The Northern Ireland production might have vivified the conflicts by way of a transitory allusiveness, but it would have falsified one truth of the script—the ancient grudge has no current basis. It just is. It is certainly not an understandable (if, in our tolerant eyes, reprehensible) result of religious differences. It is the implacability and irrationality of the feud that makes the plight of the lovers maddening and their deaths inevitable. Placing the play in contemporary contexts erases the inevitability already set in the stars.

The best setting for a script that does not call for doublet and hose is "neutral modern." The costumes would indicate social station or attitude— morning coat for York, business suit and military uniforms for Bolingbroke and his party, mod but expensive informality for Richard and his group, a la the ads in *Vanity Fair*. Such costuming would make distinctions without defining the world as, say, England in 1937, and would be the background from which the issues of the play emerged, as opposed to a "clever" concept into which the issues of the play were coerced. I think of the Ian McKellen *Richard III* as such a coercive context. (Coursen 1999, 137 ff.) In that film, the fidelity to detail was remarkable, but the detail pulled the issues of the script into the Tiffany pin. The play set in 1937 cannot take us very far into the issue of Richard's loss of soul. The play is very medieval in its premises. Pacino looked for that Richard at the Cloisters, the medieval museum of the Metropolitan and achieved a remarkable transition in his film from contemporary New York street scenes to Richard's nightmare and his sweaty awakening from it before Bosworth Field. The Ethan Hawke *Hamlet* could not accommodate a formal duel, so the pistol that had killed Polonius somehow made its way from the NYPD evidence room to the final scene of the play. (Coursen 2002, 151-56) A setting like the one suggested in the front of this book, while "modern," would not exclude the deployment of rapiers. Were that production mounted today, however, we would say that it was set in the 1920s, not in our own time. That time might be just distant enough from our own to work, though the director would have to avoid reminding us too much of Gatsby.

My prescriptions may be reactionary, but Shakespeare's plays are not products of a post-modernist sensibility. They *lose* meaning when that is what they become, whether in criticism or production. The director must somehow establish the continuum between the script and his production, not permitting the latter to smother the former. If Shakespeare "converts archetype into image, idea into action" (Bate 2009), the director must provide the sensory data and the movement that archetype and idea demand. He cannot merely substitute his concept for the intrinsic energies he inherits. He must re-imagine them in the planetarium of a mind that is his own and that is also inhabited by the script of the play. Most directors, unfortunately, do not agree with me that neutrality in face of the work the language can do to appeal to *our* imaginations is the best course. They perceive themselves as getting paid for their inventiveness and originality, not for their effective production of Shakespeare's scripts.

But, still, the director must make decisions. I once served as a dramaturge for a *Measure for Measure* and helped the director condense the final scene without eliminating necessary entrances and exits. What I did not do was ask about concept. The costumes in this blackbox production turned out to be eclectic. The Duke wore a ratty old Ike jacket. Lucio was a college boy with a shirttail out in back. Socially, he "outranked" Vincentio. The production's failure to make distinctions between the characters blurred its emphasis. As in all of the plays, the world of *Measure for Measure* is hierarchal. A virtuous person like the Provost is still subject to what authority orders. In this case, "no concept" caused just as many problems for the production as "bright idea" would have done.

The imposition of "modern" meanings on Shakespeare's scripts tends to flatten them into our own image, whether in stage versions of *Henry V* or film versions of *Romeo and Juliet*, which focus with some validity on the "separateness" of the teenage world and which feature, less legitimately, relationships that bridge economic, racial or religious gaps between the two. In those instances, we are denied the opportunity to bridge the gap ourselves between a world that is not ours and the one that is. We are denied the chance to make metaphors. And that creativity, one of the joys of childhood, should not be denied us as adults, particularly when it comes to the re-imagining of the greatest plays that have ever been written.

Notes

Introduction

1. What I remember most about that production, though, was the guy who entered the wrong row from the Barbican staircase with those doors that swing shut. "I'm in the wrong bleeping row!" emerged clearly through the darkness from a desperately seatless individual just as the curtain went up after the second interval.

2. The chapter on Ophelia is a revision of an essay in *The Myth and Madness of Ophelia*, edited by Carol Solomon Kiefer. Amherst: Mead Art Gallery, 2001.

II Local Shakespeare and Anachronism

1. It would be churlish of me not to mention that Robinson's *Measure for Measure* featured one of the most luminous Isabellas I have ever seen, in Kathleen Lewis. I add her to a list of splendid Isabellas that includes Estelle Kohler, Elizabeth Marvell, Kate Nelligan, Anna Carteret, Penelope Wilton, Juliet Aubrey and Anna Soloway.

2. As Morven Christie did in Sam Mendes's version at the Brooklyn Academy of Music in 2009.

III *Richard II* as Script

1. The same qualification would not apply to a priest who renders communion. The priest does not claim to be a ruler. Nor is his transmission of the sacrament conditioned by the fact that he himself may be a notorious evil liver. Richard actively interferes with the mechanisms of kingship and rule.

2. When John Barton's meretricious *Richard II* arrived in New York in 1972 it picked up a lot of unearned energy from the episode of our own history known as Watergate. In this case, latent cultural energy pushed forward to obscure the gimmicks in which Barton indulged. Richard Nixon may have been a transitional figure, but his fall was not that of a world order tumbling to ashes like a star. A too-specific linkage to an increasingly desperate cover up might have obscured the profound issues that *Richard II* depicts, but, here, it was the production itself that trivialized its content. See my *Shakespearean*

Performance as Interpretation (Newark: University of Delaware Press: 1992): 140-146 on the contrast between Barton's production and Terry Hands' superb *Henry V*.

3. I count some forty-four instances of the use of "un" as a prefix for a noun, verb or adjective in the play.

4. The prayer from the Elizabethan "Visitacioun of the Sicke" (1558): "Heare us almighty, and most mercifull God, and saviour, extend thy accustomed goodnes, to this thy servaunt whice his greved with syckeness, visit him O Lorde…and restore unto this sicke person his former health (if it bee thy will)."

5. Mowbray's career emulates that of the generic knight described by Johan Huizinga: he is the "literary type of the ideal knight (85-6)… painted in the colors of piety and restraint, simplicity and virtue (79…[H]istoriography employed the fiction of the ideal of knighthood and thus traced everything back to a beautiful image of princely honor and knightly virtue." (72) *The Autumn of the Middle Ages*. Trans. Rodney J. Paton and Ulrich Mammitzsch. Chicago: University of Chicago Press, 1996.

6. On Mowbray and the sources of *Richard II*, see my discussion. *The Leasing Out of England*. Washington: University Press of America, 1982, pp. 16-45.

7. Keith Gregor, in describing the first *Richard II* to be performed in Spain (Adrian Daumas' 1998 production), mentions the "particularly powerful" doubling of the prophets Gaunt and Carlisle. (Gregor 2004, 216)

8. On doubling see Ralph Berry, "Doubling: Theory and Practice," *Shakespeare in Production*. London: Macmillan, 1993, pp. 15-26. On which characters are in which scenes see the useful charts in T. J. King, *Casting Shakespeare's Plays*. Cambridge: Cambridge University Press, 1992.

9. For a detailed discussion of Robert Egan's *Richard II* with Kelsey Grammer at the Mark Taper Forum in 1994, see my *Reading Shakespeare on Stage* (Madison, N.J.: Fairleigh Dickinson University Press, 1995), pp. 185-91. For comments on other televised *Richard II*s, including that of Maurice Evans, see James Bulman and H. R. Coursen, *Shakespeare on Television* Hanover, N. H.: University of New England Press, 1988: 239, 253-55. William Woodman directed a profoundly forgettable version for Bard in 1982, with David Birney. It was designed for students who have trouble with that "hard to understand English accent" said to inhibit listening to the BBC productions.

IV *Henry V* in Performance

1. On the Hands' production, see Sally Beauman. *The Royal Shakespeare Company's Production of* Henry V. Oxford: Permagon Press, 1976, and my *Shakespearean Performance as Interpretation*. Newark: University of Delaware Press, 1992, pp. 140-46.

2. On the scene with the traitors, see Karl P. Wentersdorf. "The Conspiracy of Silence in *Henry V*." *Shakespeare Quarterly* 26 (1976): 264-87.

3. For an extension of this version of *Henry V*, see my *The Leasing Out of England*. Washington: University Press of America, 1982, chapters VI-VIII.

4. I am indebted to my student, Pamela Wilcox, for bringing the equation between the two Katherines to my attention.

VI Reading *The Tempest* toward Production

1. For more on *The Tempest* in performance, see my *The Tempest: A Guide*, Westport, Ct.: Greenwood, 2000, pp. 141-195, Anthony Dawson, *Watching Shakespeare: A Playgoer's Guide*. London: Macmillan, 1988, pp. 231-241, Romana Beyenburg, *"The Tempest." Shakespeare in Performance*, edited by Pamela Mason and Keith Parsons. London: Salamander Books, 1995, pp. 202-208, and Stephen Orgel, editor, *The Tempest*. Oxford: Oxford University Press, 1984, pp. 64-87. On film and television versions, see Kenneth Rothwell and Anabelle Melzer, *Shakespeare on Screen*. New York: Neal-Schuman, 1990, pp. 282-293. On television productions, see James Bulman and H.R. Coursen, editors, *Shakespeare on Television*. Hanover, N.H.: University Press of New England, 1988, pp. 163 and 241. On the BBC-TV version, see John Wilders, editor, *The Tempest*. New York: Mayflower Books, 1980. For a complete discussion of text, sources, intellectual background, the dynamics of the play itself, and *The Tempest* in performance, see my *Guide to 'The Tempest'*. Greenwood, 2000.

2. In addition to the South Bank documentary (1988) see Roger Warren's meticulous analysis of these productions: *Staging Shakespeare's Late Plays*. Oxford: Clarendon Press, 1990.

3. On this production, see my review, "Shakespeare in Maine, Summer, 1970." *Shakespeare Quarterly* XXI (1970): 487-490.

VII Shakespeare on Film: The Web of Allusion

1. *Shakespeare Translated: Derivatives on Film and TV*. New York: Peter Lang, 2004 deals primarily with two versions of *The Goodbye Girl*, with manifestations of *Romeo and Juliet* (*Stagedoor Canteen, Perry Mason, In and Out, Andy Hardy Gets Spring Fever, The Little Rascals, Romeo, Juliet, and Darkness, Romanov and Juliet, Los Tarantos, Shakespeare Wallah, Everytime We Say Goodbye, China Girl, Pocahantas, The Lion King, Wishbone, Titanic, The Cosby Show, Romeo Must Die, The Gilmore Girls, Clueless*, and *Save the Last Dance*); of *Hamlet*, (*Strange Illusion, My Darling Clementine, Prince of Players, The Bad Sleep Well, Willie and Phil, Strange Brew, Outrageous Fortune, Hamlet Goes Business, Rosencrantz and Guildenstern Are Dead, Star Trek, The Trial of Hamlet, The Lion King, A Midwinter's Tale*, and *A Killing Kindness*); of *Othello* (*A Double Life, Cheers, The Animated Othello, O*, and the BBC *Othello*); and *King Lear* (*Harry and Tonto, House of Strangers, Broken Lance, Godfather III*, and *King of Texas*).

2. For recent personal experiences of women passing as men, see Susannah Kaysen, *Girl, Interrupted*, New York: Vintage, 1994 and Norah Vincent, *Self-made Man: One Woman's Year Disguised as a Man*. New York: Bantam, 2006.

VIII. Three Recent Productions

1. The eminent film critic, Samuel Crowl, informs me that the earlier vision of ring and monkey was, indeed, Shylock's hallucination. The technique is similar to that used by Oliver Parker in this film of *Othello*, where Othello voyeuristically glimpses Desdemona's infidelity on the basis of Iago's insinuations. In *Merchant*, however, Tubal, Shylock's confidant, claims actually to have seen a bartered ring: "One of them show'd me a ring he had of your daughter for a monkey." We must surmise that, if Tubal is telling the truth, Shylock leaps to the conclusion that the ring was his turquoise. For me, the imposition of a flashback to something that is untrue represents another of Radford's bad decisions. I note that Crowl's *Norton Guide to Shakespeare and Film* has just appeared. It will quickly become the standard text in the field.

2. An "Official Teacher's Guide" for this production was available. It was full of good background material, but it cannot enhance the artistic product for which it was a guide.

3. For my approach to other productions of *King Lear*, see Coursen 1992, pp. 122-139; 1995, pp. 134-154; 2002, pp. 54-57.

Works Cited

Hilton Als, "Kingdom Come." *The New Yorker* (2 October 2006): 94-95.

Alan Armstrong, "Shakespeare in Ashland: 2001." *Shakespeare Bulletin* XX (Spring 2002): 25.

Robert Hamilton Ball, *Shakespeare on Silent Film*. London: George Allen and Unwin, 1968.

Clive Barnes, "Taking B'way by Storm." *New York Post* (2 November 1995): 27.

Frances Barber. "Ophelia in *Hamlet.*" *Players of Shakespeare 2*. Russell Jackson and Robert Smallwood, editors. Cambridge: Cambridge University Press, 1988: 137-49.

Sylvan Barnet, editor, *The Tempest*. New York: Signet, 1987, revised 1998.

Kate Bassett, "Review of *The Tempest.*" *Independent on Sunday* (8 August 2006).

Jonathan Bate, *Soul of the Age: A Biography of the Mind of William Shakespeare.* New York: Random House, 2009.

Sally Beauman, *The RSC 'Henry V.'* Oxford: Pergamon, 1976.

Bernard Beckerman, "*Tempest* in a Loft." *Shakespeare Quarterly* 27 (1976): 57.

Gerald Berkowitz, "*Richard II.*" *Shakespeare Bulletin* 14/2 (1996): 9.

Ralph Berry. *Shakespeare in Performance*. London: Macmillan, 1993.

David Bevington, *The Complete Works of Shakespeare*, 3ed edition. Glenview: Scott, Foresman, 1980.

Romana Beyenburg, "*The Tempest.*" *Shakespeare in Performance*, edited by Pamela Mason and Keith Parsons. London: Salamander, 1995.

Michael Billington, "*The Tempest.*" *Guardian* (15 July 1994): 26.

http://www.guardian.co.uk/stage/theatreblog/2007/oct/08/doesshake-spearebelonginthe

James Black. "Shakespeare's *Henry V* and the Dreams of History." *English Studies in Canada* 1 (1975).

Harold Bloom, editor, *William Shakespeare's* Henry V. New York: Chelsea House, 1988.

Jay Bobbin, "Shakespeare's *Tempest* Brews Anew on NBC." *TV Week* (13-19 December 1998): 2.

A. C. Bradley, *Shakespearean Tragedy.* London: Macmillan, 1904.

____. *Oxford Lectures on Poetry.* Oxford: Oxford University Press, 1909.

Kenneth Branagh, editor. *Hamlet.* New York: W. W. Norton, 1996.

Bertrand H. Bronson, editor. *Samuel Johnson: 'Rasselas,' Poems, and Selected Prose.* New York: Holt, Rinehart and Winston, 1952.

Reuben Brower, *The Fields of Light.* Oxford: Oxford University Press, 1951.

Robert Brustein. "Twenty-First Century *Hamlet.*" *The New Republic.* 18-25 July 1988: 28.

James Bulman, "*As You Like It* and the Perils of Pastoral," *Shakespeare on Television,* ed. J.C. Bulman and H.R. Coursen. Amherst: University of Massachusetts Press, 1988, pp. 174-78.

____ and H. R. Coursen, editors. *Shakespeare on Television.* Hanover: University of New England Press, 1988.

Vincent Canby, "Jarman's *Tempest.*" *New York Times* (22 September 1980): C20.

Maurice Charney, "Shakespearean Anglophilia." *Shakespeare Quarterly* 31(1980): 287-292.

Karin S. Coddon. "'Suche Strange Dessygns': Madness, Subjectivity, and Treason in *Hamlet* and Elizabethan Culture." *Hamlet,* edited by Susan L. Wofford. Boston: Bedford, 1994: 380-402.

Judith Cook, *Shakespeare's Players.* London: Harrap, 1985.

Michael Collins, "*Hamlet.*" *Shakespeare Bulletin* 20/1 (Winter 2002): 11-12.

____. "*The Tempest*: Shakespeare's Globe Theatre." *Shakespeare Bulletin* 23/4 (Winter 2005): 63-66.

Linda Cookson and Brian Loughrey, editors. *Hamlet.* London: Longman, 1988.

Michael Cohen. *'Hamlet': In My Mind's Eye.* Athens: University of Georgia Press, 1989.

Walter Coppedge, "Jarman's *The Tempest.*" *Creative Screenwriting* 5 (1998): 12.

H. R. Coursen. *Christian Ritual and the World of Shakespeare's Tragedies.* Cranbury, N.J.: Associated University Presses, 1978.

____. *The Leasing Out of England.* Washington: University Press of America, 1983.

A Jungian Approach to Shakespeare. Washington: University Press of America, 1986.

____. "Theories of History in *Richard II.*" *The Upstart Crow* VIII (1988): 42-53.

___. "'Must There No More Be Done?' Images of Ophelia." *Shakespearean Performance as Interpretation*. Newark: University of Delaware Press, 1992: 85-102.

___. *Reading Shakespeare on Stage*. Madison: Fairleigh Dickinson University Press, 1995.

___. *Shakespeare in Production: Whose History?* Athens: Ohio University Press, 1996.

___. "The Closet Scene." *Approaches to Teaching 'Hamlet.'* Edited by Bernice W. Kliman. New York: Modern Language Association, 2001.

___. *"Titus* and the Genre of Revenge," *Shakespeare in Space: Recent Shakespeare on Screen*. New York: Peter Lang, 2002. pp. 129-41.

___. *Shakespeare Translated*. New York: Peter Lang, 2005.

___. "Margreta de Grazia's *Hamlet* without Hamlet." *Shakespeare Newsletter* 57:3 No. 273 (Winter 07-08): 85-86.

Samuel Crowl, "A World Elsewhere: The Roman Plays on Film and Television." *Shakespeare and the Moving Image*. Cambridge: Cambridge University Press, 1994. 146-162.

___. "Review," *Shakespeare Bulletin* 19/3 (Fall 2001): 42.

___. *Shakespeare at the Cineplex: The Kenneth Branagh Era*. Athens: Ohio University Press, 2003.

___. *Shakespeare on Film: A Norton Guide*. New York: Norton, 2008.

Lawrence Danson, *"Henry V:* King, Chorus, and Critics." *Shakespeare Quarterly* 34/1 (Spring, 1983): 27-43.

Peter Davison, *Hamlet: Text & Performance*. London: Macmillan, 1983.

Anthony Dawson, *Watching Shakespeare: A Playgoer's Guide*. London: Macmillan, 1988.

___. *Shakespeare in Performance:' Hamlet.'* Manchester: Manchester University Press, 1995.

Patty S. Derrick, 'Richard Mansfield's *Henry V*: The Making of an America Hero," *Theatre History Studies* XIX (1999): 3-16.

Alan Dessen, "The Supernatural on Television." *Shakespeare on Film* XI (1986): 1, 8.

___. *Rescripting Shakespeare: The Text, the Director, and Modern Production*. Cambridge: Cambridge University Press, 2002.

Bonamy Dobree, "The Last Plays." *Living Shakespeare*, Edited by Robert Gittings. New York: Fawcett, 1963.

Peter Donaldson. "Kenneth Branagh's *Henry V* ." *Shakespeare Quarterly* 42 (1991): 60-70.

Jennifer Drougin, *Shakespeare Re-Dressed: Cross-Gender Casting in Contemporary Performance*, edited by James Bulman (Madison: Fairleigh Dickinson University Press, 2008, p. 51).

Halina Filipowicz and Gary Mead, "A Polish Pantomime *Hamlet*," *Shakespeare Quarterly* 32/3 (Autumn 1981): 376-78.

Michel Foucault, *Surveiller et punir: Naissance de la Prison*. Paris: Gallimard, 1975.

R. M. Frye. *The Renaissance 'Hamlet': Issues and Responses in 1600*. Princeton: Princeton University Press, 1984.

H.H. Furness, editor, *The New Variorum 'Tempest.'* Philadelphia: Lippincott, 1892.

Helen Gardner, *The Buisness of Criticism*. (Oxford: Oxford University Press, 1963.)

Harold Goddard, *The Meaning of Shakespeare* (Chicago: University of Chicago Press, 1951).

Jack Gould, "Review," *New York Times* (4 February 1960): 63.

Harley Granville Barker. *Preface to 'Hamlet.'* London: Nick Hern, 1993.

Stephen Greenblatt, editor. *The Norton Shakespeare*. New York: W.W. Norton, 1997.

____. *Will in the World: How Shakespeare Became Shakespeare*. New York: Norton, 2004.

____. "Shakespeare & the Uses of Power," *New York Review of Books* (12 April 2007): 75-80.

Keith Gregor, "The Spanish Premier of *Richard II, Shakespeare's History Plays: Performance, Translation, and Adaptation in Britain and Abroad*, edited by Ton Hoensellaars. Cambridge, CBU 2004.

Andrew Gurr, *The Shakespearean Stage: 1574-1642*. Cambridge: Cambridge University Press, 1970. Revised, 1980.

Jay L. Halio, *Understanding Shakespeare's Plays in Performance*. Manchester: Manchester University Press, 1988.

Donna Hamilton, "The State of Law in *Richard II*." *Shakespeare Quarterly* 34/1 (Winter, 1983): 5-17.

Robert Hanks, "*The Tempest*," *Independent on Sunday* (17 July 1994): Sec. 6, 1.

Robert Hapgood. "Shakespeare and the Included Spectator." *Reinterpretations of Renaissance Drama*, edited by Norman Rabkin. New York: Columbia University Press, 1969: 117-36.

O. B. Hardison, "Three Types of Renaissance Catharsis." *Renaissance Drama* (1969): 3-22.

Paul J. Hecht, "Review." *Shakespeare Bulletin* 23/4 (Winter, 2005): 125-27.

Virginia Heffernan, "*As You Like It.*" *New York Times* (21 August 2007).

G.R. Hibbard, editor. *Hamlet.* Oxford: Oxford University Press, 1987.

David Hirst, '*The Tempest': Text and Performance.* London: Macmillan, 1984.

Barbara Hodgdon, "Viewing Acts," *Shakespeare Bulletin* 25/3 (Fall 2007): 3).

Peter Holland. "*Hamlet:* Text in Performance." *Hamlet.* Edited by Peter J. Smith and Nigel Wood. Buckingham: Open University Press, 1996: 55-82.

___ and William Worthen, eds. *Theorizing Practice: Redefining Theatre History.* London: Palgrave Macmillan, 2003.

John Houseman, *Run-Through.* New York: Simon and Schuster, 1972.

Kathy M. Howlett, *Shakespeare Framed* and *Reframed.* Athens: Ohio University Press, 2000.

Johna Huizinga, *The Autumn of the Middle Ages.* trans. Rodney J. Payton and Ulrich Mammitzsch. Chicago: University of Chicago Press, 1996.

Charles Isherwood, "A Leader Abandoned, Overthrown, and Humbled." *New York Times* (19 September 2006).

Harold Jenkins, editor. *Hamlet.* London: Metheun, 1982.

Nicholas Jones, "Review," *Shakespeare Bulletin* 24/3 (Fall, 2006): 72.

David Kastan, "'The Duke of Milan / And His Brave Son': Dynastic Politics in *The Tempest.*" *Critical Essays on 'The Tempest.'* New York: G.K. Hall, 1998, pp. 93-101.

Dennis Kennedy, *Looking at Shakespeare: A Visual History of Twentieth-Century Performance.* Cambridge: Cambridge University Press, 1993.

Bob Keyes, "They come not to bury 'Caesar,' but to praise it." *Maine Sunday Telegram* (19 Oct 2008):1 and 7.

Frank Kermode, editor, *The Tempest.* New York: Random House, 1964.

Carol Solomon Kiefer, ed. *The Myth and Madness of Ophelia.* Amherst: Mead Art Museum, 2001.

T.J. King, *Casting Shakespeare's Plays: London Actors and Their Roles: 1590-1642.* Cambridge: Cambridge University Press, 1992.

George Lyman Kittredge, *The Tempest.* Boston: Ginn & Company, 1939.

Bernice W. Kliman, *Approaches to Teaching 'Hamlet.'* New York: Modern Language Association, 2001.

Robert Kole, "Review" *Shakespeare Bulletin* (Spring 2001): 12.

Grigori Kozintsev, *Shakespeare: Time and Conscience*. Translated by Joyce Vining. London: Dennis Dobson, 1967.

John Lahr, "Big and Bad Wolfe." *New Yorker* (14 May 1995): 121.

Thomas Larque, "Review," *Shakespeare Bulletin* 21/ 1 (Winter 2003): 17.

Christopher Lasch, *Culture of Narcissism: American Life in an age of Diminishing Expectations*. New York: Norton, 1979.

Ernest Law, *Shakespeare's 'Tempest' as Originally Produced at Court*. London: Shakespeare Association, 1920.

Cynthia Lewis, "Review." *Shakespeare Bulletin* 23/4 (Winter, 2005): 121-24.

Pia Lindstrom, "Review," WABC (2 November 1995).

James Loehlin, *Henry V*. Manchester: Manchester University Press, 1997.

Molly Mahood, *Bit Parts in Shakespeare*. Cambridge: Cambridge University Press, 1992.

Derek Marsh, "Shakespeare in Perth." *Shakespeare Quarterly* 30/2 (Spring 1979): 271-72.

Katherine Eisaman Maus, "Introduction to *Richard II*." *The Norton Shakespeare*. Edited by Stephen Greenblatt (New York: Norton, 1997).

Kathleen McLuskie. "The Patriachal Bard." *Political Shakespeare*. Edited by Jonathan Dollimore and Alan Sinfield Manchester Manchester University Press, 1985.

Barbara Mowat. *The Dramaturgy of Shakespeare's Romances*. Athens: University of Georgia Press, 1976.

Anna Nardo. "Hamlet: A Man to Double Business Bound." *Shakespeare Quarterly* 34 (1983): 181-199.

Paul Nelson and June Schlueter, eds. *Acts of Criticism: Performance of Shakespeare and His Contemporaries: Essays in Honor of James Lusardi* Madison: Fairleigh Dickinson University Press, 2006.

A. M. Nagler, *Shakespeare's Stage*. New Haven: Yale University Press, 1958.

Benedict Nightingale, "Lively Under the Plastic." *The Times* (11 February 1999): 36.

Stephen Orgel, editor, *The Tempest*. Oxford: Clarendon Press, 1984.

Laurie Osborne, "Poetry in Motion: Animating Shakespeare." *Shakespeare: the Movie*, edited by Lynda Boose and Richard Burt. London: Routledge, 1997.

____. "Mixing Media in Shakespeare: Animating Tales and Colliding Modes of Production." *Post Script* (Winter/Spring 1998): 73-89.

Malcolm Page, *Richard II*. London: Macmillan, 1987.

John Palmer. *Political and Comic Characters of Shakespeare*. Macmillan: London, 1961.

___. *Shakespeare: The Tempest*. London: Macmillan, 1968.

Keith Parsons and Pamela Mason, editors. *Shakespeare in Performance*, London: Salamander, 1995.

Michael Pennington. *Hamlet: A User's Guide*. New York: Limelight, 1996.

"Peter Hall Directs the Final Plays." Southbank Documentary. Bravo Channel, 1988.

Lois Potter, "A Brave New Tempest." *Shakespeare Quarterly* 43 (1992).

Susan L. Powell, "Richard II," *Shakespeare in Performance* edited by Keith Parsons and Pamela Mason. London: Salamander, 1995.

Marian Pringle, *"The Tempest: A Stage History."* *Program*, Royal Shakespeare Company (1998).

Moody Prior, *The Drama of Power*. Evanston: University of Illinois Press, 1973.

Diane Purkiss. *The Witch in History: Early Modern and Twentieth-Century Interpretations*. London: Routledge, 1996.

Norman Rabkin. *"Rabbits, Ducks, and* Henry V." *Shakespeare Quarterly* 28 (1977): 279-96.

Hugh M. Richmond. *Shakespeare's Political Plays*. (New York: Random House, 1967).

Ron Rosenbaum, "The Crucial First Clue to 'Henry V.'" *New York Times* (29 June 2003): AR 5-6.

Marvin Rosenberg, *The Masks of 'Hamlet.'* Newark: University of Delaware Press, 1992.

___. "The Myth of Shakespeare's Squeaking Boy Actor—Or Who Played Cleopatra?" SB 19/2 (Spring 2001): 5-6.

Hanna Rosin, "A Boy's Life" What Would You Do If Your Son Wanted to be a Girl?" *The Atlantic* (November 2008).

Kenneth S. Rothwell and Annabelle H. Melzer. *Shakespeare on Screen*. New York: Neal-Schuman, 1990.

___. *A History of Shakespeare on Screen*, 2nd ed. Cambridge: Cambridge University Press, 2004.

Carol Rutter, "Fiona Shaw's Richard II." *Shakespeare Quarterly* 48/3 (1997): 214-24.

Justin Shaltz, "Review," *Shakespeare Bulletin* 14/4 (Fall 1996): 29

___. "Review," *Shakespeare Bulletin* 2/2 (Spring 2002): 33.

Levin Schucking. *Character Problems in Shakespeare's Plays*. Berlin, 1917. English Translation, New York, 1922.

Charles H. Shattuck. *Shakespeare on the American Stage*. II. Cranbury, N.J.: Associated University Presses, 1987.

Margaret Shewing, *Shakespeare in Performance:* Richard II. Manchester: Manchester University Press, 1996.

Samuel Schoenbaum, "*Richard II* and the Realities of Power." *Shakespeare Survey* 28 (1975): 1-13.

Michael Shurgot, "'Get you a place': Staging the Mousetrap at the Globe Theatre." *Shakespeare Bulletin* 21/3 (Summer, 1994): 5-9.

Elaine Showalter. "Representing Ophelia: Women, Madness, and the Responsibilities of Feminist Criticism." *Shakespeare and the Question of Theory*. Edited by Patricia Parker and Geoffrey Hartman. London: Metheun, 1985: 77-94.

Robert Smallwood, "Director's Theatre," *Shakespeare: An Illustrated Stage History*, edited by Jonathan Bate and Russell Jackson. Oxford: Oxford University Press, 1996.

___. "Shakespeare Performances in England.' *Shakespeare Survey* 52 (1999).

Susan Snyder, "*Romeo and Juliet*: Comedy into Tragedy." *Essays in Criticism* 20 (1970): 391-402.

Bert O. States. *Hamlet and the Concept of Character*. Baltimore: Johns Hopkins University Press, 1992.

Zdenek Stribrny, "Recent *Hamlet*s in Prague." *Shakespeare Quarterly* 35/2 (Summer 1984): 208-214.

John Styan, *Shakespeare's Stagecraft*. Cambridge: Cambridge University Press, 1970.

Patricia Tatspaugh, "Review," *Shakespeare Quarterly* 57/3 (Fall 2006).

Paul Taylor, "*The Tempest*," *Independent* (15 July 1994): 38.

Francis Teague, "Review." *Shakespeare Bulletin* 19/2 (Spring 2001): 21.

Sidney Thomas. *The Antic Hamlet and Richard III*. London: King Crown's Press, 1943.

Peter Thompson, *The Cambridge Companion to Shakespeare on Stage*, edited by Sarah Stanton and Stanley Wells, Cambridge: Cambridge University Press,

2002. pp. 137-154.

D. Traister, "Review," *Choice*, 1999.

J. C. Trewin. *Going to Shakespeare*. London: Allen & Unwin, 1978.

____. *Five and Eighty Hamlets*. London: Hutchinson, 1987.

John Updike. *Gertrude and Claudius*. New York: Knopf: 1998.

Alden and Virginia Vaughan, editors, *The Tempest*. New York: Routledge, 1999.

Roger Warren, *Staging Shakespeare's Late Plays*. Oxford: Clarendon Press, 1990.

Robert Weimann, "Bi-Fold Authority in Shakespeare." *Shakespeare Quarterly* 39/4 (Winter, 1988): 401-17.

Karl P. Wentersdorf, "The Conspiracy of Silence in *Henry V*," *Shakespeare Quarterly* 26 (1976): 264-87.

Rebecca West. *The Court and the Castle*. New Haven: Yale University Press, 1947.

Wendy Williams, "Fonda Takes on 'The Tempest'." *Satellite TV Week* (22-28 November 1998): 2.

Robert Willson, Jr. *Shakespeare in Hollywood*. Madison, N.J.: Fairleigh Dickinson U.P., 2000.

William Worthen, "Staging 'Shakespeare': Acting, Authority, and the Rhetoric of Performance," *Shakespeare, Theory, and Performance*, ed. James C. Bulman. London and New York, 1996, pp. 12-28.

____. *Shakespeare and the Authority of Performance*. Cambridge: Cambridge University Press, 1997.

Index

STUDIES IN SHAKESPEARE

Edited by Robert F. Willson, Jr.

This series deals with all aspects of Shakespearean drama and poetry. Studies of dramatic structure, verse and prose style, major themes, stage or performance history, and film treatments are welcomed. The editor is particularly interested in manuscripts that examine Shakespeare's work in its American setting—in the academy, on stage, and in popular culture. Inquiries and manuscripts should be sent to the series editor:

Robert F. Willson, Jr.
Department of English
University of Missouri-Kansas City
College of Arts & Sciences
106 Cockefair Hall
Kansas City, MO 64110-2499

To order other books in this series, please contact our Customer Service Department at:

(800) 770-LANG (within the U.S.)
(212) 647-7706 (outside the U.S.)
(212) 647-7707 FAX

or browse online by series at:
WWW.PETERLANG.COM